Rechtstheorie · Legal Theory

herausgegeben von

Thomas Gutmann, Tatjana Hörnle und Matthias Jestaedt

5

Trevor N. Wedman

Inverting the Norm

Law as the Form of Common Practice

Mohr Siebeck

Trevor N. Wedman, born 1981 in Oklahoma, USA; he obtained his Juris Doctor degree at the University of San Diego School of Law and his PhD at the Institute for Philosophy of the University of Leipzig; he currently researches at the University of Vienna and practices international commercial law.
orcid.org/0000-0001-5027-3531

ISBN 978-3-16-161691-4 / eISBN 978-3-16-161717-1
DOI 10.1628/978-3-16-161717-1

ISSN 2629-723X / eISSN 2629-7248 (Rechtstheorie · Legal Theory)

The Deutsche Nationalbibliothek lists this publication in the Deutsche Nationalbibliographie; detailed bibliographic data are available at *http://dnb.dnb.de.*

The book was typeset using Times typeface and printed on non-aging paper by Gulde Druck in Tübingen. It was bound by Buchbinderei Spinner in Ottersweier.

Printed in Germany.

Preface

I am feeling the weight of the war much more since I came back here – one is made so terribly aware of the waste when one is here. And Rupert Brooke's death brought it home to me. It is deadly to be here now, with all the usual life stopped. There will be other generations – yet I keep fearing that something of civilization will be lost for good, as something was lost when Greece perished in just this way. Strange how one values civilization – more than all one's friends or anything – the slow achievement of men emerging from the brute – it seems the ultimate thing one lives for. I don't live for human happiness, but for some kind of struggling emergence of mind. And here, at most times, that is being helped on – and what has been done is given to new generations, who travel on from where we have stopped. And now it is all arrested, and no one knows if it will start again at anything like the point where it stopped.[1]

When this project began fifteen years ago, the two primary sources were John Searle's theory of institutional reality and Friedrich Hayek's analysis of the spontaneous development of order found in his monumental *Law, Legislation and Liberty*. The idea was to show how an understanding of the deontic structure of institutions, informed by Hayek's insights into the natural development of these rights and obligations within societies, could inform the contemporary debate about the nature of law. My ignorance of the historical depth of these topics made me believe that this would be a feasible project. Yet, over the course of this research, I have not only had the opportunity to explore an institutional world that is long since gone, but have also witnessed during these years the gradual, yet significant arrest of many of our own institutions. While, to my knowledge, the literati of Cambridge no longer go bathing in Grantchester as they once did, and while the educational, political and civic institutions of 2022 no longer reflect the status quo that was even two decades ago, the keynote of hope remains in the normativity that abides in each of us. These norms persist through the practice of law, in which we all engage, and through canon, to which all have access, even after each of us is gone.

Thanks to particularly persistent advisors, as well as intervening professional duties which have kept extending the project's timeline into the future, I was given occasion to wander back in time from the world of John Searle, Raimo

[1] Bertrand Russell in a letter written in Cambridge in 1915, displayed at the Orchard in Grantchester.

Tuomela and Margaret Gilbert to Weber, Durkheim, then Hegel, Hobbes, Spinoza, and Bodin. Moving from Hayek and Richard Posner, Hart, Dworkin and Raz, I had time to study enough of Hans Kelsen's work such that the Pure Theory of Law no longer seemed to be an obscure perspective of a continental jurist informed by a code law tradition, but rather the result of years of study immersed in an intellectual world which no longer exists for us today. And Kelsen was by no means the only of his generation, though the present work focuses mainly on Kelsen's contribution to the theory of law with significant assistance towards the end from the thoughts of Kelsen's early contemporary, Felix Somlo. There were dozens of jurisprudes from the turn of the 20th century up until the Great War who, though not as well received in the Anglophone world as Kelsen, were just as learned and sophisticated in their approach to the law.[2] Many of those who did not die in the first war, were either silenced in exile, such as Hermann Heller, or succumbed to either the ideology or careerist ambitions of National Socialism, such as Carl Schmitt.[3] As such, we now mostly have Kelsen in the world of law as a lucky specimen of one who escaped, just as in philosophy we came to have Kelsen's Viennese colleague, Carnap.

Kelsen's *Hauptprobleme der Staatsrechtslehre*, first published in 1911 at the age of 30, represents a standard of legal theoretical inquiry which in breadth and depth is unmatched today. As such, it is from my perspective not the result of historical inquiry that I have essentially started with Kelsen and worked backwards in time, but rather a matter of systematic and conceptual exigency:

Hans Kelsen developed a theory of the legal norm as it exists within a legal system. The legal norm which Kelsen conceives is that of a hypothetical imperative directed at officials: if citizen a does x, then official b shall respond by doing y. Through his postulate of the basic norm, Kelsen refuses to address the issue of how, why or wherein the normative force behind such norms exists. Kelsen also refuses to account for the agency of non-officials (i. e. citizens) in their interactions with the legal norm. Accordingly, the legal system for Kelsen is narrowly conceived and, within this delimitation, the legal norm enjoys a sphere of perfect ideality where it always fits perfectly within a hierarchy of norms and is always executed without fail. Kelsen refuses to inquire further into the basic norm, i. e. the issue of sovereignty, and refuses to account for legal norms being directly addressed to subjects because, in his reasoning, no norm can justify the legal system, or sovereignty, itself. For Kelsen, the existence of a legal system as well

---

2 One key example is František Weyr, who developed a 'normological' theory of the law in Brno. See Kubeš and Weinberger, *Die Brünner Rechtstheoretische Schule*.

3 An important step in the preservation of the legacy of Heller and the contextualization of the contributions of Schmitt was made by Dyzenhaus, *Legality and Legitimacy: Carl Schmitt, Hans Kelsen, and Hermann Heller in Weimar*.

as the obedience of its subjects to its legal norms is not reducible to a norm, but rather is a matter of fact and thus beyond the scope of a legal theory. Thus, he develops his Pure Theory with conspicuous brackets at each end. I believe it is possible to break-open these brackets within the ambit of a theory of law. I also believe that it is imperative to do so, for, without the sovereign and the subject, there is not much left to the concept of law.

I hope to show that sovereignty, subjectivity and normativity, or the sovereign, the subject and the (legal) norm are three wholly interdependent concepts: the meaning of each of these concepts entails the other two. The five chapters of this work seek to explore this relationship. Chapter I commences with an analysis of the legal norm. It is an open question whether Kelsen subscribed to an expressivist or hyletic conception of norms, or perhaps both at different times. Only with an hyletic conception does it make sense to speak of inherent relations between norms. However, von Wright suggests that even when working with an expressivist conception of legal norms, it is possible to consider norms within a broader context that includes the issuer and the addressee. Issuers and addressees, however, are facts. Relying on the is-ought distinction, Kelsen asserted that the arbitrary nature of legal norms is fundamentally different from the causal necessity of scientific (natural) laws: legal norms express an 'ought' whereas scientific laws describe an 'is'. I propose that for legal theory the core issue of the is-ought distinction can be more clearly perceived through Anscombe's distinction of directions of fit. Scientific laws would thus have a mind-to-world direction of fit and therefore primarily require reason, legal norms a world-to-mind direction of fit and therefore primarily require the will (of a sovereign). However, both the descriptive nature of scientific laws and the prescriptive nature of legal norms begins to blur on closer inspection, just as do the respective priorities of reason and will. Kelsen subscribed to the requirement of rationality in the law at the atomic level, but denied it at the systemic level once the big issues of the nature of sovereignty and the state came into question. In order to further develop this rational element of the law, it is necessary to determine the object of our knowledge at the level of the state.

Thus, in Chapter II, I seek to understand the modern concept of state that underlies most of legal theory as it has developed in the past 250 years. The key touchstone here is the concept of the absolute state and the figure of Leviathan. I seek to avoid interpreting the rise of Leviathan as a result of a 'social contract' according to which a strong man or group of men agree to establish peace and order in a society in exchange for total subservience. In contrast, I argue that Leviathan is not a great protector, but rather an actor, a fictive person who exercises authority on behalf of the many. Accordingly, Leviathan must be conceived as being normatively (legally) constituted as a function of the desire independent rationality that is afforded by human reason. Since Hobbes shows that desire independent rationality can only exist within a system of laws, human beings can only exist as persons, subjects, within the affordance of the state. Despite the severe limitations that Kelsen placed on his theory, this aspect of the legal order having priority to the legal subject is nonetheless a very Kelsenian point – at the heart of the Kelsenian theory is the unity of the whole of the legal order.

In Chapter II I argue, with Kelsen, that the sovereign cannot be conceived as a physical person but that it nonetheless must be conceived as a unity. However, if the sovereign is not a physical person, then it, like the law, is just a construct. Of the three necessarily interdependent concepts, sovereign, law, and subject, the first two turn out to have no existence as natural facts. The question is whether the constructed existence of the sovereign and the law is just make-believe or whether it is actual (*wirklich*). In Chapter III I explore this issue through the lens of 'political theology'. Here, I argue again with Kelsen that legal theory and theology are basically two different discourses describing one common issue: what is the relationship between the individual and the collective? Kelsen and I diverge, however, when characterizing the nature of this relationship. Kelsen maintains that while the individual used to be actually bound to the collective (or God or state) on the basis of an actual, though mistaken, belief in a supernatural entity, modern (legal) science no longer needs to resort to such superstition in accounting for the normativity of a legal order. In contrast, I argue that the relationship between the individual and the collective, whether in the religious or political realms, never actually had much to do with belief in a supernatural being. Instead, the actuality of this relationship between the individual and the collective is based on a normative stance, a categorical 'leap of faith', not unlike that which forms Leviathan, in which the individual recognizes that it is something in the collective, i. e. a rational being, which it could never be without it. As a result, sovereignty and the law are not mistaken notions that are holdovers of a bygone era, but rather essentially constituent components of individual subjectivity.

If the sovereign, the subject and the law are concepts that are dependent on one another, how does this relationship come to be? The scholastics might have said that God creates the order and places a sovereign in charge of the order to ensure that it functions properly. However, without a divine architect, is the relation between sovereign and subject through the law merely random? Have we established a necessary theoretical role of the collective in the subjectivity of the individual only to realize that the actual normative relations between individuals are just the result of arbitrary power relations? Chapters IV and V take account of these issues. In Chapter IV, I look to the theory of one of Kelsen's early contemporaries, Felix Somlo. One of the difficulties in accounting for the content of the law lies in explaining its hierarchical, top-down, nature. Yet, Somlo points out that the concept of sovereignty, i. e. that which enjoys a generalized habit of obedience, in no way entails the existence of a hierarchical legal order. Instead, sovereignty only requires that there be a source which (implicitly or explicitly) issues norms covering a broad range of human conduct and that these norms are generally obeyed. Nothing in the concept of sovereignty requires that a particular government have a monopoly on legislation and, even if we would stipulate that the sovereign authorizes the government to enact laws, no sovereign can ever authorize another (secondary source) to counteract the laws of itself (the primary source). Because Somlo rejects the hierarchical model of a master imposing duties, there is no clear way for him to identify that which is the law. As a result, Somlo insists that legal norms exist only as logical sentences in context (*Satz im Zusammenhang*) and thus, since the context of each sentence depends on all other legal norms, that they can actually only exist in the form of a *plurale tantum*.

Chapter V takes its inspiration from Brian Leiter's legal naturalism, according to which facts are that which actually matters in a theory of adjudication. I agree that facts are of primary relevance for the law, but, following on the previous chapters and especially Chapter IV, the relevance of fact begins to play out very differently than how Leiter envisions. Whereas Leiter conceives of factual relevance as ultimately detracting from law's normativity, I appeal to the American Legal Realists and the idea of the generic form in order to argue that it is fact, or rather matters of fact, which are actually the source of law's normativity. This serves to indicate the proper 'logic' of norms, according to which norms arise out of general patterns of conduct among individuals as they act in groups, classes and institutions. The law, especially adjudication, plays a crucial role in reflecting upon this reality and then expressing it in the form of rules.

In the Conclusion I consider the role of this reflected normativity on the constitution of the individual and the constitution of the state. On the one hand, such normativity is essential for a common political existence even though, at the individual level, foreordained normativity can also be restrictive. On the other hand, the fact that normativity is derived from the generic forms of conduct means that there is always a critical moment that injects itself into law's normativity, thereby allowing for critical reflection.

The title, *Inverting the Norm – Law as the Form of Common Practice*, refers not only to an attempt at switching our perspective on legal normativity from top-down to bottom-up. The argument underlying such a switch reflects on an aspect of our social reality which goes beyond just legal theory: humans are not automata, but agents and agency in some way always depends on inverting the norm. This, importantly, is not the same as rejecting the norm. We are always already constituted by the law and as such cannot escape it. At the same time, the law is our reflected, and thus sovereign, form of common practice.

I am greatly thankful to the many mentors and colleagues who, over the years, have contributed their time and insights towards the realization of this project. I thank Pirmin Stekeler-Weithofer for generously agreeing to act as the advisor for the dissertation and for welcoming my project at the University of Leipzig. However, more important than the administrative affiliation was the theoretical contribution which serves, in my mind, as the chief influence in the text, even if the ideas expressed herein are all too imperfectly executed by its author. I also thank Georg Meggle, whose insights on language, meaning and social ontology have been indispensable for the work. I thank John Searle, Nikos Psarros, Christian Schmidt, Hans-Bernhard Schmid and Åsa Burman for the many valuable philosophical discussions over the years. I thank Tom Smith, Laurence Claus and Larry Alexander from the University of San Diego, who propelled me to engage in the following legal theoretical investigation. Especially the law of contract, as taught to me in San Diego, has been relentless in leading me to repeatedly consider the nature of it all. Further thanks are due to Nigel Simmonds, David Dyzenhaus, Torben Spaak, Mauro Zamboni and Benno Zabel who have provided valuable comments on passages of the text.

I dedicate the book to Beatrice … *che mi fa andare*.

Vienna, May 2022 Trevor N. Wedman

Table of Contents

Introduction

The following is an attempt to investigate the law on its own terms, not as a sociological, critical or meta-ethical study, but rather as a legal theoretical project in the narrowest sense. While each other approach must be recognized for its contribution to the understanding of and even shaping what the law is today, no consideration of the law from the outside can yield the perspective that can singularly be won through an examination of the law as law.[1] The task is not to deconstruct and contextualize, but to lay a foundation, ὑπόθεσις, which may prove fruitful for future endeavors.

This project conceives of the law as a set of norms that places legal subjects in relation to the legal sovereign, though certainly the main task for any legal theory lies in exploring just what is meant by each of these concepts, the legal subject (or citizen), the legal sovereign (or state) and their normative relation. The upshot of focusing on the relational aspect of the law, as opposed to, for example, the aspect of commands or exclusive state power, is first and foremost to pledge allegiance to the approach of Hans Kelsen, who viewed the legal norm as connecting different points of attribution, even if in substance and outcome I will ultimately arrive at the opposite theoretical pole of Kelsen's theory, at least in its late phase. Beyond being a Kelsenian partisan though, my defining the law as a

[1] Here in common with Kelsen, who states in *Der soziologische und der juristische Staatsbegriff*, p. 93, in the context of the theory of the state: "Was bedeutet nun diese Tatsache, dass nur eine wenigstens bis zu einem gewissen Grade wirksame Staats- oder Rechtsideologie Relevanz behauptet? In welchem Verhältnis steht dieses Minimum an Wirksamkeit zu der Geltung, steht die Normativität der Staats- und Rechtsordnung, d. i. ihre spezifische Geltungsexistenz, zu ihrer Faktizität, richtiger: zur Faktizität, d. i. der Wirksamkeit des Vorstellens, Fühlens, Wollens, kurz des Erlebens dieser Ordnung? Zunächst sicherlich in keinem anderen Verhältnis als jenem, in dem sonst ein psychischer Akt zu dem ihm zugeordneten geistigen Inhalt steht! So wie wenn man, z. B. zu sagen pflegt, es könnte keinen pythagoräischen Lehrsatz geben, wenn es keine Menschen gäbe, die ihn denken, das heißt, dass der psychische Akt des Denkens zwar die conditio sine qua non, nicht aber die conditio per quam ist für den geistigen Inhalt, den man als pythagoräischen Lehrsatz bezeichnet. Dessen Geltung findet ihren spezifischen Grund nicht in der Tatsache, dass er gedacht wird, sondern in irgendwelchen letzten Axiomen. So findet auch die als 'Staat' bezeichnete Zwangsordnung den Grund ihrer Geltung durchaus nicht in der Wirklichkeit der Wollungen und Handlungen, die sie zum Inhalt haben." If law is to persist as a science unto itself, its foundation must correspondingly lie within the law, and not outside of it.

relation positions the legal norm squarely within the realm of institutional, or man-made, reality.

Importantly with the definition above, this approach is committed to considering the relations between legal sovereigns and legal subjects as normative in nature, corresponding to rights (and correlative duties) on the parts of legal subjects and legal sovereigns. Though this is clearly inherent in the concept of a *legal* subject and *legal* sovereign, it is also not trivial to note that neither the legal subject nor the legal sovereign can be similarly situated *without* the law as they are *within* it. If this is the case, then individual laws, and law in general, are not merely descriptive of a present state of affairs, but rather constitutive thereof, presuming of course that legal subjects and legal sovereigns indeed have something to do with states of affairs. Legal norms, i. e. laws, do not have a mind-to-world, but rather a world-to-mind direction of fit. Because the 'world' in this case, i. e. the addressees of the law, consists of volitional subjects who through the law are meant to conform their actions to the 'mind' of the sovereign, these individual laws must therefore be considered normative, or action-guiding.

If the law is normative, then we must be able to account for why we should follow the law. In other words, how does the law function to make the world match the mind (or many minds) of the sovereign? The following text postulates that a legal subject (or legal sovereign) cannot but follow the law. Both the legal subject and the legal sovereign are fictions (constructs) whose sole and formal function in the legal system is to follow the law and whose function in legal science is to serve as points of attribution without which the normativity of legal norms cannot be understood. A legal subject, as an abstraction, has no free will and cannot violate the law. Indeed, the legal subject is purely ideal and does not exist in space and time. As an ideal entity the legal subject can only act according to the idea which creates it and the idea which creates the legal subject is the law itself.

However, what is the relationship between legal subjects (or legal sovereigns) and subjects more generally? Subjectivity and therewith agency do not exist outside of the universe of valid statements that also, in one form or another, comprise the law. Of course, a legal system does not tie sanctions to all potential actions that a subject can undertake, just as a legal system does not contain a listing of all potential valid statements of law. However, all potential actions and all potentially valid statements that can be made are nonetheless possible only within and therefore are encompassed by the legal system, the law. Thus, in this conception, the subject (or sovereign) is identical to the legal subject (or legal sovereign) and as a result cannot but follow the law.[2]

[2] Cf. Stekeler, *Hegels Phänomenologie des Geistes*, pp. 27, 28: "Denn die eigentliche Ein-

Stating that a subject must necessarily follow the law still does not function as a satisfactory response to the traditional problem of obligation in the law. The issue of obligation on the part of an ideal subject can only be resolved once we understand the ideal subject, as well as the legal subject and the law itself as ideal entities of a generic kind, the existence of which is derived entirely from actual situations in fact brought on by the conduct of real (factual) individuals. The question, why should I, as a flesh and blood individual, follow the law, can thus be answered with the reply that I, as an individual, follow the law to the extent that I *am* actually a subject and, in a derivative sense to be explored in greater detail, a sovereign. The categorical imperative of subjectivity is that any individual can only act according to norms which should become a universal law or, in other words, which constitute the universe of valid norms comprising the law. This brings us to the fundamental issue of the relation between individuals and collectives – legal theory is not possible without political theory, and more specifically social ontology.

As with many theoretical debates, the discourse regarding the nature of law is fraught with many ambiguous terms. The following initial introduction to some of the concepts used in this text may serve to indicate the contours of the argument which I set forth:

'Norm' and 'value' are roughly synonymous in the present text and can be taken to mean that which is action-guiding (*handlungsleitend*). The connotation of 'value' is more abstract and general than that of 'norm'. A norm is especially an expressed or implied legal norm, although values which exist outside of the legal realm can also be expressed or implied as norms. Only a norm or value can be action-guiding, which indicates that the present text employs a Kantian understanding of action – I can only act according to a norm. Conduct that occurs on the basis of brute desires or instincts is not an action, but a re-action to stimulus.

As with 'norm' and 'value', 'normativity' is roughly synonymous with 'validity'. A legal theoretical project in a social ontological vein seeks precisely to explain the equivalence of these two terms, one being of ethical, the other of legal provenance. To say that a norm is valid is to say that it is binding, to say that a key feature of the law is its normativity is to say that legal norms at some level must guide the subjects' actions. It is clear that in using normativity and validity as synonyms, the normal boundary of a positivistic legal theory is thereby erased. As will be set forth in further detail below, the following is nonetheless an expo-

sicht (der *Phänomenologie des Geistes*) ist die, dass wir erst vermöge der Teilnahme an einer allgemeinen Praxis zu personalen Subjekten werden, dass also das emphatische Selbstbewusstsein des Ich sich erst aus einem diffusen transzendentalen Wir oder Man entwickelt."

sition of positivistic legal theory and does not entail a natural law conception, at least not within the conventional, Aristotle's, Thomas' or Finnis', sense.

The present text seeks to avoid the terms 'moral' and 'morality'. The universe of all values or norms that exist are relevant for the legal system and, as will be argued in Chapter IV, form part of the legal order, even if the great majority of these norms and values would never be subject to sanction or codification in many if not most legal systems. I reject both (i) the notion (as supported by some natural law theorists) that there could be a set of (proper legal or even divine) norms against which individual norms within a given legal order can be judged and (ii) the notion (as supported by some legal positivists) that the value of a legal system itself can be judged by an external or my own internal moral compass.

A 'human' is an individual in its natural, brute state. A 'person' is a human in its normative relation to other humans, who are thus presumed to be capable of entering into reciprocal normative relations and are so recognized as persons themselves. A 'people' is a group of persons with a common normative background or which participate in the same society. A 'society' forms the common normative background of a people.

With Austin, 'sovereignty' or 'sovereign' relates to a highest power that enjoys a general habit of obedience on the part of a people. Rousseau's *pouvoir constitué* is synonymous with sovereignty and *pouvoir constituant* (nation) is integrally related to the concepts of highest power and generalized habit of obedience. As is familiar with the distinction between the President of the United States and the Presidency of the United States, the sovereign is never identical with a given individual, though in some legal theories and in some legal systems the sovereign may be fully embodied by a given individual, for example an absolute monarch. For the purpose of the following text, sovereignty is solely an attribute of the state, never of an individual alone, and carries with it the competency of creating and perpetuating laws. Accordingly, 'l'etat c'est moi' could never be the case, except perhaps for Robinson Crusoe before Friday.

The 'constitution' is the political form of the state (*determinans* of *status*). The state is identical to the legal order (see Kelsen).

1. A Man at Rest

Mais il suffisait que, dans mon lit même, mon sommeil fut profond et détendit entièrement mon esprit; alors celui-ci lâchait le plan du lieu où je m'étais endormi, et quand je m'éveillais au milieu de la nuit, comme j'ignorais où je me trouvais, je ne savais même pas au premier instant qui j'étais; j'avais seulement dans sa simplicité première, le sentiment de l'existence comme il peut frémir au fond d'un animal; j'étais plus dénué que l'homme des cavernes; mais alors le souvenir – non encore de lieu où j'étais, mais de quelques-uns de ceux que j'avais habités et où j'aurais pu être – venait à moi comme un secours d'en haut pour me tirer du néant d'où je n'aurais pu sortir tout seul; je passais en une seconde par-dessus des siècles de civilisation, et l'image confusément entrevue de lampes à pétrole, puis des chemises à col rabattu, recomposaient peu à peu les traits originaux de mon moi.[3]

Donoso Cortes imagines the state as the great protector of the people, corrupted by original sin, in desperate need of guidance on its eschatological path to spiritual and political glory. Carl Schmitt views the state as the product of an existential, political struggle. For Rudolf Smend, the state best serves as an instrument for integrating a people into a unity. Hans Kelsen thinks that the state should best be conceived as nothing but the legal order, comprised of formal rules that clearly and transparently guide officials in the conduct of their public affairs. Proudhon sees the state itself as corrupt and Karl Marx sees it as an enabler of a particular class.

The concept of law can hardly be divorced from the concept of state. Deriving our understanding of law from an understanding of the state necessarily presupposes a consensus about the nature, purpose or scope of the state which, as evidenced by the sampling of theorists above, should not be taken for granted. As will be discussed, the state, like the legal order, is an institutional fact, a construct that is capable of taking a plethora of forms, of persistently resisting creation, doggedly persisting throughout time, or transforming quite unexpectedly. It is possible to create a legal theory on the basis of any given or conceived state, but choosing such a particular state as the legal theoretical starting point results in a concept of law that is equally particular, local in its scope. This is inherently problematic if the desire is not to create a particular, but rather a general, foundational legal theory.

Thus, instead of focusing on a necessarily local conception of the state as can be found throughout the 19th and 20th centuries in the works of their legal and political theorists, I would rather start by focusing on that other *sine qua non* of the law that is not the state, namely the social human being, the generic man. In doing so, we might take as an initial image a specimen far more *local* in nature than any of the conceptions of state listed above, i. e. a fin-de-siècle Parisian man lying in his bed, which can serve as an icon into the state of man most generally. Just like with our conception of state, our conception of man will prejudice our conception of law if we conceive of man, the legal person, too narrowly. Thus, if we take man already compromised in his legal status, like Dostoevsky's Raskolnikov, subject to law's sanction, or Mann's Thomas Buddenbrook, enjoying the privilege of property, or if we take a pre-legal man in a state of nature, whether this be Hobbes' warrior, Locke's nascent proprietor or Rousseau's noble savage,

[3] Proust, *Du cote de chez Swann*, p. 14.

then our legal theory will be equally biased toward the interests of criminal law, property law, human rights et cetera. Even if any such a man ever really existed as that abstract person imagined by Hobbes, Locke or Rousseau, such a figure, though real, is much less relevant (*wirklich*) for our present purposes than the figure of pure fiction described by Proust above that reflects itself in the ready imagination of an everyday modern man.

In his own perception, the man in question is at first in the depths of sleep, unconscious of his own identity, his place, even himself. On the verge of waking, he perceives a very basic, brute existence, perhaps equal to, but certainly weaker than that of a normal animal. A rational creature, this waking man is still more depraved of reason than a cave man. But then memories enter his mind of places where he has been or maybe imagined himself to be. These memories save, distract, him from the initial brute and carnal impressions of his waking self. The memory, or impression, of 'centuries of civilization' transform our man from a scared individual to a man with a ruffled collar, lying at rest in his bed with the full imaginary arsenal of a person of privilege in the most cultivated place in the world at the most developed time of our history. In locating the baseline for a general theory of law, we cannot look for a man in his 'natural' state because the law has precious little to do with nature. A man in action is likewise overdetermined as being necessarily either legal or illegal in his actions. A man at rest, however, at the moment of waking, stands before the entirety of the legal system as a child upon the threshold of a playground. The legal order constitutes the entirety of his potential and, as he embarks on his day, he will make thousands of decisions each of which determines his relation to the law, his legal status. Our man is not alone in this endeavor though, but rather has centuries of civilization at his disposal, guiding him on his path. He is homo oeconomicus, but he is also Moses on the mount. He is the good Samaritan, he is a Southern slave, he is a battered woman and a starving immigrant. He is Ebenezer Scrooge, he is a consummate debtor. Once he gets out of bed, our man at rest, who is none other than the ordinary reasonable prudent person, will act not on his own in the face of the law, but rather on the precedent of these and millions of other agents and figures of agency that constitute the centuries of civilization forming his horizon of action, without which our man is just an outcast, naked boy faced with an arbitrary system of coercion.

2. Regarding 2.061

Die Sachverhalte sind von einander nicht unabhängig, sondern *abhängig.*[4]

3. Empiricism or Positivism

Eugenio Bulygin identifies a conflict at the core of Hans Kelsen's Pure Theory of Law which comes from what Bulygin describes as fundamentally opposed philosophical traditions, i.e. Kantianism and Positivism.[5] As Kantian influences in the Pure Theory, Bulygin identifies: (i) "the characterization of legal norms as ideal entities belonging to the world of Sollen ('ought'), distinct from the world of natural reality or the world of Sein ('is')"; (ii) "the conception of validity qua binding force"; (iii) "the normativity of legal science"; and (iv) the basic norm as a transcendental category. As positivistic influences in the Pure Theory, Bulygin identifies: (a) "a sharp separation between 'is' and 'ought'"; (b) "the non-cognitivist conception of norms and value judgments as prescriptions that are neither true nor false"; (c) "the positivity of law, the thesis that all law is positive, that is to say, is created and destroyed by human acts"; and (d) "a sharp distinction between description and prescription (or evaluation), between reason and volition, between cognition of law and the creation of law, between the sciences of law and legal politics".[6]

Among these two sets, none of the Kantian influences fit very easily into the 'positivist' set while, interestingly, the only influence within the 'positivist' set that fits neatly into the Kantian set is precisely that of the positivity of the law, i.e. that law (and legal norms) are created and destroyed by human acts. As a result, there is reason for an inchoate suspicion that the tenet that is the namesake of legal positivism, i.e. the positivity of the law, is actually not adverse to Kantianism, or at least to Kant's critiques of pure and practical reason, and may well even originate in it. Meanwhile the other three 'positivist' characteristics – (a) the is-ought distinction, (b) the non-cognitivist conception, and (d) the distinction between descriptions and prescriptions – are indeed antithetical to Kantianism and must originate from a different source. I would posit that it is this dichotomy, more so than any of the ideas that are properly 'original' to the Pure Theory of Law, that makes Kelsen's work so rich. This is not, as Bulygin would imply, a conflict between metaphysical idealism on the one hand and the aspirations of

[4] Cf. Wittgenstein, *Tractatus*, 2.061: "Die Sachverhalte sind von einander unabhängig."

[5] Bulygin (1998).

[6] Id. at pp. 299, 300.

positivism (meaning: science) on the other, but rather between dueling scientific conceptions on either side of the development of *logical empiricism* at the beginning of the 20th century. It is not so much Kantianism vs. Positivism that is the threshhold issue in Kelsen's oeuvre, but rather Positivism as the form that (Neo-) Kantianism had taken by 1911 and Empiricism as the set of background assumptions that would be adopted by the Vienna Circle within the next two decades and which would continue to accompany Kelsen throughout the remainder of his career.

The import of Kelsen's theory is thus not just emblematic of the transition undertaken by the concept of law in the 20th century, but that of philosophy and society generally from the Neo-Kantian synthesis that had obtained in Central Europe prior to World War I to the value-free logical empiricism of the Anglo-American centered, post-World War II world. The current work begins on the assumption that this rupture has occurred and that an exploration of the conceptual dimensions of this turn towards a value-free science is nowhere better placed than in an analysis of the normative science par excellence, i. e. a theory of law.

In science there are no depths, everywhere is surface[7] – this slogan of the logically empiricist Vienna Circle serves as a frame for understanding the project of legal reductivism and simultaneously indicates its limitations:

Wenn jemand behauptet: 'es gibt keinen Gott', 'der Urgrund der Welt ist das Unbewußte', 'es gibt eine Entelechie als leitendes Prinzip im Lebewesen', so sagen wir ihm nicht: 'was du sagst, ist falsch'; sondern wir fragen ihn: 'was meinst du mit deinen Aussagen?' Und dann zeigt es sich, daß es eine scharfe Grenze gibt zwischen zwei Arten von Aussagen. Zu der einen gehören die Aussagen, wie sie in der empirischen Wissenschaft gemacht werden; ihr Sinn läßt sich feststellen durch logische Analyse, genauer: durch Rückführung auf einfachste Aussagen über empirisch Gegebenes. Die anderen Aussagen, zu denen die vorhin genannten gehören, erweisen sich als völlig bedeutungsleer, wenn man sie so nimmt, wie der Metaphysiker sie meint. Man kann sie freilich häufig in empirische Aussagen umdeuten; dann verlieren sie aber den Gefühlsgehalt, der dem Metaphysiker meist gerade wesentlich ist.[8]

It is of course possible to cull as 'meaningless statements of a metaphysician' all statements of our expression that refer to something beyond the simplest empirical facts. Indeed, precisely this approach has often succeeded as a force of disruption in the face of mistaken preconceptions, yielding tremendous results in many of the sciences. This includes the law – some of Bentham's critiques against Blackstone were indeed legitimate. The issue with the quote from the Vienna Circle above is that scientific inquiry cannot be engaged-in merely through tearing down the building of science as it has been handed down up to a

[7] Damböck, Der Wiener Kreis. Ausgewählte Texte: "Wissenschaftliche Weltauffassung: Der Wiener Kreis": "In der Wissenschaft gibt es keine Tiefen, überall ist Oberfläche."

[8] Ibid.

certain point. It is clear that all of our impressions can be reduced to the elemental phenomena of the empirical world. However, this alone does not characterize the human experience. In addition to *Gefühlsgehalt*, also knowledge, thought, community and meaning, all core aspects of the human existence, may be lost when transitioning from the given statement to its empirical equivalent. None of these are directly *given to*, but rather *constituted by*, us as a function of our rational, logical apparatus.[9]

It may be necessary to return to the 'surface' of empirical reality every now and again in order to critically examine the conceptions which pre-determine our knowledge. However, this knowledge itself does not exist at the surface, but rather in the depths. Social reality, including all of the sciences, is deep, with iterations upon iterations of institutional construction, designed with the blueprint of normativity. Some of this is superfluous, and if we assign the moniker of 'metaphysics' to that which is superfluous, then we should all be able to agree to the banishment of metaphysics from our sciences. However, not everything that constitutes our society, or that is not directly perceptible as a matter of empirical fact, is metaphysics in this derogative sense. Thus, a further differentiation is needed between the depths of human knowledge made by and for ourselves and the surface of empirical phenomena: between positivism and empiricism.

A similar sentiment to that of the Vienna Circle above can be found already with Bentham:

> Common law,…, that fictitious composition which has no known person for its author, no known assemblage of words for its substance, forms every where the main body of the legal fabric: like that fancied ether, which, in default of sensible matter, fills up the measure of the universe. Shreds and scraps of real law, stuck upon that imaginary ground, compose the furniture of every national code. What follows? – that he who, for the purpose just mentioned or for any other, wants an example of a complete body of law to refer to, must begin with making one.[10]

Bentham says that if there is to be a legal system built on a solid basis then, one (i.e. Bentham) must make one himself. In doing so, Bentham operates on the basis of a logic of the will according to a principle of utility – meaning, basically, that which makes sense.[11] As Montague suggests in the footnote below, the prin-

---

[9] Probably the most eloquent formulation is John Searle's: x counts as y in c. Cf. Carnap's *Der logische Aufbau der Welt.*

[10] Bentham, *An Introduction to the Principles of Morals and Legislation*, Preface.

[11] See id. at Ch. I, Sec. 2.: "By the principle of utility is meant that principle which approves or disapproves of every action whatsoever, according to the tendency which it appears to have to augment or diminish the happiness of the party whose interest is in question: or, what is the same thing in other words, to promote or to oppose that happiness." See also Montague's introduction to *The Fragment on Government* (Clarendon Press 1891), p. 43: "The truth is that such a principle as the principle of utility is valuable not as a creative, but as a critical principle. It is valuable as a test, not as a germ. Its true potency is negative, a potency to lay bare injustice, to

ciple of utility, like the Vienna Circle's reduction of statements to the empirically given, works first and foremost as a critical principle. However, Bentham, and then his pupil Austin, moved beyond the reductive aspect to focus on the positive, thereby attempting to develop, in some ways from scratch, a system of law. This is also a form of positivism, but not the kind to be expounded here.

Justice Holmes cautions us that the life of the law is not logic, but experience. A perusal of his opinions suggests that this experience is not that of the cold facts of life or a cynical understanding of how judges decide cases based on party affiliation or ideology, but rather it is an experience of the law as it is lived in practice, both in harmony and discord. This understanding of the law in practice suggests that there are practice 'forms' underlying our social endeavors and that the science of law consists in the understanding and determination of these forms, i. e. norms. As such, the life of the law must be both experience and logic – this, so the assumption of this work, must be the basis for any legal positivism.

4. Radical Legal Positivism

The following presents a defense of a radical version of legal positivism. As a radical version, it will affirm many of the core tenets of the doctrine while arguing that it has sometimes gone astray by focusing too much on certain peripheral aspects. The touchstone on which this analysis is based is the core attribute of legal positivism – the separability thesis. It is this touchstone which has succeeded in both guiding and misguiding the debate within the Oxonian vein. The separability thesis has afforded great progress in the field of analytical jurisprudence insofar as it correctly suggests that the law, as an objective, jurisprudentially verifiable social fact, is logically distinct and independent from morality. Understood as a separate normative system, any such 'moral' system, being separate from the law, is necessarily subjective and unverifiable from the jurisprudential perspective. However, the separability thesis has hindered progress in the field insofar as, along with morality, it has eschewed value altogether, for, as will be

---

unravel sophistry, to cancel verbiage. For such purposes it is most efficacious. Is a law really and not merely apparently partial? Is it an instrument for aggrandizing a class of citizens without any reference to the common weal? If so, it will not bear to be tried by a standard which requires the legislator to seek the happiness of the greatest number and of each individual equally with every other individual. Is a law incapable of being explained or justified except by merely technical arguments, by professional petitio principii or professional pedantry? If so, it will not bear to be tried by a standard which makes happiness the object of all legislation."

claimed, value in some form must be the logical basis of the law, namely that without which there is no viable concept of law.[12]

The *radicality* of the version of legal positivism presented here consists not just in providing a countervailing interpretation of legal positivism, but in seeking a return to the 'roots' of the doctrine. These roots of legal positivism are to be found in a concerted effort of creating a scientific approach to law. While these efforts have been quite explicit in the fifty years since *The Concept of Law*, they did not just begin in the twentieth century. Austin set out to scientifically determine the field of jurisprudence as did, before him, Bentham seek to revolutionize the practice of law and legislation according to the principle (i. e. value) of utility. Even Blackstone, the primary recipient of Bentham's ire, had himself sought to systematize the amorphous body of English common law precedents as an object of study and professionalization. A cursory study of Pufendorf, Grotius or Suarez will reveal theorists who, far from blindly accepting natural law tendencies or divine revelations into their models, were extremely concerned with developing a rational conception of the law. Even Thomas Aquinas, one of the most natural law oriented or 'metaphysical' legal theorists, held scientific rigor to be a core principle of his investigations.

Indeed, the primary difference between legal theories in the twentieth century and the legal theories which preceded them is not a newly found commitment to a scientific approach to the law, but rather the shift which occurred throughout all sciences in the first half of the twentieth century from a rationalist to an empiricist understanding of the world.[13] The consequences of this shift, both positive and negative, have been felt in all fields. However, nowhere has this shift been more fundamental to our understanding of the field itself than in the science of law.

---

[12] See Kramer, *In Defense of Legal Positivism*. Part of the difficulty of the separability thesis lies in the ambiguity of that which is to be considered separately from the law. Matthew Kramer insists that law should be separable, though not necessarily separate, from morality and contraposes "morality" to "evil", facticity and prudence. The preceding paragraph maintains, however, that the separability thesis has gone astray when refusing to consider questions of value *in* the law. Kramer conflates the two terms when he says that moral considerations can creep into legal analysis when we consider how the law can be seen to have an inherent "value" through considerations of procedure or outcomes (see 5–7). However, to say that the law is of value *to us* is once again quite different than saying that value is essential to or constituent of the law. For the countervailing position to Kramer's, see Nigel Simmonds' *Law as a Moral Idea*. And in contrast to Simmonds' maximalist idea of morality in the law, see also Alexy's *Begriff und Geltung des Rechts*.

[13] See, for example, the first sentence of *The Concept of Law*: "My aim in this book has been to further the understanding of law, coercion, and morality as different but related social phenomena."

The contemporary form of legal positivism which seeks to divorce the concept of law from any inherent form of value may best be seen as resulting from a certain interpretation of Kelsen's theory of law, according to which Kelsen, in seeking to lay the foundation for a scientific approach to law, restricted the question of normative value to mere secondary norms which then led him to postulate a purely formal and thus entirely valueless basic norm.[14] Kelsen constructed his theory with the dual objectives of being both normative and scientific. However, whether due to conflicts within Kelsen's own world view, failings on the part of his interpreters or the failings of Kelsen's exposition itself, the normative has mostly been forgotten and replaced with a kind of naive empiricism with regard to how we determine the content of the law.

While the effects of Kelsen's Pure Theory of Law may have been counterproductive on this view, there is no denying that the theory itself is stunning in its elegance. In what follows, I will pursue what I consider to be Kelsen's core idea which is found at the beginning of his *Allgemeine Staatslehre*: the state and the individuals in it can be conceived as belonging (i) to the natural order governed by laws of causality or (ii) to a normative order governed by human laws.[15] While

---

[14] See Paulson in introduction to *Normativity and Norms*, xxix–xxx for the discussion of secondary (hierarchical) norms and xliii ff. regarding the value-less basic norm. Though Paulson attributes Kelsen's skepticism toward normativity only to the 'late' phase, there are certainly elements thereof in the early writings as well, especially with regard to the Vaihingerian fictions as can be seen in Kelsen's introduction to the 2nd edition of the Hauptprobleme as well as Kelsen's article "Zur Theorie der juristischen Fiktionen. Mit besonderer Berücksichtigung von Vaihingers Philosophie des Als Ob" (1919).

[15] There are two passages from the first chapter of the *Allgemeine Staatslehre* that deserve quoting here: "Dabei ist es durchaus nicht etwa bloß das Faktum, dass Menschen den Staat für eine Autorität halten, das von den Rechtssoziologen konstatiert wird; diese begnügen sich nicht mit der Feststellung, dass Menschen von irgendwelchen, Autorität zum Inhalte habenden, Vorstellungen motiviert werden, sondern sie machen den Inhalt dieser Vorstellung zu ihrem Gegenstand, indem sie den Staat wesentlich als verpflichtende Autorität charakterisieren. Damit statten sie ihn aber mit einem Wertelement aus, das in einer kausalwissenschaftlich orientierten Sozialpsychologie oder Soziologie keinen Platz finden kann. Der Staat als verpflichtende Autorität – und anders kann sein Wesen nicht ausgedruckt werden – ist aber ein Wert oder – sofern der satzmäßige Ausdruck des Wertes ausgedruckt wird – eine Norm, bzw. ein System von Normen und als solches wesensverschieden von der wertindifferenten, spezifisch-realen Tatsache des Vorstellens oder Wollens einer Norm" (14–15). Then, at pp. 18, 19, Kelsen continues: "Unbeschadet der grundsätzlichen und uneingeschränkten Disparität der beiden Systeme wird man ohne weiteres die Tatsache zugestehen müssen, dass der Inhalt der Normen, und speziell der Rechtsnormen, die man als gültig voraussetzt, dem Inhalt des tatsächlichen Verhaltens bis zu einem gewissen Grade entspricht, dass tatsächlich nur Rechtsnormen als gültig vorausgesetzt werden, deren Vorstellungen wirksam sind [...] Diese durch ein Maximum und ein Minimum bestimmte Beziehung zwischen dem Inhalt des als Sollordnung geltenden Rechts oder Staates und dem Inhalt der korrespondierenden Seinsordnung tatsächlichen Geschehens (als

a natural or social scientist may concern himself with the former, the problem of law only exists with the latter. This basic insight, now often ignored, seems to have been largely accepted in the initial flurry of legal theoretical publishing following the release of Kelsen's *Allgemeine Staatslehre* and leading up to the dissolution of the Weimar Republic, and goes back to the neo-Kantian tradition which came to a pinnacle at the *fin de siècle*. Moreover, Kelsen's theory of the state as being identical with the legal order has the potential to revolutionize the Anglo-American understanding of the relationship between individuals, law and the state.

---

eines Stückes der Natur) ist es, die sich im Begriff der Positivität ausdrückt. Das Problem der Positivität erscheint demnach als das – keineswegs auf das Gebiet der Rechts- und Staatstheorie beschränkte – Problem der inhaltlichen Beziehungen zwischen einem System des Wertes und dem ihm korrespondierenden System der Wirklichkeit, d. h. als das Problem der sogenannten Wertverwirklichung."

Chapter I

Logic of Norms I

The investigation begins from the standpoint of a logic of norms as typically presupposed within the school of analytical legal philosophy. Here, I will address the issue of normativity as it pertains to the legal norm. The paradigmatic point of departure lies in the traditional separation of 'is' from 'ought' and to what extent this separation may nonetheless be overcome. Following in the tradition of Kelsen, the task is to conceive of the state and its individuals as belonging to a normative order comprised of laws of human making. However, in seeking to avoid the vacuity (and implicit nihilism) of Kelsen's free-standing basic norm,[1] I will attempt to account for the existence of the state on the one hand and the role of individual legal norms in guiding the action of individuals on the other. The thought of Georg Henrik von Wright provides a clue with which to develop such a framework which is capable of commenting on the contents of legal norms within a legal system, i.e. given the full context of legal sovereign, legal norm, and legal subject, as opposed to merely commenting on the contents of norms in the abstract.

1. A Normative State of Affairs

One can either have a cognitivist or a non-cognitivist conception of legal norms. To have a cognitivist conception of legal norms is to hold that there is something essential about norms, normative relations or normativity that can be known. If such knowledge can exist, then "one can truthfully say that something or other ought to or may be".[2] The cognitivist view entails that norms have an inherent relation to each other and is generally associated with a natural law position[3], though, depending on how natural law is defined, this need not be the case.

---

[1] Kletzer (2013), see Chapter III below.

[2] von Wright (1998, p. 369).

[3] Here Pufendorf may serve as a classic example of a natural law theorist in his *De Officio* preface (p. 13): "Es liegt auf der Hand, dass die Menschen die Kenntnis ihrer Pflichten, bestimmte Dinge in diesem Leben, weil sie ehrenhaft sind, zu tun und andere wegen ihrer Schändlichkeit zu unterlassen, aus drei Quellen schöpfen. Nämlich aus dem Lichte der Vernunft, aus

Perhaps because of this association with natural law, most legal theorists in the past couple of generations have been non-cognitivists and therefore have tended toward the expressivist conception of legal norms.[4] For von Wright, the non-cognitivist position "follows the pattern of a master imposing duties."[5] Likewise for Alchourrón and Bulygin, non-cognitivism entails that nothing is essential about

---

den staatlichen Gesetzen und aus der besonderen Offenbarung Gottes. Aus der ersten Quelle entspringen die allgemeinsten Pflichten des Menschen, besonders die, die ihn dazu befähigen, mit den anderen Menschen in Gemeinschaft zu leben. Aus der zweiten entspringen die Pflichten des Menschen, soweit er sein Leben als Untertan eines ganz bestimmten Staates führt. Und aus der dritten fließen schließlich die menschlichen Pflichten, die den Menschen als Christ treffen. Daraus ergeben sich auch drei verschiedene wissenschaftliche Disziplinen. Die erste ist die Wissenschaft des Naturrechts, das allen Völkern gemeinsam ist. Die zweite ist die Disziplin des positiven Rechts der einzelnen Staaten, die so vielfältig ist oder sein kann, wie es Staaten gibt, in die die Menschheit sich geteilt hat. Und die dritte Wissenschaft ist die Moraltheologie, die von dem Teil der Theologie zu unterscheiden ist, in dem die Glaubenswahrheiten dargelegt werden." Of interest is that while Pufendorf separates positive law (and divine law) from natural law, this does not mean that positive law, whether of a state or of God, is therefore to be understood as a set of non-cognitive expressions, since Pufendorf grounds the positive law of a state on the pre-existence of natural law and states that divine law only adds to natural law to the extent that revelation contains precepts that humans alone, without divine intervention, could not grasp. In contrast to Pufendorf, the present work assumes that there is only one source of law, i. e. positive law, which comprises norms of a cognitive quality. Just how norms with a cognitive quality come to exist within a state is a key question going forward.

[4] See Alchourrón and Bulygin (1998, p. 387 ff.). Alchourrón and Bulygin divide legal theories into hyletic conceptions entailing that legal norms have meanings and expressive conceptions entailing that they have no such meanings. "Most legal and moral philosophers as well as deontic logicians share the expressive conception of norms", which means that they hold that "there can be no logic of norms, because there can be no logical relations among norms" (388). This can be contrasted with von Kutschera (2021): "Die nichtkognitivistischen Deutungen erweisen sich alle als unhaltbar und werden gegenwärtig auch kaum mehr vertreten." In his *Grundlagen der Ethik*, von Kutschera pursues the clearer distinction on the one hand between cognitivism and non-cognitivism, which is whether or not normative statements can be true or false, and on the other between the performative modes of statements, i. e. the expressive, evocative and descriptive, which refer to whether the illocutionary focus of the statement is on the speaker, the listener or the matter of fact contained in the statement. As such, depending on the context, the statement "It is time to go to bed" can be an expression of the desire or will on the part of the speaker for himself or others to retire, it can also be a command or request for the listener to go to sleep, it can also be a statement about the time of day relative to the need to sleep, or importantly it can include two or all three of these aspects. While an expressivist conception of norms could therefore also permit a descriptive aspect, this certainly need not be the case. Indeed, the expressivism on which Alchourrón and Bulygin focus explicitly rejects the necessity of a descriptive mode and therefore is non-hyletic / non-cognitive, instead focusing solely on the will of the legislator which is expressed. On Alchourrón's and Bulygin's expressivist conception, a child would certainly be missing the point if he responds: "no, it is not time for bed!"

[5] von Wright (1998, p. 370).

legal norms in themselves, that they are completely contingent upon, and nothing but expressions of, the will of a sovereign. Since such norms cannot be known (independently of the command-propositions in which they exist), there can be no logic of norms, but merely of normative propositions. In other words, it is not possible to examine relations of 'ought' propositions to each other. However, it is possible to examine the relations of 'is' statements about such 'ought' propositions, i. e. describing various normative relations as expressed by an authority.

Assuming that norms do not contain truth values, and further assuming that the law of non-contradiction therefore does not apply to norms, then there cannot be a logic of non-contradiction with respect to norms in the traditionally received sense.[6] However, this does not mean that there are no rational, as opposed to merely prudential, constraints on norm giving activity.[7]

Von Wright states:

A normative code envisages, I shall say, an ideal state of affairs. This ideal state obtains in the real world when everything which the norms of the code pronounce obligatory always is the case, everything which they prohibit never is the case, and those things which it permits can be the case without obligations being neglected or prohibitions violated. If this ideal state is not logically possible then there is something wrong or rotten with the normative code itself. It either imposes demands which cannot be all of them satisfied or it permits things which cannot

---

[6] The original formulation of this argument appears to originate with Jørgensen (originally in 1937) as attributed by Weinberger (1998): "I. Imperative sentences are not capable of being either true or false. According to the logical positivists' testability criterion of meaning they therefore must be considered meaningless. However, they are nevertheless capable of being understood or misunderstood and seem also to be able to function as premises as well as conclusions in logical inferences. II. This puzzle may be dealt with by analyzing the imperative sentences into two factors: an imperative and an indicative factor, the first being merely an expression of the speaker's state of mind (his willing, wishing, commanding, etc.) and therefore of no logical consequence, whereas the last may be formulated in an indicative sentence describing the contents of the imperative sentences and therefore being capable of having a meaning and of being governed by the ordinary rules of logic. III. The ordinary rules of logic being valid for the indicative sentences which can be derived from the imperative ones, and no specific rules for the imperatives being known (unless it should be the rule governing the derivation of the indicative sentence from the imperative one), there seems to be no reason for, indeed hardly any possibility of, constructing a specific 'logic of imperatives'."

[7] It seems a matter of common sense that there are in any case *prudential* constraints to norm-giving. For example, it may not be prudent for a King to demand that his subjects pay inordinately high rates of tax, for this could lead to the King's laws becoming ineffective or to strong discontent within the kingdom. However, such prudential considerations are not *rational* considerations as they do not derive from the concept of the norm itself, but rather from instrumental considerations of effectiveness, political expediency etc. In contrast to the question of prudential considerations of norm-giving, views are more divided regarding the potential of rational constraints. Reductivists, for example, tend to reduce legal norms merely to a matter of social fact without regard to any considerations of rationality. For an illustrative defense of this position, see Kramer's, *In Defense of Legal Positivism.*

consistently with these demands be realized. Logic cannot exclude such demands from being made and licenses from being given; but giving them *intentionally* would surely be irrational, contrary to reason, purposeless.[8]

Even if any two norms, compared abstractly, cannot technically contradict each other, von Wright's scenario of an ideal state of affairs is meant to point out that there are at least some rational (or logical) requirements for legal systems if considered within a fuller context. In the passage above, von Wright invites his readers to imagine legal norms from the perspective of a subject who always follows the law or a legislator whose will in enacting the law is always perfectly obeyed. If, within a given context, a subject's course of action is both commanded and prohibited (or a legislator both commands and prohibits the course of action), then the legal system, in which the subject (and legislator) exist, is in some way faulty. Moreover, the faultiness of such a legal system would not only have to do with practical considerations of motivation or administration, i. e. what should the subject do or how should the court adjudicate the action in question given conflicting norms. Rather, the legal system would, as a matter of fact, be at odds with itself. It being the case that the legal system would contain both the norm φ and $\neg\varphi$ for identical contexts, such a system would be contradictory, even if the norm φ, given a certain degree of abstraction, cannot contradict $\neg\varphi$.

If von Wright takes us this far in understanding the necessary success conditions for a rational legal system, it may make sense to venture further down this path of understanding legal norms within their proper context. Excluding a symbolic logic of legal norms as traditionally understood should not necessarily exclude the possibility of a logic of the legal system. Phrased differently, the impossibility of a logic of legal norms in the abstract does not exclude the possibility of a logic of normative relations between an individual and a collective, a subject and sovereign, as expressed in the totality of a legal framework, i. e. a logic of norms in the world.[9]

---

[8] von Wright (1993, p. 109). In reference to FN 4 above, von Wright seems to be making the point that, in contrast to norms considered more generally, legal norms necessarily have both an expressive and an evocative mode. Since the legal subject, i. e. the recipient of the norm, is always also subject to a plethora of other norms, the expressive and evocative modes must always be conditioned by the state of legal affairs more generally and the state of affairs expressed in the given norm, i. e. the descriptive mode. See also Chapter V below.

[9] Von Wright, himself, eventually moved away from the strictures of his earlier deontic logic by incorporating the notion of the self-understanding of an agent's reasons for action into his theory of action. See Meggle (2016).

2. Is and Ought

A radical positivism should pose a challenge to the received understanding of the nature of legal norms including the understanding of the nature of those from whom the norms issue and those to whom the norms are addressed. It has become a core position among legal positivists that it is not possible to derive statements expressing what ought to be the case from statements expressing what is the case. This distinction is sometimes attributed to Hume's assertion that morals are not derived from reason[10], Moore's discussion of the naturalistic fallacy[11], or Hare's warning[12] against making prescriptive judgments on the basis of descriptive premises.[13] Taken together and in their proper context, these predecessors of legal theory seem to share in admonishing against attributing values to the natural world, i. e. against a naturalist cognitivism. An interesting concurrence to this position is found with Hermann Cohen in his *Ethik des Reinen Willens* in which he discusses Kant's distinction of *Sein* and *Sollen* in stating: "…die Ethik will nicht in erster Linie von den Bäumen lernen, sondern von den Menschen in der Stadt."[14] He explains:

> Das ist der tiefe, der keusche Sinn in der dem Ausdruck nach freilich nicht ganz klaren Formel von dem Unterschiede zwischen Sein und Sollen: dass das Problem der Ethik selbstständig gemacht, von dem der theoretischen Vernunft unterschieden werde, und doch nichtsdestoweniger als ein Problem der Vernunft anerkannt bleibe.[15]

It would be counter-productive to legislate based on constellations of the stars, adjudicate on the basis of an approaching thunderstorm or fell a tree as punishment for one of its limbs injuring a child.[16] Each such scenario (astrology, divi-

[10] Hume, *Treatise of Human Nature*, Book III, Part I, § 1: "In every system of morality, which I have hitherto met with, I have always remarked, that the author proceeds for some time in the ordinary way of reasoning, and establishes the being of a God, or makes observations concerning human affairs; when of a sudden I am surprised to find, that instead of the usual copulations of propositions, is, and is not, I meet with no proposition that is not connected with an ought, or an ought not. This change is imperceptible; but is, however, of the last consequence. For as this ought, or ought not, expresses some new relation or affirmation, it is necessary that it should be observed and explained; and at the same time that a reason should be given, for what seems altogether inconceivable, how this new relation can be a deduction from others, which are entirely different from it."

[11] See Moore, *Principia Ethica*, § 10.

[12] Hare, *The Language of Morals*.

[13] See, for example, von Wright (1998)

[14] Cohen, *Ethik des Reinen Willens*, p. 13.

[15] Id. at p. 21.

[16] See Oliver Wendall Holmes, *The Common Law*. For example, Holmes cites a passage from Aeschines: "we banish beyond our borders stocks and stones and steel, voiceless and mindless things, if they chance to kill a man."

nation and animism) would involve sourcing a norm, which is a reason for human action, from a realm independent of human agency. While it is certainly valid to criticize such invalid normative judgments, it is much likelier that the primary concern of Hume and Kant in focusing on this distinction was not to combat an animistic tendency, but rather to call into question the hidden normative assumptions of the scholastic positions which at times served as the basis for moral teaching. Thus, it would be worth pointing out that Adam giving a rib to Eve provides in itself no justification for a religious fundamentalist approach to a certain arrangement of familial life or, to use a more modern example, the fact that humans find themselves in a process of evolution in no way entails that social policies should be enacted to promote this development in one way or another (i. e. Social Darwinism). There may very well be relevant values underlying the discourse when applying norms to or deriving them from natural, historical or mythical phenomena.[17] However, as long as these underlying values are not explicated and critically examined, there is no way to evaluate the resulting norm.

Beyond naturalist cognitivism, legal positivism in the 20th century has defended the logical rigor of its methods against versions of non-naturalist cognitivist theories as well, theories which, so the positivists argue, equally violate this distinction between 'is' and 'ought' and between the natural sciences and the human sciences. For many legal positivists, such non-naturalist (i. e. non-empirically inclined) natural lawyers would be understood to derive their legal norms from objective and immutable Platonic forms or from a puerile imagination of God handing out commands from on high. Legal positivists often go further than this, however, by eschewing all explanations of the normativity of law which make reference to the factual whatsoever, whether human or natural. The result of this is the refusal to accept legal justifications or explanations outside of the legal norms, the *explananda,* themselves.

The main consequence for this approach has been that legal positivists have had no means by which to explain, contextualize or criticize a legal norm from the perspective of a legal system. Either the positivist must accept the legal norm in question as a non-normative matter of fact with no actual bearing on the actions of its addressees as actions or, much more precariously, as a normative

[17] On its surface, it does not make sense to punish a tree for committing a tort since the tree is not capable of acting. Thus, such a practice may seem primitive. However, even if everyone speaks of punishing the tree for its "malfeasance", it is entirely possible that such a practice could actually develop as a means of causing an economic harm for the tree's owner in order to deter the occurrence of future accidents or perhaps to prevent the victim from seeking vengeance on his own against the tree's owner. See a similar discussion in Chapter V. The point of insisting on the is-ought distinction then would be to not be satisfied with explanations which serve to hide the proper normative significance of moral or legal practices.

matter of fact with an actual and absolute bearing on the actions of its addressees as *legal* subjects, but not as *human* (or moral) subjects. Thus, ironically, the well-meaning legal positivist must either accept that legal norms are not norms at all (but rather predictions of punishment) or, at the end of the day, blindly accept the normative force of the factual.[18]

The third way relative to these unsatisfactory solutions is to attempt to (rationally) reconstruct the legal norm within a system of norms. While it is precisely Kelsen who stands accused by Schmitt of abiding by the 'normative force of the factual', there are nonetheless glimpses in Kelsen's early writings of a more nuanced approach of understanding the normativity of the law in such a way that espouses a rational reconstruction of the legal norm within a system of norms *in order* to try to understand the facticity of the law in the fullness of its normative context.[19] Though we will see that Kelsen himself falls short of realizing this endeavor, in what follows we can begin to see how to make sense of such a rational reconstruction of legal systems.

---

[18] See Schmitt, *Politische Theologie*, p. 8: "Der sogenannte Positivismus und Normativismus der deutschen Staatsrechtslehre der Wilhelminischen und der Weimarer Zeit ist nur ein degenerierter – weil statt auf ein Naturrecht oder Vernunftrecht begründeter, an bloß faktisch 'geltende' Normen angehängter – daher in sich widerspruchsvoller Normativismus, vermischt mit einem Positivismus, der nur ein rechtsblinder, an die 'normative Kraft des faktischen' statt an eine echte Entscheidung sich haltender, degenerierter Dezisionismus war." However, for a more contemporary, mainstream positivist perspective, see: Kletzer (2013): "Anglo-American Positivism … mainly consists in not making explicit the radical thought already implicit in relative positivism. Its main claim thus is that all law is 'source based.' However, it does not draw the conclusion or make explicit that by maintaining that the law is 'source based' it has already claimed that the law is law-based or, which is the same, that the law is, in an important respect, base-less."

[19] Kelsen, *Das Problem der Souveränität und die Theorie des Völkerrechts*, vi: "Die logische 'Erzeugung' des Rechts aus der Ursprungsnorm vollzieht sich stufenweise in stetem Bezug auf ein paralleles Faktum, das aber doch nur – wie die psychologischen Tatsachen im Verhältnis zu den logischen Geltungen – die conditio sine qua non, nicht aber die conditio per quam des Rechts auf seinen verschiedenen Stufen, in seinem für den Juristen entscheidenden Geltungsaspekte ist." This necessary relationship (*sine qua non*) between the facticity of the legal system and its normativity would seem to suggest that, while the law is not defined by its facticity (*conditio per quam*), it is nonetheless dependent on it. However, the relation, at least in this passage, is not one of the 'normative force of the factual' in the sense that whatever the state might say then becomes automatically normatively binding. Rather, the relation is one of the law being informed, but not defined, by matters of fact.

3. Laws, Scientific and Legal

If we want to understand the legal norm as it exists within a legal system, we must understand what a norm is generally, i. e. an expression of a normative relation between an individual and the world (whether this world consists of other individuals or objects). Analyzing the legal norm as a normative relation in this sense, we are forced to look beyond the limits of a formal law, viewed in the abstract, and instead consider that law as it relates to its subject and object, judging what would constitute success for such a law in its relationality in any given context.

Instead of confining our analysis to the 'is' / 'ought' paradigm, it would be fruitful for enhancing our understanding of the legal norm to rephrase the debate above in terms of the direction of fit of different kinds of statements. In contrast to the distinction between 'is' and 'ought' which focuses solely on the quality of a statement in the abstract, the distinction of *direction of fit* introduces the notion of success conditions for when the 'world' fits the 'mind' (in the case of a norm which succeeds in motivating an action) or when the 'mind' fits the 'world' (in the case of a statement of fact accurately depicting the world).[20] As with the lack of relation between 'is' and 'ought' statements, a statement with a mind-to-world direction of fit, without any other qualifications, has no bearing on a statement with a world-to-mind direction of fit. In contrast to 'is' and 'ought' statements, however, an analysis in terms of direction of fit is useful because doing so removes the given statement from a merely formal and abstract consideration and forces us to analyze it within the context of a human action, whether seeking to change the world in the future or to describe the world as it presently is. Thus, prescriptive, or normative, statements succeed when the addressee of the prescription or norm acts according to the norm. Descriptive statements, also statements of fact or assertions, succeed when the statement in question adequately (accurately, coherently, functionally, or pragmatically) reflects the matter of fact.

Importantly, this clear delineation between world-to-mind and mind-to-world directions of fit, or prescriptive and descriptive statements, or 'ought' and 'is', begins to blur whenever we map the various uses of the term 'law' onto this framework. The laws of a legal system are thought by many, and are certainly thought by Kelsen, to consist of prescriptive norms, whereas the laws of nature, meaning the laws which one uses when engaging with the natural sciences, are generally thought to consist of descriptions of how the world is. In the standard

[20] Anscombe, *Intention*. To paraphrase her famous example, a statement with a world-to-mind direction of fit would be found on a grocery list in which a man is ordered to go to the store to fetch some milk and eggs. The statement could take on a mind-to-world direction of fit if the man, upon returning home and having forgotten the eggs, simply deleted "and eggs".

analysis, the problem with natural *law*, meaning that branch of legal science which seeks to derive legal precepts from the nature of man or human community, is that it tries to derive 'ought's from 'is's or prescriptive norms from descriptive statements of fact.

The laws of morality and grammar are similar to 'legal' laws in that the chief components both of a moral code and of the rules of grammar are normative. Yet, both the norms of grammar and of morality are in some important way (also) grounded in the world – they are not arbitrary in their respective contexts even if one could abstractly conceive of a great number of functional grammars or moral codes. Kelsen cites Simmel who describes this phenomenon of how the law is used in all of these areas: "einmal dessen, was allgemein, generisch geschieht 'i. e. natural sciences', dann dessen, was geschehen soll, wenngleich es vielleicht nicht geschieht 'i. e. moral sciences or law'."[21] In the midst of this 'double' usage of the term 'law', there are nonetheless key ambivalences in the usage of the term which show how the law of legal science differs from and shares commonality with other kinds.

Kelsen maintains in the *Hauptprobleme* that our usage (and understanding) of the concept of 'law' in legal science, but also the laws of morals, grammar and aesthetics, historically derives from the usage of the term 'law' in the natural sciences, which in turn borrowed the concept from the political realm much earlier in history.[22] On Kelsen's reconstruction, the order of nature was thought to be analogous to the political order, but instead of an absolute political ruler issuing commands to its subjects and thus determining the relationships within a society, nature had the absolute rule of a *divine will* which invariably subjected the natural elements to God's eternal command.[23] For Kelsen, the two uses of the concept 'law' may have been strongly related at one time through analogy. However, with the Enlightenment came the emancipation of the natural sciences from this idea of God as supreme author such that now the two concepts can be understood as having little in common. On the one hand, the laws of the natural sciences now seek to show the actual relationships of things in the world and explain their being, i. e. are purely descriptive. On the other hand, the laws of legal science, as

---

[21] Simmel, *Einleitung in die Moralwissenschaft*, Berlin 1892, cited in *Hauptprobleme*, p. 4. English translation: "(the use of law is) sometimes that which occurs generally and generically and sometimes that which should occur, though sometimes it does not."

[22] Id. at p. 4 ff. See also, *Die Rechtswissenschaft als Norm oder als Kulturwissenschaft*, 1916, p. 97: "Gründet man den Begriff der Wissenschaft aber auf den der Gesetzmäßigkeit, dann muss man sich bewusst bleiben, dass 'Gesetz' im Sinne von Kausal-(Natur-)Gesetz etwas wesentlich anderes bedeutet als Gesetz im Sinne von Norm. Gesetzmäßigkeit ist Kausalität oder Normalität."

[23] Ibid.

well as grammar, morals and aesthetics, are purely prescriptive in that they regulate how subjects *should* relate to each other, the basis of this 'ought' in each case lying in the will of an authority. In other words, the natural sciences borrowed their concept of 'law' from the properly normative disciplines under a false understanding of their own nature. Now that the natural sciences have corrected this misunderstanding, the two uses of the term 'law' have little in common with each other. This characterization may seem satisfactory at first glance. However, on closer inspection, this Kelsenian differentiation begs two questions deserving of a closer analysis, (i) as to the nature of *generic occurrences* and our ability to describe them and (ii) as to the nature of a will which Kelsen identifies as providing the source of the (normative) law in the understanding of primitive society above.

A description of a generic occurrence does not just have a mind-to-world direction of fit. A generic occurrence is an occurrence that is within a certain *genus*, or kind. It does not lie solely within the thing itself that something is described as generic, but rather also within the understanding, the apperception, of the observer. Certainly, that a billiard ball falls when released from one's hand is dependent on the thing itself – and the same is true of each of a thousand balls treated in a similar way. That each of these thousand drops is a *generic* occurrence, however, is dependent not on the thing, but rather on the observer who classifies the drops as being sufficiently similar so as to build a class. The scientist observes data sets, looks for relevant similarities and expresses these similarities in general laws and concepts.[24] General laws are formed from individual perceptions and then are used to *inform* future perceptions (*ad* + *percipere*) in a conceptualized way – identification and subsumption are thus key elements of scientific inquiry.[25] Con-

[24] Here Kelsen agrees: "Versucht man näher zu präzisieren, welcher Art jener Akt ist, durch welchen ein Objekt – seiner besonderen Bedeutung, Wichtigkeit oder Interessantheit wegen – zum Gegenstand einer Wissenschaft gemacht wird, so muss man ihn als 'Wertung' characterisieren; Wertung, sei es im subjektiven oder objektiven Sinne. Ohne hier schon auf die sehr wichtige Unterscheidung einzugehen, sei bemerkt, dass es gleichgültig ist, ob das Objekt wissenschaftlicher Erkenntnis sich bestimmt nach dem subjektiven Werte, das heißt dem Interesse, der Bedeutung und Wichtigkeit, die es für den speziellen Forscher tatsächlich hat, oder nach dem objektiven Werte, den der Forscher als allgemeingültig voraussetzt." *Rechtswissenschaft als Norm oder Kulturwissenschaft*, p. 100.

[25] See Vaihinger, pp. 21–22: "Das natürliche Verfahren bei der wissenschaftlichen Denktätigkeit besteht darin, dass wir den unmittelbaren und ohne Reflexion gewonnenen Inhalt der Wahrnehmung zu bestimmten Begriffen und zu ihres Grundes sich bewussten und folgerichtig verbundenen Gedanken entwickeln. Der nächste Weg ist die Induktion. Man sucht aus den einzelnen Wahrnehmungen allgemeine Begriffe und Urteile vermittelst gültiger Schlüße und Beweise zu gewinnen. Man geht dabei vom Gegebenen aus, verbindet es mit anderem anderwärts Gegebenen, sucht hier die Gleichförmigkeiten, welche in allgemeinen Gesetzen und Begriffen zu Ausdruck gelangen. Es beruht dieser Weg eben auf den gewöhnlichen Apperzep-

trary to the Kelsenian picture above, scientific laws are therefore doubly normative, twice having a *world-to-mind* direction of fit in addition to the commonly accepted mind-to-world direction of fit. First, the law is normative as a result of the process of identification, matching likes with likes to form laws which are normative in the sense that similarity is never given in the world, but rather constructed as a category of understanding subject to a certain interest. Second, scientific laws are normative as a result of the process of subsumption in which the observer must decide whether new data falls within the ambit of the given law. These two elements of scientific method, i. e. identification and subsumption, are indeed closely related to the method of adjudication in customary law in which lawyers identify legal rules based on common patterns of previous cases and then apply those rules through subsumption to individual cases at hand (see Chapter V below). Far from being an unrelated namesake of the legal norm, the scientific law within this framework seems to be a close cousin to at least one kind of legal norm, i. e. customary law. There is, however, reason to believe that there is a deep relation between scientific laws and other kinds of legal laws as well.

Regarding the issue of the will, there would be some basis for claiming that the laws of the state fundamentally differ from the laws of science insofar as legal norms are considered to issue as commands from a sovereign to a subject. There is nothing generic at all about such commands and whatever normativity they may have would most likely derive from threats of sanction. There is a wide gulf between a law which expresses an essential relation between two objects (as in the law of gravity) and a law which arbitrarily leads a subject to change its pattern of behavior out of fear of personal harm. However, Kelsen rejects both that the normativity of the state consists in motivating subjects through fear of sanction[26] and that the will of a state can be conceived as a psychological will.[27]

Legal normativity does not arise out of a paternalistic ruler binding howsoever his subjects to his will. Even if a state has an absolute monarch with absolute power, it is never the monarch as individual human being who embodies the will of the state. Instead, for Kelsen the will of the state is nothing but the final point of attribution for all agents acting on behalf of the state.[28] Just as the state itself is a construct representing the unity of the legal order, the 'will' of the state is a construct without which it is impossible to understand how the actions of offi-

tionen der Identifikation und Subsumption. Die Induktion … apperzipiert das Allgemeine indem sie es aus dem Einzelnen schafft, also mittels des Einzelnen, und apperzipiert in demselben Akte durch dieses Allgemeine das Einzelne."

26 Kelsen, *Hauptprobleme*, pp. 212–215.

27 Id. at p. 170 ff.

28 Id. at p. 183: "… der gemeinsame Treffpunkt aller Zurechnungslinien, die von den als Organhandlungen qualifizierten Tatbeständen ausgehen, ist der Staatswille."

cials can be 'on behalf of' the state and can bind subjects. However, if the essence of the legal norm is not adequately captured by the picture of a sovereign ruler issuing his commands for his subjects to obediently follow, what is the essence of the legal norm? How are we to understand the law within the context of a legal system?

4. Beyond Prescriptions

In his work *Norm and Action*, von Wright follows many prominent theorists in considering legal norms to be a class of prescriptions which he defines as norms that are (i) issued by someone with authority, (ii) addressed to an agent or subject, (iii) publicly promulgated, and (iv) connected with a sanction which at least in part assures compliance with the norm on the part of the subject.[29] This conception is open-ended in the sense that there are no restraints on which kinds of norms can be promulgated, there is no reference to the kind of relationship that must exist between authority and subject in order for the promulgation to succeed, and there are no limits regarding the severity of sanctions which can be levied against subjects in the case of violation of a norm. This follows a reductivist understanding of legal norms according to which legal norms are determined solely by and reducible entirely to social fact, without any regard to considerations of natural law or morality.[30] It also follows the basic pattern of a master, or Rex[31], imposing his will on a people. This is a linear relation in which the law originates in the will of an individual, becomes externalized through a speech act, and then is accepted or not by the subject.

Von Wright's analysis is useful and surely correct with regard to empirically verifiable legal prescriptions. These would include hierarchical legal norms of a second order (such as 'the county shall have the authority to levy local taxes') as well as publicly promulgated primary norms (such as a notice affixed to the city hall stating 'all new residents must forthwith register with the city hall in order to qualify for health services'). These kinds of laws form what is often the standard case of analysis within the legal positivist tradition and primarily include the areas of the law known as procedural and administrative law. This view is plausible in these contexts, though not necessarily compulsory.

However, there are two important kinds of law, existing at each end of the procedural and administrative law spectrum, in which the prescription criteria

---

[29] von Wright. *Norm and Action*, Ch. 1 Sec. 5.

[30] See Paulson in preface to *Reine Rechtslehre*, iii.

[31] As stylized by Hart in Chapter IV of *The Concept of Law*.

listed above either do not manifest or manifest in a fundamentally different manner from the standard case of procedural or administrative law. The first kind includes the civil law and parts of modern criminal law: even in jurisdictions in which civil and criminal law have long been codified through parliamentary enactment, the great majority of these norms within the civil and criminal law derive from customary norms which have formed the basis of social cohesion for these peoples for centuries. The second kind of law which differs significantly from the procedural and administrative law paradigm is constitutional law, by which I mean the norms which actually constitute the state in the form of the Kelsenian basic norm[32] or the Rousseauian *volonté générale*[33].

While it is possible to consider these kinds of law within the prescription framework above, there is a distinct sense in which the satisfaction of these criteria would be merely superficial. For the case of customary law, the act of codification by the state in which the first three criteria of authorship, subjectivity and promulgation are most identifiable is more *symptomatic* of previously existing norms than *constitutive* of new ones. Likewise for constitutional law, a written constitutional document could better be said to memorialize the constitution of a political entity than to constitute it, itself.[34] This we see repeatedly in the case of fledgling democracies which would seek to constitute political institutions from scratch, and in doing so fail to match the provisions of the formal constitution with the underlying political reality of the society.[35]

I suggest that these cases highlight something essential about the concept of law which is not captured by the standard view of norms as prescriptions which von Wright seems to have endorsed. By investigating how viewing norms as prescriptions in the manner above misses some of the essential aspects of law, we may be able to arrive at a point at which we can broaden the scope of our analysis.

---

[32] Kelsen. *Reine Rechtslehre*, p. 67.

[33] Rousseau. *Du contrat social*, p. 28.

[34] See Hegel's *Grundlinien der Philosophie des Rechts*, § 273: "Eine andere Frage bietet sich leicht dar: wer die Verfassung machen soll? Diese Frage scheint deutlich, zeigt sich aber bei näherer Betrachtung sogleich sinnlos. Denn sie setzt voraus, dass keine Verfassung vorhanden, somit ein bloßer atomistischer Haufen von Individuen beisammen sei. Wie ein Haufen, ob durch sich oder andere, durch Güte, Gedanken oder Gewalt, zu einer Verfassung kommen würde, müßte ihm überlassen bleiben, denn mit einem Haufen hat es der Begriff nicht zu tun."

[35] For example, a document which seeks to establish a representative democracy in a state following the end of a dictatorship would be merely aspirational as long as the society does not have civic institutions in place (such as a free press along with a politically interested electorate) which would allow for the democratic provisions to properly function.

5. The Normative Relation

In his article "Is and Ought", von Wright argues that Kelsen was a non-cognitivist with regard to legal norms, meaning that directives or prescriptions can neither be true nor false.[36] This position has its origin in the impossibility of deriving an 'ought' from an 'is' since any cognitive discoverability or verifiability of a legal norm is taken to imply that there is some kind of factual existence in the world from which the legal norm is derived, or obtained. To use the cases of civil and constitutional law just mentioned, this would mean that no constellation of civil or political custom as social fact could ever be taken to entail, or necessarily involve, legal norms.

As a result, we could imagine that legal norms are merely those prescriptions that are issued by a person in a position of *authority*, namely a sovereign, to a person in a position of *obedience*, i. e. a subject. Because such legal norms can neither be true nor false, there is no limitation on what the content of such norms could be from the normative perspective, even if practical expedience and issues of factual efficacy do nonetheless impose certain limits on what legislatures can 'get away with' in enforcing norms. Depending on how such a theory of norms with regard to actually existing legal systems is construed, I believe that this conception of legal norms fails in two respects.

First, the concepts of authority and obedience are themselves normatively laden. In order to figure out which person is the proper authority in a legal system, we have to ask ourselves questions such as 'who is the rightful heir to the king' or 'does the military junta have the authority to depose the democratically elected, but corrupt president'? Such questions may or may not be directly addressed by a written constitution and, even if they are, there is no guarantee that in such situations the formal provisions of a constitution will enjoy the force of law at the end of the day. Likewise for the issue of obedience, there is a real sense in which a statement such as 'all Canadians are hereby subject to the laws of the United States of America' would be misplaced or wrong. The legal authority and legal subject are thus at least two concepts which are tied to success conditions, in such a way that they do not seem to be completely arbitrary, even if we would grant for the moment that, abstractly, the contents of the particular primary prescriptions which the authority issues to its subject *could* be completely arbitrary. Moreover, these two concepts, legal authority and legal subject, seem to be correlative. One can only have legal authority if others are subject to one's prescriptions and one is only a legal subject if one's actions are subject to the prescriptions of another person in a position of authority.

---

[36] von Wright (1998, p. 366).

Of course, we could solve this problem of success conditions restricting our conception of legal norms by simply revising the standard definition, doing away with any 'normative' vestiges in our language such that we could say that legal norms are prescriptions issued by a person, or a human being, in a position of power to another human being in a position of weakness. Accordingly, we would call the sovereign that human being who is the strongest or who has the most power and the subject would be the opposite. However, this conception also fails. Even Hobbes in Chapter 13 of *Leviathan* sees that such a power structure is pure chaos, that power relations are always in flux.[37] If we look at a modern state, we see that all of us, including those who hold the highest governmental positions, both are subject to the power of others and are exerting power over others in a variety of ways at any given time and that, over time, these relations are likely to change. The very fabric of our social order is grounded in the law in a way that prescriptions based on mere power relations cannot fully explain. Without the concepts of legal authority and legal subject, it would be difficult to make any sense of these structures.

When we talk about a person in a position of authority, namely a sovereign, and a person in a position of obedience, namely a subject, we are talking about a relation with two clear points of reference. This is not a power relation with the references being the powerful and the weak, but a normative relation with the references considered as agents in the normative context. In considering such references to be agents, we presuppose that these persons are capable of acting freely and within the realm of reason in a way that extends beyond the technical means-to-end rationality of hypothetical imperatives. Accordingly, while sanctions may well serve an important role in maximizing the efficacy of legal systems, they are not at the heart of the normative relationship between sovereign and subject. The subject obeys the sovereign freely and primarily *without* recourse to means-end rationality and the sovereign has complete authority over the subject, bound by the limits of the concept of authority itself.

In order to have an adequate account of legal norms, it is thus imperative to consider how the requirements of normativity condition the existence of legal norms. Just because legal norms as 'ought' expressions may not be derivable from 'is' expressions or even other 'ought' expressions[38], it does not therefore hold that legal norms in a legal system exist within a normative vacuum. What is required is a conception of the law which transcends any linear relationship of command between sovereign and subject and which forbears a normative relation through which subjects follow the law in order to maximize individual pref-

---

37 Hobbes. *Leviathan*, p. 183 ff.

38 von Wright (1993, p. 110).

erences, whether this be in the avoidance of sanction or realization of social recognition. In order to develop this full conception of agency in the law, a categorical change is required in our conception of the individual and its relationship with others.

6. Power in Reason

The voluntarism debate of the Middle Ages revolved around the question of whether God's will or God's intellect is prior. If God's will is prior, then God is free to will anything with the result that God, and by extension creation, will recognize that thing as good; if God's intellect is prior, then God is only capable of willing the (Aristotelian) good or that which is according to reason. Of course, since intellect and will are one in the scholastic conception of God, this debate was carried out with a certain degree of theoretical abstraction. Even in the political realm during the divine right of kings, the sovereign was thought to embody both divine power and wisdom within the territory. It seems that only with the death of God witnessed in modernity (compounded by the exultation of reason by the sciences on the one hand and the propagation of political power concomitant with the nation state on the other) does the issue arise regarding the nature of law when divorced from the 'divine' foundation of reason. Yet, the message of the modern political theorists prior to the 20th century, especially those within the positivist tradition such as Hobbes, Spinoza, Rousseau, Bentham and even Austin, has been that it is not only possible to divorce *power* from a literal god, i. e. a literal belief in scripture, while maintaining it in the realm of the political, but that it is also possible to maintain reason in the political realm without recourse to a divine mind.

Thus, Hobbes founds his state not on the principle of 'might makes right', but on the idea that the state has inherent authority for a reason, i. e. because it is the guarantor of security and order. Spinoza recognizes that the force of the law is formed by reason and common sentiment. Rousseau bases the absolute authority of the state in the *volonté générale*, which in turn is derived from common custom.[39] Bentham argues that the principle of utility or reason should be used in developing the positive law as a reform to the metaphysics of natural law which he claimed were nothing but fictions used to disguise the naked power interests of the ruling class.[40] Austin, in addition to defining laws as commands of the

---

39 Rousseau. *Discours sur l'economie politique*, pp. 49, 50.

40 Bentham (1823, xlii): "Now then, with respect to actions in general, there is no property in them that is calculated so readily to engage, and so firmly to fix the attention of an observer, as the tendency they may have to, or divergency (if one may so say) from, that which maybe

sovereign, refers to the positive law which obtains in all nations (*ius omnium gentium*) as a law that must be based on intelligence since it appears not to be random and that this is the measure by which all positive laws are tested.[41]

Despite von Wright's classification to the contrary, Kelsen, too, *partially* falls into this line of positive law cognitivists, not because he thought that truth could be predicated of legal norms, which he did not, but because he considered it essential to the normativity of law that legal norms be understood through the frame of reason. In his letter to Treves in 1933, Kelsen affirms that he seeks through his theory to apply the Kantian transcendental method to a theory of positive law. Kelsen understood Kant to have developed a theory which helps us to better understand empirical reality: understanding positive law as empirical law or law in experience, Kelsen sees his Pure Theory of Law to be a theory of how we can come to *understand* this empirical reality.[42]

Kant rejects the metaphysics of natural law as it relates to the physical world by asserting that concepts such as causation and time are merely categories of our understanding and yet that these categories are nonetheless essential in order for us to understand the world as ordered and to act up to our potential as rational creatures. Likewise, Kelsen rejected the metaphysics of natural law within the realm of law by showing that the normativity and order of the law exist not because of the inherent goodness of particular prescriptions or the states which issue them, but rather because of our understanding of these prescriptions as *legal norms* or, in other words, within a normative context. This is a consequence of Kelsen's identification of the state with the law. All state action must be legal and any action which does not fit within the legal order is no state action at all.

By identifying the state with the legal order, Kelsen takes a step towards reestablishing with the visor of categorical certainty the supposed unity between power and reason that had been lost with the advent of modernity. By definition for Kelsen, the sovereign is the source of both the power and the reason of the law. Moreover, because the legal order is prior to the state, the sovereign is bound to the legal order in his actions – the power of the law must necessarily flow from its reason. Whereas in the past power and reason were unified in the existence of the one God, only to be interpreted by the king, now power and reason are united

---

styled the common end of all of them. The end I mean is Happiness: and this tendency in any act is what we style its utility: as this divergency is that to which we give the name of mischievousness. With respect then to such actions in particular as are among the objects of the Law, to point out to a man the utility of them or the mischievousness, is the only way to make him see clearly that property of them which every man is in search of; the only way, in short, to give him satisfaction."

41 Austin. *The Province of Jurisprudence Determined*, p. 13.

42 Kelsen (1998, p. 171).

in the concept of the legal norm which is constituted by us in our relation with one another. With this construction, Kelsen is able to accomplish his own Copernican turn and indeed, as with many of the neo-Kantians, becomes more Kantian with respect to the concept of law than Kant himself.

7. Fact and Fiction

The problem with this Kelsenian turn is that, for Kelsen, the priority of the legal order, and thus the priority of reason, is a priority by definition only. On some accounts of Kelsen's theory, it would seem that the normativity of the law, with its hierarchy of norms ending in the basic norm, is a mere artifice which we use in order to pretend *as if* the structures which exist between the powerful and the weak are actually valid norms, obligating us to act in compliance. Kelsen even says in his *Allgemeine Theorie der Normen* that the basic norm is just a fiction and that it does not correspond to reality.[43] If this were the case, if the basic norm were merely a way for Kelsen to pretend to ground the legal system in a normative source, then all veneer of normative / rational context for the legal system would be lost, as we will see in Chapter IV below. Then there would be no further context into which we could place the open-ended conception of norms as prescriptions, i. e. that which I described von Wright adhering to at the outset. Kelsen would effectively become a non-cognitivist in the end thereby betraying the goal of developing a normative theory of the law, just as many serious Kelsenians have indeed concluded.[44]

However, while much attention has been paid to this statement of Kelsen's late, supposedly 'sceptical' phase, little attention has been paid to the kind of fiction which he said his basic norm was, i. e. a Vaihingerian fiction.[45] Far from Kelsen merely pretending to ground his legal theory in a basic norm as a kind of *deus ex machina*, Kelsen here as well as elsewhere explicitly references Vaihinger as providing the conceptual framework which he is seeking.[46] According

---

43 Kelsen. *Allgemeine Theorie der Normen*, pp. 206–207.

44 For example, Bulygin (1998) and von Wright (1998).

45 For an informative analysis of Kelsen's relationship to the Vaihingerian fiction, see Christophe Bouriau's *Le "Comme Si"*.

46 For example, see *Hauptprobleme*, xvii) as well as "Zur Theorie der juristischen Fiktionen." See Vaihinger, *Die Philosophie des Als-Ob*, p. 174: "Ein weiteres wesentliches Merkmal der Fiktionen, d. h. der wissenschaftlichen, ist, dass sie Mittel zu bestimmten Zwecken sind; also ihre Zweckmässigkeit. Wo eine solche nicht zu sehen ist, da ist die Fiktion eben unwissenschaftlich. Wenn also Hume die Kategorien Fiktionen nennt, so hat er damit zwar faktisch das Richtige erkannt, allein sein Begriff der Fiktion war ein ganz anderer als der unsrige. Sein Begriff der 'fiction of thought' ist, dass diese Gebilde bloss subjektive Einbildungen seien; unser

to this framework, the basic norm and the *normativity* of the law as a whole would, as fictions, be considered consciously false, but nonetheless goal oriented – false in the sense that they do not correspond to the facticity of the physical world (which is obvious given the is-ought distinction), goal oriented in the sense that their function is self-referential and self-constituting. It is not logically necessary to conceive of the political realm as a legal order or of concrete prescriptions as being normatively binding on the actions of subjects, but if one wishes to do so – and there are of course many good reasons for doing so, then it must be done with (some version of) the Pure Theory of Law and the help of the basic norm.

Moreover, to discount the basic norm as a fiction without taking into account its Vaihingerian provenance is to ignore important insights which Vaihinger gained regarding knowledge generally in his *Philosophie des Als-Ob*. In the same passage in the *Allgemeine Theorie der Normen*, Kelsen says that his use of the Vaihingerian fiction is similar to the concept of hypothesis. However, in contrast to an hypothesis, a fiction is, or at least should be, accompanied by an awareness of its lack of correspondence to reality.[47] However, we should not understand this distinction between fiction and hypothesis as one between make believe and reality, since fictions, in Vaihinger's sense, are simply a means of representing (as opposed to corresponding to) reality in way that assists the agent in thinking about and dealing with it.[48] Thus, for Vaihinger, not only the basic norm would be a fiction, but also Adam Smith's homo oeconomicus[49], Linnaeus' botanical classification[50], laws of theoretical physics[51], or schema within psychology.[52]

The content of the legal norms under Kelsen's conception *is* at the outset open – unlike with the natural law, there is no pre-determined set of legal norms which all legal systems should enact. In this sense, it is largely correct to follow

Begriff (entlehnt aus dem Gebrauch der Mathematik und Rechtswissenschaft) schliesst ein, dass sie zweckmässige Einbildungen seien. Hierin liegt eigentlich der Schwerpunkt unserer Auffassung, durch den sie sich von den bisherigen Auffassungen wesentlich unterscheidet."

47 Kelsen. *Allgemeine Theorie der Normen*, p. 207.

48 See Vaihinger, p. 29: "Wenn also das Material zu kompliziert und verworren ist, um dem Denken zu gestatten, es allmählich bis auf seine einzelnen Faden zu entwirren, wenn die gesuchten kausalen Faktoren wahrscheinlich komplizierterer Natur sind, als dass sie unmittelbar zu bestimmen sind, so wendet das Denken den Kunstgriff an, vorläufig und einstweilen eine ganze Reihe von Merkmalen zu vernachlässigen und nur die wichtigsten Erscheinungen herauszugreifen."

49 See Ibid.

50 Ibid.

51 Id. at p. 30.

52 Id. at p. 32.

the definition above and describe legal norms as prescriptions being (i) issued by someone with authority, (ii) addressed to an agent or subject, (iii) publicly promulgated, and (iv) connected with a sanction which at least in part assures compliance with the norm on the part of the subject. However, Kelsen was also aware that a legal system cannot be merely bootstrapped into existence. The conscious self-constitution of the legal system as a Vaihingerian fiction means that a certain functionality inheres within the legal system. Even if, as will be shown, Kelsen does not follow through to this conclusion himself, the end which this functionality defines is the conscious self-constitution of the legal subject as a reference point (Kelsen's *Zurechnungspunkt*) for rights and obligations – the creation itself of a personhood and the very possibility for normative agency.

8. Summary – The Law as Common Ground

One of the core problems of legal theory is that, since 'ought' statements are assumed to not be subject to the law of non-contradiction, it is, at least with the expressivist conception of legal norms, difficult to create anything like a legal science which can account for such norms. Nonetheless, I have pointed to a passage from von Wright which opens the door to a scientific discussion of norms, not on the basis of non-contradiction, but rather on the basis of the relation which norm-giving activity requires between the sovereign and the subject. While on the expressive view it is not a strict contradiction for the sovereign to command his subject to φ and $\neg \varphi$ in the same time, place and context, it nonetheless is quite useless and nonsensical to do so if the sovereign assumes that both commands should be obeyed.

I also claimed above that a radical legal positivism must challenge the received understanding of legal norms, that the strict division of 'is' and 'ought' within the context of a legal system either leads to a denial of legal normativity in principle or to a blind acceptance of the normative force of the factual. Given the direction provided by von Wright regarding the relational aspect of the law, together with the dilemma arising from the strict separation of 'is' and 'ought' judgments, I have sought to reformulate the issue from the qualities of statements in the abstract (is-ought) to the success conditions of statements as they relate to a respective subject and object (direction of fit). Rephrasing the debate in this way, I have argued that the general concept of law is neither primarily normative nor descriptive. Scientific laws, while purporting to describe a matter of fact, nonetheless have a doubly world-to-mind aspect, first in the quality of identification (categorization) of phenomena and second through their subsumption into already existing rules. Likewise, law and grammar, while ostensibly normative, are nonetheless grounded in objective reality in an important way, thereby exhibiting a mind-to-world direction of fit.

As for legal prescriptions, i. e. the standard case of legal norm for much of the legal positivist debate, we have seen, at least within the Kelsenian system, that legal norms are not normatively binding through coercion (fear of sanctions) and also do not emanate from any factual / psychological will. Moreover, both prescriptions themselves and the authority from which they originate are normatively thick – sheer force or violence cannot explain why subjects obey, but also cannot explain why some persons get to issue legal norms and others do not. I argue that the key for understanding how legal prescriptions function within legal systems is to focus not just on their compulsory aspect (i. e. power) but on their rational aspect as well. I tried to identify a line of political and legal theorists who have also done so up until the first part of the 20th century, including, *partially*, Hans Kelsen. I include Kelsen in this group of legal rationalists because of his commitment to understanding the normativity of the law within the frame of a legal science. I claim that the skeptical reading of Kelsen according to which Kelsen states that 'the basis of the normativity of the law is nothing but a fiction' is itself based on a misunderstanding of the role that Vaihingerian fictions play in our knowledge and judgments of the world. I only *reservedly* include Kelsen in this group of legal rationalists because it is not clear in Kelsen's references to Vaihinger that Kelsen himself understood this constitutive aspect of the Vaihingerian fiction. It is quite possible that even the early Kelsen saw the basic norm as a mere veneer that would allow one to think of the legal order as normative, if one was so inclined. It is possible that Kelsen, as a jurist, did completely accept the normative force of the factual, that laws are binding on individuals simply as a result of the fact that they have been promulgated by the sovereign, meaning nothing but the one who is in power.

In discussing the concept of law above, I cite Kelsen's account of how scientific laws were once thought of as the commands issued by God to nature, similar to the commands of a sovereign to its subject. On Kelsen's characterization, the Enlightenment represented a revolution for the sciences which could not be matched in the legal / political realm, thus resulting in a permanent chasm in the meaning of the term 'law' in the scientific and legal fields – whereas science would be governed by reason, law would always be governed by the will of the sovereign.[53] Regardless of Kelsen's very prominent attempts to rationalize the law in a system of normativity, it would seem that Kelsen nonetheless always reverted to the voluntarist model of legislation.

53 See Kelsen, *Hauptprobleme*, pp. 4, 5.

However, it is also possible to understand this history not through the lens of voluntarism, but through the lens of rationalism.[54] In the Middle Ages, instead of the laws of science being analogous to the laws of the state, the laws of the state could be conceived as being analogous to the laws of God, both divine (religious) and natural (scientific). The laws of the state could be analogous to the laws of God not in the sense that the state is all powerful in the political realm just as God is (thought to be) all powerful absolutely, but rather in the sense that the state is the source of reason for the political as God is (thought to be) the source of reason for creation. If this historical terminological development is seen through the rational lens, then the scientific Enlightenment would not represent a fundamental turn away from the 'will' of God, but rather a progression (albeit significant) in the method of understanding the world, not unlike the impressive developments in our understanding of law and the state simultaneously taking place with Bodin, Hobbes, Spinoza, Leibniz, Locke and Rousseau.

On this understanding, the laws of the state would share one essential feature with the laws of science – each kind would be subject to rationality constraints. The principal difference between the two would not be that one is descriptive and one is normative, but rather that scientific laws have immutable objects in a way that laws of the state do not. Each kind of law is judged on how well it functions in its respective context. However, while suitability with respect to immutable objects is typically defined in terms of how adequately the object is described, suitability with respect to persons or agents must have another measure.

Kelsen's development of his theory of points of attribution in the *Hauptprobleme* in 1911 was in many ways a culmination of a development of such a measure that had begun in the 18th century with Rousseau and more explicitly in Kant, but also implicitly even with Hobbes. Far from legal science being left deserted in its voluntarist purgatory having watched its cousin, natural science, ascend to heavenly enlightenment, the law for its part also made immense strides in its self-conception following on the Reformation, the development of the modern nation state, and the French and then Industrial revolutions. Kelsen's aspirations to a Pure Theory of Law as legal science should therefore not automatically be dismissed as a misguided or ill-fated aspiration of a lawyer seeking to apply scientific principles to an utterly arbitrary legal system.[55] Instead, understanding Kelsen's (especially early) work as thoroughly grounded in the fin de siècle intellectual framework can bring us toward insights about the reality of law as a

---

[54] See Bolzano, § 25, p. 139: "Es ist nicht etwas wahr, weil es Gott so erkennet, sondern im Gegenteil Gott erkennet es, weil es so ist."

[55] See Ross, Alf (1998, p. 161) and Raz, Joseph (1998, p. 67).

rational construct which have since either been lost or quietly dismissed in the post-war period.

One way of understanding this core Kelsenian aspiration of law as legal science is to claim that legal science, just like natural science, does not just provide the artifice of order, but that it actually provides order itself. Whereas the order established by the natural sciences presumes a correspondence between theory and the relations of inanimate objects in the world, the order established by legal science must presume a correspondence between legal / normative theory and the relations of rationally animate individuals. Without an adequate legal theory we can conceive neither of order within the law nor of order in the social relations of individuals (i. e. that which is the subject of the law) – prior to being ordered through a theory, such relations can be nothing but random, non-normative occurrences of fact. With law being reflected through an adequate legal theory though, the random, non-normative occurrences of fact that exist within human interactions become normative actions on the part of agents. Having an adequate legal theory thus allows for a full accounting of individuals as agents of the law and, in connecting the legal theory to the legal agency, the legal norm functions as a medium between the two poles and obtains its meaning in this relation. In this way, the legal order is not a mere artifice of order, making actors within a legal system believe in a circumstance which does not actually hold true. Rather, it creates the order itself in a self-constituting fashion.[56] The order of a legal theory must depend upon the agency of the individuals within a legal order – all agency bottoms out in the minds of individuals and every legal theory must presume rationality and the potential for agency on the part of individuals. However, this individual agency is itself first afforded by a legal order, a categorical leap from the means-end instrumentality of a natural state to the rationality of desire-independence based on meaning, or value. Such agency takes the form of a norm according to which each individual can only properly act to the extent that such norm can serve as a reason for action for every other individual. To say that I can only act rationally whenever my action can be re-enacted universally is to say that individual preferences are universally subservient to collective rationality. The individual can only be rational, can only be an agent, a subject, in the state.

[56] For an example of the prevalence of this idea in the 19th century, see Hegel's *Grundlinien der Philosophie des Rechts*, § 276: "Die Grundbestimmung des politischen Staats ist die substantielle Einheit als Idealität seiner Momente, in welcher die besonderen Gewalten und Geschäfte desselben eben so aufgelöst als erhalten, und nur so erhalten sind, als sie keine unabhängige, sondern allein eine solche und so weit gehende Berechtigung haben, als in der Idee des Ganzen bestimmt ist, von seiner Macht ausgehen und flüßige Glieder desselben als ihres einfachen Selbsts sind."

We will see that Hobbes made a first contribution toward this claim by positing a relation not between individuals and a physical king, but rather between individuals and a constructed state or commonwealth, the sovereignty of which could be embodied in any number of ways. Given this construction, given that the sovereign must be much more complex than just a physical human being with a merely psychological will, the normative relation between sovereign and subject cannot be fully encompassed by the putative definition of prescriptions offered by von Wright above. On this reading, Hobbes' contribution to the modern conception of law is his conception of the commonwealth. However, Rousseau, as we will see, aptly succeeds Hobbes by placing in the sovereign, which is the abstract general will, the interests of all individuals in the state. Again, Rousseau also does not provide much additional analysis as to what the *volonté générale* as a convention or institution means for the conception of law. However, if we use as a foil the idea of a simple physical individual, Hart's Rex, who voluntaristically enacts laws as prescriptions for his subjects to follow, we certainly have with Rousseau (and probably already with Hobbes), a strong alteration of the medieval (and, as described below, late 20th century reductivist) paradigm regarding the relationship between the sovereign and the subject.

It is then not until Kant's *Grundlegung zur Metaphysik der Sitten* that the abstract political principles outlined in the great political theories of the previous two centuries begin to take on a legal character through the formulation of the categorical imperative, which, in positing that each individual should only be moved in his practical reason by that which can generally be the case, succeeds in providing the core *normative* relation between the individual and the collective that Hobbes and Rousseau could previously only allude to. The contribution of the categorical imperative for legal theory is that it provides the frame according to which individuals can be considered as acting according to the law, as opposed to the means-end rationality of the hypothetical imperative.

With this analysis of the self-constitution of the legal order and its legal subjects now in mind, I believe it is much easier to re-approach the issue of prescriptions within the legal order in order to gain a more complete appreciation of how they come about and how they are determined by success conditions for their functional ends. When we look at prescriptions as legal norms, we are looking at elements of a self-constituting system which is not arbitrary and which should not be interpreted by the lawyer, or anyone else, as arbitrary. Rather, prescriptions must be seen as norms which are directed to legal subjects in their normative capacity, which is to say in their capacity as agents capable of acting on the basis of norms. Such prescriptions are not issued in a vacuum, but rather in a pre-determined normative context, a legal language game, outside of which the normative content of prescriptions becomes incomprehensible.

Chapter II

A Positive Conception of the State

The focus of the following analysis is the addressor of the legal norm, i. e. the sovereign, and the addressee of the legal norm, i. e. the legal subject. The previous chapter sought to show that a logic of legal norms must not merely focus on the norm in the abstract, but rather on the legal norm in its entire context. Here, the focus lies on the relationship between the state and the individual, each as represented by the legal norm. The state is not something that requires the mere tolerance of the individual, but rather that actually constitutes the individual in its legal personhood.

1. Commands of the Sovereign

On its most basic definition, the law is comprised of commands of the sovereign. While this description enjoys widespread affirmation, the elements of the definition already contain the seeds of much controversy which has often run its course through legal theory. What is a command? Does the validity of the command depend on its content or is the validity content neutral? Must commands be backed by sanctions? What are the differences between enabling and prohibiting commands? Which formal criteria must commands fulfill in order to be law? What reasons for action do commands imply? These questions and many others relating to commands are at the heart of legal theory as it has been investigated for the last half century, largely under the heading of legal positivism or analytical jurisprudence.

However, considering law as the commands of the sovereign also entails a whole other set of questions relating not directly to commands as such, but to the nature of the sovereign which is qualified to issue the commands. Questions focusing on this second aspect include: Which conditions must obtain for a sovereign to exist? How does the relationship between sovereign and subject persist over time? To whom does the sovereign address its commands? Who is the sovereign? Is the concept of sovereignty compatible with the concept of self-government? Whereas the first set of questions is firmly within the line of inquiry of legal theory, the second set of questions may rather be considered part of political theory. However, the legal and political sciences have not always been so bifurcated. Montesquieu's *Esprit des Lois* treats the nature of government at length and Bentham's *Fragment on Government* deals extensively with the idea of law as fiction. In addition, many of the major German legal theorists of the late 19th and early 20th centuries wrote general theories of state and / or constitutional theories which at the very least presumed that questions about the nature of the state and the nature of the law were part of a single field of inquiry.

Lars Vinx has pointed out that Hans Kelsen's Pure Theory of Law is inextricably tied to an underlying liberal democratic theory of the state.[1] It is, however, true of all legal theories that they presuppose something about the nature and identity of the state and, since the commands must issue from some source, they therefore presuppose something about the sovereign as well. The definition of laws as commands of the sovereign creates a co-relation: whichever position one takes on the nature of commands will entail a relative position on the nature of the sovereign, and vice versa. Even the most adamantly analytical legal theories, ones which attempt to describe law at its most abstract level, make particular assumptions about which kinds of regimes can be responsible for enacting laws which satisfy the formal criteria of validity.[2] With a penchant for focusing on the worst case of the political, such theories either seek to show that (i) even evil laws are law or that (ii) the legal character of a norm says nothing about whether a subject is morally justified in following it, or both.[3] The common thread of this kind of abstract legal theory is that the job of the lawyer as a lawyer is to simply apply the commands of the sovereign regardless of their normative context. This, of course, says a lot about the theory's view of the legal profession as well as its view of citizen / subjects in their relation to lawyers and laws in general.

---

[1] Vinx. *Hans Kelsen's Pure Theory of Law*. For a variation on this theme of placing Kelsen's legal theory within a broader political theory, see also Elif Özmen, *Hans Kelsens Politische Philosophie*.

[2] See Matthew Kramer's *In Defense of Legal Positivism*, in which Kramer repeatedly envisions evil regimes enacting evil norms which, despite their depravity, fit within the class of laws abstractly understood.

[3] Even if Hart, in relation to more contemporary analytical jurisprudence, represents a relatively modest form of this position, Joseph Raz adequately captures this general stance in describing Hart's project as follows: "His analysis of the concept of law is part of the enterprise of demythologizing the law, of instilling rational critical attitudes to it. Right from his inaugural lecture in Oxford he was anxious to dispel the philosophical mist which he found in both legal culture and legal theory. In recent years he has shown time and again how much the rejection of the moralizing myths which accumulated around the law is central to his outlook. His essays on "Bentham and the Demystification of the Law" and on "The Nightmare and the Noble Dream" showed him to be consciously sharing the Benthamite sense of the excessive veneration in which the law is held in Common Law countries, and its deleterious moral consequences." "Authority, Law and Morality", p. 295.

Legal theory necessarily presupposes political theory. If we do not have a clear understanding of the nature of the sovereign, our understanding of its commands will necessarily be indeterminate and vague, if not over-broad and misleading. Of course, attempts at legal theory which are indeterminate and vague need not necessarily arise from a lack of political theory, but can also result from a concept of the political according to which the sovereign itself is indeterminate and vague. If the people, as opposed to a king, are the sovereign, it is much more difficult to develop a unified theory of how this sovereignty is expressed and, more importantly for legal theory, what the content of this expression is. The discourse theories of Rawls and Habermas are one kind of attempt at establishing the formal conditions under which democratic or majoritarian expression can succeed as a political order. However, as long as we conceive of this expression as being democratic in nature and we understand this to entail neutrality relative to content, the formal success conditions of such a system are the most to which we can aspire. Legal theory, or at least its most prominent strands, has followed a similar course over the past half century and, like its political counterpart, has had success despite the indeterminacy of its subject. One prominent example of this success is in Fuller's enunciation of eight principles of legality, in which he set forth the minimum success conditions for a legal system.[4] In this case, the Fullerian legal theory, or something like it, would be the best that we can do given the indeterminacy of the political concept at its base.

The openness of democratic theory, though, along with the formal nature of analytical jurisprudence, can also be attributed to a theory of the political which is thoroughly apolitical. If we are truly free as a people, there may not be much need in conceiving of a sovereign at all, for self-governance (autonomy) can easily entail non-governance (i. e. a lack of heteronomy). Accordingly, liberty would be achieved by limiting government or any 'sovereign' in the traditional sense and the lion's share of society would then occur outside of the political realm in voluntary interactions between private individuals. Under such a view, legal theory can easily view the political and its laws as perhaps unavoidable, but yet something with which normal individuals need not necessarily concern themselves in their day-to-day dealings. Much like death and taxes, it is best for normal people to leave questions of law to experts to the extent possible and focus instead on the moral aspects of social and familial circumstance. Interpreting the political in such an apolitical manner is a second justification for taking a reserved approach toward questions regarding the meaning of law. Namely, all meaning in society should be derived from morality and any legal requirements should be seen as mere super-impositions upon the properly normative framework of the moral.

---

[4] See Fuller, *The Morality of Law*.

A second apolitical strain of legal theory can be found in a libertarian frame of reason according to which the commands from a sovereign *above* are likely to disturb both the absolute freedom of the individual and the order of society as it organically exists *below*. This kind of argument, which runs through the work of Friedrich Hayek, Robert Nozick and Richard Epstein, also denies the moral bindingness of the political. However, instead of resigning itself to commands of the sovereign as a matter of social fact, the libertarian frame asserts that such commands can be parasitic on the normativity of the properly social order. As such, legislated law would then not be a necessary evil to be tolerated, but rather a pernicious evil to be eradicated.

In the face of such political theoretical influences upon contemporary legal theory (either the indeterminacy of the sovereign or a very minimalist or contrarian interpretation of sovereignty itself), we are nonetheless left with the unrelenting idea that law, in its most basic form, *is* the command of the sovereign and that this command of the sovereign retains its validity regardless of the strength of the sovereign (i. e. a minimalist or absolutist state) or the democratic legitimacy of its origin. This relationship between the sovereign, its command and the addressee to whom the sovereign communicates the command has become clouded over the past century, perhaps in part due to civil society having increasingly sought to emancipate itself from political authority. However, even if it is not in vogue for the average individual to consider himself subject to the political order, we still must acknowledge this relationship if we consider the lawyer, who, *as a lawyer*, must commit to defending the law and being its champion in practice. To defend the law is to defend its norms and to defend its norms is to defend the sovereign. This defense entails more than a mere recognition of valid rules and the subsequent technical subsumption thereof to facts, as Kelsen might have envisioned it. Instead, as Hart corrected with the Rule of Recognition, it requires acknowledgement of the sovereign as the *rightful* author of the command.

If we understand why this relationship exists between the lawyer and the sovereign, then we will understand that the legal profession does not represent a special case of an 'internal' perspective on the law, but that rather the lawyerly case is prototypical of the general. The qualification of the lawyer does not lie in a special agency relationship with the sovereign, nor is it the result of a special deal in which the lawyer has agreed to uncritically follow the sovereign's commands in exchange for certain privileges. Rather, through education and training the lawyer is meant to have gained extra insight into and understanding of the legal order. This understanding requires exercise in the art of legal reasoning, which is a reasoning within a system of principles and rules. This system of norms, here Kelsen would agree, must be comprehensible as a system unto itself.

The lawyer, or law student, must learn how the norms make sense in relation to each other and that a 'lawyerly' appeal to supposedly extra-legal norms (such as those of morality) is not only a sign of professional incompetence but a contradiction in terms. However, this indication of incompetence or contradiction is importantly not due to a supposed non-existence of the claimed moral norm. Instead, it is due to the inability of the lawyer to formulate his claim within the valid argumentative framework which the respective legal system provides – the presumption being that such an integrative formulation would be possible for a lawyer with sufficient mastery of the legal order.

The cry of unfairness which the novice student is wont to utter is invalid for the reason that, faced with the inability to justify his sentiment within the legal order, the only recourse left for the student is to seek justification in an alternative order. However, the sovereign, as the highest authority within the order, permits of no such alternative. If one is committed to being a subject of the legal system, one must also commit to the order which the system provides; this is true of both lawyers and laymen.

The law does not require the normative commitment of each legal subject to every legal norm. However, the law does require the normative commitment of each legal subject to the legal system itself. In this respect, law is just like language. It may make sense to cull certain concepts from our language and to introduce others, but it is not possible in any normal state of affairs to opt out of language itself. Likewise, I may not prefer the particular set of norms that my legal system offers me, but I am nonetheless bound to the law in two particular aspects. First, I am bound to the jurisdiction of the law in the trivial sense – as long as I am within a legal system's jurisdiction, I am compelled on threat of sanction to follow the law. Second, though, I am also bound to the order of the law in a normative, desire-independent sense. The law constitutes the entirety of the normative framework in which I can act. As a result, it is possible to attribute a legal meaning to any relevant action such that my entire personhood is ultimately constituted in the legal order.

2. Leviathan, not Rex

I argued in Chapter I that the law should not be conceived as mere prescriptions and that the very idea of a singular will is inherently problematic when referring to the state. Yet, the primary frame in which the 'commands of the sovereign' have been viewed in the last sixty years is that of a singular King, who issues his edicts for his subjects to follow. Of course, theorists have merely used Rex as a simplification of the concept of sovereignty in order to analyze the necessary and sufficient qualities of the law. Nonetheless, this very simplification calls into question the nature of sovereignty itself. Is Rex a big man with power over others? This is not necessarily or even essentially the case.

The problem is that if one posits that Rex is simply presupposed, then this necessarily glosses over issues of authority and legislation. Most perniciously, we then imagine a man carrying the title of Rex, we imagine that the law exists because of something which has occurred in the world – we derive an 'ought' from an 'is' and reduce the legal norm to a matter of social fact. However, if we want to conceive the law as a norm, then our Rex cannot be physical in his essence at all, but rather spiritual, mental, normative. Sovereignty cannot attach to any *thing* in the world, but rather is an *idea* of authority that is exercised absolutely over others. The sovereign must be an absolute normative order, a basic condition of society, a first convention, *volonté générale*, a Leviathan.

3. Political Agency

If laws are the commands of the sovereign and these commands entail a relationship between the sovereign and the subject, the question arises as to the generality of this relationship. Am I as a human agent generally under the authority of the law or is the scope of my legal obedience particular to specific commands? Does obedience to the law constitute and explain only a portion of my action or, as provisionally claimed above, does the law constitute me as an agent more generally?

Implicit in Austin's (partial) definition of the law as commands of a sovereign is that sanctions comprise at least part of law's normativity.[5] Without the threat of sanction, a legal subject may or may not be inclined to follow the sovereign's prescriptions. However, *with* the threat of sanction, the subject always has a reason to comply and, if the sanction is calibrated correctly, this reason to comply will be sufficient to bind the subject to the sovereign's prescribed course of action

[5] See Austin, pp. 29–30: "Superiority is often synonymous with precedence or excellence. We talk of superiors in rank; of superiors in wealth; or superiors in virtue: comparing certain persons with certain other persons; and meaning that the former precede or excel the latter in rank, in wealth, or in virtue. But, taken with the meaning wherein I here understand it, the term superiority signifies might: the power of affecting others with evil or pain, and of forcing them, through fear of that evil, to fashion their conduct to one's wishes. For example, God is emphatically the superior of man. For his power of affecting us with pain, and of forcing us to comply with his will, is unbounded and resistless. To a limited extent, the Sovereign One or Number is the superior of the subject or citizen: the master, of the slave or servant: the father, of the child. In short, whoever can *oblige* another to comply with his wishes, is the superior of that other, so far as the ability reaches: the party who is obnoxious to the impending evil, being, to that same extent, the inferior."

by means of hypothetical imperative – if I want to avoid the punishment associated with the violation of this norm, then I shall comply with the norm. By using the police power to tie a sanction to the violation of a legal norm, the sovereign can alter an otherwise non-obedient subject's rationale for pursuing or refraining from a course of action. The sovereign, as the highest power in the land, is in a position to create reasons for action by means of the sanction. However, the question is whether this is the sole or even an essential function of the sovereign.

In addressing this question, we must consider the kinds of human agency which exist within society and which are at the sovereign's disposal when issuing commands. There are two basic ways to think about human agency. The first is a brute, animal form of agency which consists in the actions which an individual takes that are directly or indirectly related to the satisfaction of basic, physical desires to satisfy hunger, thirst, fatigue, etc. The second is a desire-independent form of agency which has a rule-based or deontic structure. The first takes the everyday form of 'I want, I need…' and the second takes the form: 'I should, shall, must, may…,' which is to say 'I can.'

The first form is at first glance more evident and basic. The fundamental desires for food, drink, shelter and procreation seek to satisfy the minimum physiological conditions of life. In addition though, there are second and third order desires which build upon these fundamental desires. For example, the seven deadly sins signify desires which do not satisfy first order needs, but rather excesses thereof. Gluttony is the desire to have more food than one needs in an overabundance of caution to avoid hunger; greed is the desire to have more wealth than one needs in an overabundance of caution to avoid poverty; etc.

However, higher order subjective desires need not all be detrimental to personal or communal well-being, but can extend to enlightened versions of egotistical behavior / prudential self-interest as well. Kant's merchant who raises the price of his goods neither in the face of high short term demand nor when dealing with inexperienced customers is one example of a higher order, desire dependent action.[6] The fact that the merchant is perceived by his community to be honest in his prices will result in a sufficient increase in customer base to offset the loss of any short-term profits which he could have obtained through price-gouging. Indeed, by viewing civil society through such a lens of higher order, desire dependent reasons for action which extend the effectual horizon of any given action over a long term and a multitude of beneficiaries, one can develop a seemingly complete picture of social reality. Social reality and its societal order would accordingly be the result of a multitude of homines oeconomici acting in a self-interested, but prudential manner and, with Bentham, we could say that any talk of rules,

[6] Kant, *Grundlegung zur Metaphysik der Sitten*, p. 23. (Werkausgabe VII)

rights or duties removed from these considerations would be nothing but unfounded and unjustifiable metaphysics.

While it is possible to imagine social individuals acting solely on the basis of desire-dependent reasons for action, it is actually difficult to imagine a developed society consisting solely of such individuals. If the horizon of an action is relatively limited as in the case of a clan, for example, with measurable benefits of the action to be enjoyed within a lifetime and with beneficiaries not extending beyond direct relations of the agent, then prudential self-interest could conceivably account for most phenomena. However, if the horizon of actions becomes so attenuated that one can no longer point to any subjective stake which the agents have in the results of their actions, then self-interest seems no longer to suffice as an ordering principle.

In contrast to the subjectivity of self-interest, there must be a way to account for *objective* order in the actions of individuals. What is missing is an account of that invisible hand which seems to provide direction or order to the self-interested behavior of individuals. If we are to avoid a blind faith in the providence of enlightened self-interest, a *deus ex machina* of social order, the source of social cohesion must be through a set of norms which attains objectivity through (i) an appeal to a common reason or (ii) sanctions which are more or less uniformly effective across all subjects. It is not necessary at the moment to locate this source of order in either of these alternatives exclusively because each requires the other in an important way.

The validity of objectively binding rules within complex societal orders does not entail foreclosing the realm of self-interested actions. On the contrary, society provides a cornucopia of opportunities for self-interested persons who believe themselves to slyly take their own advantage of the naivety of the rule-abiding. For example, free-riding is precisely the desire-dependent act of a self-interested individual which is afforded by other individuals acting in desire-independent ways and for the common good. Of course, the conscientious bus passenger who pays for his ticket may also fit within the framework of desire-dependent reasons described above. On such an account, the conscientious passenger would also act out of mere self-interest, but this would be a self-interest of a higher order. Instead of focusing on the immediate gratification of saving money, the conscientious passenger would instead prefer the more remote gratification (i) of knowing that he could ride the bus in the same way every day without fear of suffering a fine (temporal remoteness) or indeed (ii) of knowing that his payment contributes to a bus system which would never exist without the contributions of himself and those like him (general remoteness).

At first glance, this difference between the reasons for action of the free-rider who doesn't pay his fare and those of the conscientious passenger who does pay his fare appears to be a question of degree of remoteness of the desired gratification. If this were the case, desire-independent reasons for action would simply be a more removed kind of desire-dependent reasons for action – I act in a desire independent way whenever I suspend my desires in the here and now in order to allow the fulfilment of other, superior desires in the future or in other contexts. However, if we look at the situation more closely, we see that the supposed difference in degree is actually a difference in kind, that exchanging my immediate desire for a personal gratification either in the future or in the general existence of the institution involves acting according to a generally applicable principle or norm.

If I see a ripe berry in the forest, the sight and perhaps smell of the berry will sufficiently motivate me to pick and eat the berry. However, such a sufficient motivation of a primary desire does not hold for actions based on higher order desires. In order for me to plan either for a longer term or more general good (i. e. temporal or general remoteness), I must forsake a concrete desire in the present. This forsaking, however, is a privation of motivation and can only be explained through a hypothetical imperative or norm, according to which I must have a capacity to act. For the case of the bus passenger, the hypothetical norm would be either: (i) if I am to realize the greater pleasure of riding the bus without fear of sanction, I should pay the fare now; or: (ii) if I am to realize the greater pleasure that the institution of the municipal bus system has to offer, I should pay the fare now. The first of these hypothetical norms creates a temporal remoteness relative to desire and is purely subjective in terms of motivation for action; the second hypothetical norm creates a general remoteness relative to desire and is subjective, but also *objective* in that it allows me to plan and coordinate my own action around the actions of others.

Both of these kinds of hypothetical norms build upon subjective desire as a motivating force in human behavior. However, it would be a mistake to think that hypothetical norms are simply higher forms of the same desire-dependent structure. That there is a difference in kind, as opposed to a mere difference in degree, is shown by Hobbes at the end of the first part of *Leviathan*.

The problem which Hobbes there tries to address is precisely the problem of how humans can move from desire-dependent to desire-independent reasons for action. He does this by painting a picture of man in his natural, desire-dependent state and then demonstrating that political order is the sole solution for the problem of higher order, desire-*dependent*, reasons for action. According to Hobbes' account, any attempt to forsake present for future satisfaction is likely to be frustrated due to lack of security among individual actors. The rationality which would otherwise dictate a subjective hypothetical norm (e. g. of saving some berries for additional pleasure tomorrow) therefore instead dictates maximizing the pleasure of the moment. Moreover, even if individuals would realize the usefulness of forming a voluntary collective or creating institutional reality through objective hypothetical norms as a means for enabling the pursuit of the subjective hypothetical norms, these too would be bound to failure due to desire-dependent opportunism and the resulting dissolution of trust on which the collective, institutional reality would be based. Thus, in Hobbes' account, without the intervention of an institution which itself can sanction to preserve its own existence as well as the existence of other institutions (like that of promising), there can be no progression out of this first order desire-dependent state. As a result, in postulating Leviathan, Hobbes does not just describe the origin of political reality, but of all institutional reality as well.

Interestingly though, while the need to form higher order desire-dependent reasons for action may be the impetus for the construction of the commonwealth, this is not what Leviathan can accomplish: as long as the higher order actions are desire-dependent, the higher order reason for action will always dissolve as soon as the immediate need outweighs the individual benefit in the future or in the general good. Without a desire-independent (absolute) duty on the part of the subjects to Leviathan or the commonwealth, the commonwealth would constantly be in a state of war against its subjects by seeking to create through sanction a sufficient incentive not to renege on higher order hypothetical norms. However, this is not the case for Hobbes' Leviathan. Instead of being at war with its subjects, the commonwealth represents its subjects and speaks for them as one person. Hobbes states in Chapter 17 that the construct of *Leviathan* allows all individuals:

> to conferre all their power and strength upon one Man, or upon one Assembly of men, that may reduce all their Wills, by plurality of voices, unto one Will: which is as much as to say, to appoint one man, or Assembly of men, to beare their Person; and every one to owne, and acknowledge himselfe to be Author of whatsoever he that so beareth their Person, shall Act, or cause to be Acted, in those things which concerne the Common Peace and Safetie; and therein to submit their Wills, every one to his Will, and their Judgements, to his Judgment.

Hobbes does not speak here of a wonderful tyrant who succeeds in subduing his subjects to his will, turning them into sheep to blindly follow his orders on fear of punishment. Rather, Hobbes is speaking as a first modernist, describing how individuals move beyond the instrumentalist rationality of desire-dependent reasons toward the logic of desire-independent reasons, from the calculus of the hypothetical imperative to the deonticity of the categorical imperative. The plurality of voices forms one will, one person capable of authorship, by every individual following the one general law that he may do that which, taken as a rule, would be generally applicable for every other individual.

This construction provides the foundation for desire-independent rationality which, once established, also explains why Hobbes claims that the assignment of rights to the commonwealth can never be revoked. Any revocation of the commonwealth would be a revocation of desire-independent rationality, the only alternative of which is the desire-dependent rationality of the state of nature. As such, Leviathan represents the birth of the state in the fully realized agency of the individual.

4. The Absolute State

The question of the relationship between the individual and the state is a distinctively modern issue which derives from the idea that the concretely existing political power, whether dictatorial or democratic, totalitarian or republican in nature, is fully determinate of the legal relations of social reality. This idea is first found with Jean Bodin, who, with his definition of sovereignty as the 'absolute and temporally unlimited power of a state', attempted to free political reality from the vicissitudes of divine will as interpreted by the Church or any other religious group which currently enjoyed military superiority over a certain territory. While the notion of political power flowing from divine right could be said to have secured a fairly stable state of political relations during the Middle Ages, this order fell apart in the 16th century as competing authorities began each laying claim to divine authorization and as the question of what constitutes a divine right and / or the nature of divine law itself began to be raised by politically independent parties. In the face of such difficulties, Bodin's identification of sovereignty with that which is absolute and unlimited in power within a given territory conveniently side-stepped any theological disputes and instead provided an initial, purely formal, clarification of the matter: might makes right.[7]

Although Bodin is responsible for the modern absolutist approach to sovereignty, it is Hobbes whose analysis of the commonwealth as developing out of the state of nature succeeded in finally separating political power from all forms of divine justification while still managing to uphold the claim of the commonwealth's absolute power over its subjects.[8] Only through the universal and abso-

---

[7] Although Bodin's definition of the state as a "sovereign governing power oriented to the law" still hearkens back to the medieval tension between divine law and will to a certain degree, his definition of sovereignty clearly resolves this tension in favor of voluntarism.

[8] See Strauss, p. 126: "Die Genesis von Hobbes' politischer Wissenschaft ist durch folgende Vorgänge charakterisiert: 1. die Bewegung von der Idee der Monarchie als des am meisten natürlichen Staates zur Idee der Monarchie als des vollkommensten künstlichen Staates; 2. die Bewegung von der Anerkennung einer natürlichen Verpflichtung als der Grundlage von Moral,

lute assignment of every individual's natural rights (i) does a power become absolute and obtain the status of the political and (ii) is every individual afforded the opportunity to peacefully pursue its needs as a result of the assurance of the commonwealth's sanctioning power.

However, in order to understand this idea of the commonwealth and the relationship which it entails between individuals and the state, we first must understand the idea of the premises on which this commonwealth is based. In the 17th chapter of *Leviathan* Hobbes puts forth in five parts his argument for the formation of the commonwealth. First, the final cause and end of men is their self-preservation. Second, the laws of nature, essentially the golden rule, are insufficient to bind individuals without "the terrour of some Power to cause them to be observed." Third, self-preservation is best secured when threats to such security are discouraged through the alliance of as many individuals as possible. Fourth, even when there are no threats from outside forces, if there is no central power, internal differences and strife will lead to a condition of war for the group. Fifth, because of this, each man, on the condition of the same being done by each other, gives authorisation in the following form: "I authorise and give up my Right of governing my selfe, to this Man, or to this Assembly of Men" (i. e. the commonwealth).[9]

It is not hard to understand the rationality of individuals assigning their rights to the commonwealth, for the state of nature which Hobbes describes, i. e. one in which the most basic elements of social compassion are missing, is indeed very primitive. As an alternative to an existence in which one must constantly fight for one's own life, the promise of security would be a great bargain at any cost. However, while the reasons for the formation of the commonwealth are very clear under this scenario, the analysis becomes difficult when we ask ourselves what happens following the fulfillment of Leviathan's promise to secure order. For, while the need for security may justify an absolute assignment of rights *ex initio*, there is no reason why such an assignment should be unlimited or should persist in time (as per Bodin's second requirement of sovereignty). Instead, any absolute assignment should rather create a commissarial dictatorship upon a fixed term with automatic expiration following the establishment of peace. Peace

---

Recht und Staat zu der Deduktion von Moral, Recht und Staat aus einem natürlichem Anspruch (und damit zu der Leugnung jeder natürlichen Verpflichtung); 3. Die Bewegung von der Anerkennung einer übermenschlichen Autorität – sei es der im Willen Gottes gründenden Offenbarung – sei es der im Verstand Gottes gründenden natürlichen Ordnung – zur Anerkennung allein der menschlichen Autorität des Staates; 4. Die Bewegung vom Studium der bisherigen Staaten zur freien Konstruktion des zukünftigen Staates; 5. Die Bewegung vom Prinzip der Ehre zur Prinzip der Furcht vor gewaltsamen Tod."

[9] Leviathan, Chapter 17.

having been attained, one would expect the natural rights to devolve back to the individuals who now would hopefully have been able to develop the first seeds of morality and social cohesion with the commissarial dictator waiting in the wings to once again fulfill his duty should such development fail.[10] If we consider, though, the 14 chapters which follow Hobbes' creation of the commonwealth in Chapter 17 and the institutional apparatus of the commonwealth which he therein describes, it is clear that this is not the scenario which Hobbes had in mind.

Nonetheless, it is also possible to imagine the assignment of rights as not being strictly absolute or, if absolute, subject to revision as time goes on. According to such a scenario, after an initial phase in which the commonwealth has succeeded in establishing the peace, the subjects to the commonwealth would then be afforded the opportunity to develop a new set of rights (and obligations) of a moral or civil nature. Assuming that the commonwealth would insist on being assigned the full scope of its subjects' rights and that it would not be content with an existence as a mere police state (again in line with the rest of Hobbes' argumentation), it would be plausible to think that the subjects would only make these secondary assignments subject to certain reservations or conditions. In other words, the power of the commonwealth would be unlimited in time, but no longer absolute (thus failing to fulfill Bodin's first requirement of sovereignty). Such a quasi-Lockean scenario does find a certain resonance in the modern discourse of human / constitutional rights according to which the state, in principle, has absolute power, subject to any number of identifiable rights, such as freedom of religion, speech, assembly, the right to bear arms, due process, privacy, non-incrimination, personal development, education, etc.[11] This, however, is also not the absolute assignment which Hobbes imagines in Chapter 17.

These two previous accounts ((a) power unlimited in scope, but limited in time and (b) power limited in scope, but unlimited in time) are thoroughly instrumentalist in nature envisioning the multitude of men, being weak and finding themselves in a state of war, turning to the strong man or assembly of men in order to obtain security in refuge from themselves. Such a basic account though, is very limited. If it is merely about the social contract in which the multitude of men cede their rights to a natural man, Leviathan, in return for security, there really is nothing which would prevent the multitude from claiming back their rights (for example, the Magna Carta) or in simply replacing one monarch with another.

---

[10] Carl Schmitt explores this notion in depth referring back to the commissarial dictatorships of Rome. See *Die Diktatur*.

[11] Benno Zabel (2015) argues against such a devil's bargain (i.e. the abdication of sovereignty in exchange for rights) in favor of an institutional theory of rights. See also Jean-François Kervégan, *La raison des normes – essai sur Kant*.

However, here Hobbes states in Chapter 18 that the multitude of men, being bound by covenant, can neither "lawfully make a new covenant" nor "cast off (the) Monarchy." Moreover, if Hobbes were envisioning an instrumentalist account, the following passage one paragraph later would be extremely difficult to understand:

Because the Right of bearing the Person of them all, is given to him they make Soveraigne, by Covenant onely of one to another, and not of him to any of them; there can happen no breach of Covenant on the part of the Soveraigne; and consequently none of his Subjects, by any pretence of forfeiture, can be freed from his Subjection.

In short, even if Hobbes' depiction of the natural state of man is plausible, it is difficult to see how the total and irrevocable subjection of the multitude of men to one man or assembly of men can be upheld, *if the basis of this subjection is merely a rationalistic instrumentality*. However, if we look at the passage from Chapter 17 quoted in the section above, we see that the basis for the creation of the commonwealth is not an instrumental or contractual consideration, but rather a change in *status* brought about by the multitude becoming one.

Shortly after this passage in Chapter 18, Hobbes states:

One Person, of whose Acts a great Multitude, by mutuall Covenants one with another, have made themselves every one the Author, to the end he may use the strength and means of them all, as he shall think expedient, for their Peace and Common Defence.

Hobbes states that the covenant which every man makes with every other man is more than consent, but rather a unity. Out of the multitude of wills, the covenant creates one will, one 'person', which then can authorize the one man or assembly of men, to act on its behalf. The multitude does not enter into a bargain based on a quid pro quo, but rather constitutes itself into a state. The reason why the sovereign can neither be limited nor deposed for Hobbes, is that the act of constitution presupposes this sovereign, as historically indicated by Bodin. This sovereign, in turn, must be understood not as the monarch, but as the artificial (legal) person of the state which at most can be *represented by* the monarch. The alternative to a tyrannical monarch is always another monarch or other form of government; the alternative to the state (i. e. the political order) is the dissolution of agency, that which Hobbes calls war.

Hobbes' analysis of the state of nature and the resulting assignment to the commonwealth in exchange for security must be understood as a description of the logical relation between the individual and the state and between security and sanction. The 'contract', which every individual executes with every other individual, and the resulting assignment of each individual's natural rights are figurative of the status of individuals relative to the status of the commonwealth. The essence of the Hobbesian account is that every individual exists in such a relation to the commonwealth that the commonwealth possesses every right over every individual, excepting the right to kill.

From this account we see that while natural man may be prior to the state, the state is prior to personhood; for no normative framework can be expected to exist without the state. Indeed, we can locate the first person in the artificial person of the state, which is that unity formed out of the multitude of lowly and fearful men who first submit to a first convention, a norm.

5. Volonté Générale and the Legal Concept of the Political

Beginning with Hobbes and now following up through Rousseau, we can begin to make a case for the inherent normativity of the law and state by showing how legal and political institutions can be norm (or value) driven not *in spite* but *because* of their positivist character.

Spinoza suggests that "if there is such a thing as absolute sovereignty, it is really that which is held by the people as a whole."[12] Spinoza surely does not mean that an unlimited sovereign power exists in the power being encapsulated or restrained by the multitude, as if the masses would be standing at the castle gates with pitchforks and torches, issuing directly democratic decrees (or vetoes) regarding the actions of government. Quantified brute power may succeed in providing a check on governmental actions, but could hardly be considered to enable unlimited government. Instead, there must be a qualitative or ideal aspect of the multitude which, when conformed with on the part of the sovereign, yields the greatest degree of power. Yet, a multitude in itself forms no unity and is not normatively constituted. Without such a constitution, it is difficult to see how any grouping of people can be an agent, or a sovereign. Instead, it would seem that each individual would be bound to a passive existence, to suffer the heteronomic norms of others.

This forms the point of departure for Rousseau in his *Discours sur l' économie politique.* There, Rousseau asks how it is possible to combine the interests of many individuals into one common political body: how is it possible to be free if another is capable of restricting my will or how is it possible to be master of my own well-being if my well-being is subject to the will of others? Rousseau suggests that the answer is to be found in the constitutive character of the law:

---

[12] Baruch de Spinoza, Political Treatise, Samuel Shirley (tr.). Hackett, 2000 (Spinoza, Political Treatise), Ch. 8, Sec. 3: "Nam si quod imperium absolutum datur, illud revera est, quod integra multitudo tenet."

C'est à la loi seule que les hommes doivent la justice et la liberté. C'est cet organe salutaire de la volonté de tous, qui rétablit dans le droit l'égalité naturelle entre les hommes. C'est cette voix céleste qui dicte à chaque citoyen les préceptes de la raison publique, et lui apprend à agir selon les maximes de son propre jugement, et à n'être pas en contradiction avec lui-même.[13]

For Rousseau it is the law which unifies the multitude and which thereby constitutes political authority. And already Spinoza says that, in speaking to each individual's faculty of reason, it is the reason of the law that, "as if by one mind"[14], can form the multitude into a singular force which, if complied with by the sovereign, gives the sovereign a nearly unlimited power. Spinoza adds:

For the constitution is the soul of the state; if this is preserved, the state is preserved. But a constitution cannot stay intact unless it is upheld both by reason and by the common sentiment of the people; otherwise, if for instance laws are dependent solely on the support of reason, they are likely to be weak and easily overthrown.[15]

The idea of the state requires that its positive laws conform with the *volonté générale*, or the 'soul of the state' which, in turn, is identified with a different kind of law, or as Rousseau says, the "moi commun".[16] In enacting and enforcing legal norms within a particular legal system, it is essential that the norms which are recognised are those which are based in reason and the common human affect. This provides us with a starting point for a theory of law and state which seeks to affirm, not limit the authority of the state as the *volonté générale*.

Rousseau believed that the idea of the republic requires a *volonté générale* as constitutive principle.[17] This general will, he posited, must serve as the ideal source of authority for the actions of the state, and any actions contrary to this idea (or outside of such a mandate) must necessarily be illegitimate.[18] While the *volonté générale* must be absolute in principle, Rousseau's concept of the state requires that state actions must nonetheless conform to the particular contents of the general will when the state performs its particular duties. Of course, the ostensible difficulty with this construction is that the sovereign, being the particular manifestation of the *volonté générale*, would be de facto beyond reproach in performing its duties. Without more insight into the origin and expression of the general will, this construction becomes a *carte blanche* for the arbitrary exercise of power.

---

[13] Rousseau, *Discours sur l'economie politique*, pp. 49–50.

[14] Spinoza, *Political Treatise*, Ch. 3, Sec. 2.

[15] Spinoza, *Political Treatise*, Ch. 10, Sec. 9. "Anima enim imperii jura sunt. His igitur servatis servatur necessario imperium. At jura invicta esse nequeunt, nisi et ratione et communi hominem affectu defendantur; alias, si scilicet solo rationis auxilio nituntur, invalidae sane sunt facileque vincuntur."

[16] Rousseau, *Discours sur l'economie politique*, p. 46.

[17] Rousseau, *Du contrat social*, Livre I, Ch. VI.

[18] Id., Livre II, Ch. IV.

Benjamin Constant sought to remediate this apparent design flaw of Rousseau's *volonté générale* by revamping Rousseau's theory to accommodate the exigencies of an actual democratic regime which Constant believed to have learned following the Reign of Terror. The *volonté générale*, Constant affirmed, is the sole source of authority in a republic; however, the mandate of the *volonté générale*, Constant added, must not extend beyond the social domain, it must be limited in nature.[19] In keeping with the revolutionary spirit of his time and yet wisened by the excesses of his contemporaries, Constant attested that the general will is a necessary but insufficient condition for the exercise of sovereign power. It is necessary in order to ensure that the people are the source of sovereignty; it is insufficient because there are always divisions among the people in their preferences and it is always unjust for the sovereign to give some preferences the force of law at the expense of others. Constant had no pretensions about democratic processes yielding an objective truth of society or of its laws laying claim to moral goodness by virtue of resulting from the "will of the people". For Constant, majoritarian rule is merely the least unjust among the various alternatives of government.[20] This formed a restricted, negative view of the state, according to which the state is a necessary evil that is tolerated in order to enable a social existence for individuals. As a tolerated body, its actions must be limited to the extent possible in order to protect the individual preferences of its members.

Many legal theorists have adopted a similar stance toward the state and the laws which issue from it when, in their diligent efforts to separate law from morality, they have effectively reduced legal norms to non-normative terms concerning power, habits of obedience and sanctions, even when the description of such factual habit (including the habit of being sanctioned) may be cloaked in the language of a 'rule of recognition'.[21] In making such claims, theorists have been able to disregard any normative or moral foundation to the authority of the state

---

[19] *Constant, Principes de Politique,* Livre II, Ch. I: "Il y a, au contraire, une partie de l'existence humaine qui, de nécessité, reste individuelle et indépendante et qui est, de droit, hors de toute competence sociale. La souveraineté n'existe que d'une maniere limitée et relative." See also Richard Tuck's *The Sleeping Sovereign, the Invention of Modern Democracy* and Farr and Williams (ed.), *The General Will, the Evolution of a Concept*. 2015.

[20] Constant, *Principes de Politique*, Livre II, Ch. II, p. 53.

[21] For example, see Hart, *The Concept of Law*, p. 100: "Wherever such a rule of recognition is accepted, both private persons and officials are provided with authoritative criteria for identifying primary rules of obligation." It is important that what Hart provides, in contrast to Kelsen, is not an account of the normativity of the law, but rather a description of how rules, specifically the secondary Rule of Recognition, are used by people, both private persons and officials, *as a matter of fact*, to identify those primary rules which are, *in fact*, law. Beyond the factual description that people actually behave in this way, Hart provides no *normative* justification for why this is the case.

with the result that any value pertaining to the state has been thought to derive from the limited authority of ad-hoc majoritarian decisions based on recognized democratic values, provided that the reservoir of reserved, individual rights is not thereby violated. So long as our government is elected and controlled by us, so the reasoning seems to go, we need not worry about the constitutional questions regarding the normativity, or the lack thereof, of the laws to which we are subject. Kelsen has generally been accepted into this club of mainstream legal positivists due to his strong rejection of natural law and his advocacy for liberal democratic principles, even if such recognition has often remained somewhat reserved due to the more exotic aspects of his Pure Theory, most specifically the basic norm and Kelsen's insistence on the legal system as a system entailing validity.[22]

As mentioned above, an attempt to move Kelsen further into this direction of legal theory was made in 2007 by Lars Vinx. Vinx provides an interpretation of Kelsen according to which the Pure Theory of Law is said not to set forth a normative basis or validity for the law as Kelsen explicitly claimed, but rather to explain how the law can be understood to be legitimate by ensuring a hierarchy of norms which ends in democratic discourse and mutual recognition of majoritarian rights.[23] On this interpretation, Kelsen's legal theory is specifically designed to ensure not an absolute, but relative legal validity in a democratic political order in which secondary norms serve as the logical connection between the commands of the state and their democratic origins. When asked why one should follow the law, the response according to this reading would be that the law derives its validity from a lawmaker who, at the beginning of a chain of authority ending in his enactment, was authorized to enact the law through a democratic process. The validity of this authorization itself would, in this fuller picture of the Kelsenian legal / political worldview, depend not on the validity of a higher norm, but on the legitimacy of the entirety of the political process.[24] The purpose of legal science, accordingly, would be to create a foolproof hierarchy of secondary norms that are successful in maintaining the integrity of the democratic process which is ultimately responsible for creating and implementing legally binding norms of conduct. A legal subject recognizes the legitimacy of individual legal norms because the laws are a result of the democratic process. Even if the

---

[22] For example, see Hart's "Kelsen Visited". For a discussion of Kelsen's thought in contrast to the reductivist position, see Stanley Paulson's preface in the reprint of Kelsen's *Reine Rechtslehre* (1934) (Kelsen, *Reine Rechtslehre I*). We will see below that some of Kelsen's idiosyncrasies relative to the reductivist position are concurrent with the absolute ideal of the *volonté générale* and are key in explaining the deficiencies mentioned above.

[23] Vinx, *Hans Kelsen's Pure Theory of Law: Legality and Legitimacy.*

[24] Id. at p. 59 ff.

result in a particular case is contrary to one's individual preference, one follows the law counting on the fact that others will do the same when contrary preferences are enacted following subsequent election cycles.[25] On this account, a sand-box model of the law, in which various parties take turns exercising the sovereign power for the particular interests of each, is simply the best political model we can hope for.

Kelsen's thought is subject to a wide range of interpretations[26], up to and including an interpretation of the Pure Theory as a consequentially nihilistic theory that ultimately eschews all recourse to claims of validity.[27] Moreover, Kelsen's theory is obfuscated to some degree by his insistence on rule formalism tied-in with an empirical approach toward the identification of legal norms. However, these variations on the Kelsenian theme notwithstanding, I consider the core value of the Kelsenian project not to lie in its defense of a liberal democratic political system, but rather in its attempt at explaining the legal norm as it occurs within a system of legal normativity, of ought-judgments.[28] Kelsen's assertion of the state as a normatively constituted body places him within a lineage of theorists who, without resorting to the metaphysics of natural law theorists, hold an affirmative view of the state and its laws as normative institutions, including, but not limited to, Rousseau, Hegel and Hermann Cohen.[29] In this sense, I would argue that Kelsen is important not because he was one of the first true legal positivists, but because he was one of the last.[30]

---

[25] Id. at p. 122: "The principle of revisability and the notion of community going along with it thus make it possible for the outvoted person to see her own interest in freedom reflected in a social will created according to the majority rule even if the content of that will does not, for now, match her own will."

[26] See Paulson (ed). *Normativity and Norms*. See also, Kervégan's *Variazioni kelseniane*. For a description of the various positions which Kelsen took even within his own lifetime, see Stanley L. Paulson. "Four Phases in Hans Kelsen's Legal Theory? Reflections on a Periodization". *Oxford J Legal Studies* (1998) 18 (1): 153–166.

[27] See Kletzer (2013).

[28] See Hans Kelsen, *Hauptprobleme der Staatsrechtslehre*, vi: "Darum wird für mich der Rechtssatz als der Ausdruck der spezifischen Rechtsgesetzlichkeit, als das Rechtsgesetz, zum Kernproblem, und es erscheint unter diesem Gesichtspunkt das Recht der Rechtswissenschaft als ein System von Rechtssätzen, als ein Urteilszusammenhang, so wie sich die Natur der Naturwissenschaft für die Transzendentalphilosophie als ein System von Urteilen darstellt: nur dass diese Urteile die Kausalgesetzlichkeit des Naturzusammenhanges ausdrücken, während sich im Rechtssatze die spezifische Gesetzlichkeit des Rechts manifestiert."

[29] With respect to the shared vantagepoint of Kelsen and Cohen, see Wolfgang Kersting, "Neukantianische Rechtsbegründung. Rechtsbegriff und richtiges Recht bei Cohen, Stammler und Kelsen", in: R. Alexy et al. (ed.) *Neukantianismus und Rechtsphilosophie*. Nomos Verlag, Baden-Baden 2002.

[30] In addition to Rousseau, Hegel, Cohen and Kelsen, others in this list could include Hugo, Thibaut and Savigny from the 19th century and Rudolf Stammler (*Wirtschaft und Recht nach*

6. The Unity of the State

Legal reductivism identifies the law with the actions of the state as an empirical matter of fact. In doing so, it devalues any issue of legal validity and instead focuses the discourse on sociological questions concerning sources of law on the one hand and moral philosophy (such as questions concerning duties and reasons) on the other. In contrast to that project, Kelsen, in identifying the state with the law, created a logical prerequisite, *Grundlegung* or *Hypothesis*[31], by which it becomes possible to categorize (or posit) all state action in terms of its positioning within a normative framework. Instead of identifying the law as that which is commanded by the state, Kelsen identified the state as that which issues commands in conformity with the law.[32]

Although Kelsen's requirement of conformity to law on the part of the state would appear to be similar to the standard natural law position (*lex iniusta non est lex*), Kelsen gives the principle a positivist turn by postulating the basic norm which itself serves as the source of validity for the entire legal system and yet is

---

der materialistischen Geschichtsauffassung, Die Lehre von dem richtigen Rechte), Adolf Reinach (*Zur Phänomenologie des Rechts. Die apriorischen Grundlagen des bürgerlichen Rechts*), Felix Somlo (*Juristische Grundlehre*) and at least the early Carl Schmitt (*Der Wert des Staates und die Bedeutung des Einzelnen*) from the turn of the century. Bentham, insofar as he sought to move away what he viewed as an undue formalism and metaphysical entanglement on the part of Blackstone and toward creating law endowed with utilitarian value (see *A Fragment on Government*), was also a positivist in this mode. As for Austin, his theory is significantly more complex than the mere identification of law with commands backed by sanctions often claimed by reductivists today (see Kramer, *In Defense of Legal Positivism*, pp. 98 ff.) as contrasted with Austin's disciple Somlo, above.

[31] Cohen, *Ethik des Reinen Willens*, pp. 99 ff. "Alle Theorie, alles Gesetz kann keinen anderen Grund haben, als den die Grundlegung legt."

[32] Kelsen's position on this question is one of the key sources of conflict in the debate carried out with Carl Schmitt regarding the role of a constitutional court and culminating in dueling monographs in 1931. Within this framework, the question of who is the guardian of the constitution revolves around the issue of whether the political is based on the legal (Kelsen) or whether the legal is based on the political (Schmitt). For a detailed and clear analysis, see Dyzenhaus, *Legality and Legitimacy, Oxford 1999*, and Vinx (tr.), *The Guardian of the Constitution, Cambridge 2015.* Schmitt would appear to agree with Kelsen that the state can only be understood on normative terms, i.e. that the state is constituted by the law and not the law by the state (see *Der Wert des Staates und die Bedeutung des Einzelnen, 1914*. The difference between the two theorists is that whereas Kelsen seems to see the normativity of the state being contained entirely in empirically verifiable legal norms which can form the basis of judicial review, Schmitt doubts that such norms are properly constitutional in a material sense and that it is therefore up to the sovereign to decide upon the proper constitution of the state in cases involving constitutional disputes.

void of any particular normative content regarding justice, authority, etc.[33] Some legal positivists such as Stanley Paulson, Eugenio Bulygin and Joseph Raz have been reasonable in concluding that, if the basic norm is effectively void of content, the Kelsenian construct must be a purely formal one which would necessarily result in a blanket identification of commands with laws, yielding a system which would be non-reductivist in name only.[34]

However, the basic norm as the source of validity in Kelsen's system need not, merely as a result of it being an abstract construct, be necessarily void of content. Rather, the basic norm can be conceived as being the source of its own content as the foundation (*Grundlegung*) for the legal system.[35] The natural law theorists have always sought the source of normativity in something other, either exterior to or within the state (e.g. in divine ordinance or the inherent justice of the state's laws). The reductivists have been skeptical of such an endeavor and therefore have denied that the law has any necessary claim to validity in the first place. Kelsen recognizes the reductivists' skepticism of justifying the laws of the state in something which is either exterior to, or within, the state, but transcends this skepticism by positing that the state, by definition, is the source of its own normativity.[36] Attempting to base the legal system's normativity in anything else, whether in external values, habits of obedience, patterns of recognition, etc. could only serve to diminish the internal validity which derives from the unity of the system itself, a unity that is required by the concept of sovereignty and which excludes the possibility of two highest powers existing at the same place and time: i.e. لا إله إلا الله.[37]

---

[33] See Kelsen, *Reine Rechtslehre I*, p. 66.

[34] For clear expositions by each of these authors regarding their views of Kelsen's basic norm, see *Normativity and Norms* above.

[35] See Geert Edel, "The Hypothesis of the Basic Norm: Hans Kelsen and Hermann Cohen", in: Paulson (ed.) *Normativity and Norms* as well as "Zum Problem der Rechtsgeltung. Kelsens Lehre von der Grundnorm und das Hypothesis-Theorem Cohens", in: Simone Zurbuchen and Peter A. Schmid (ed.) *Grenzen der kritischen Vernunft. Festschrift für Helmut Holzhey*. Schwabe & Co, Basel 1997.

[36] Ibid. See also Hegel, *Grundlinien der Philosophie des Rechts*, § 278: "Diese beiden Bestimmungen, dass die besonderen Geschäfte und Gewalten des Staats weder für sich, noch in dem besonderen Willen von Individuen selbständig und fest sind, sondern in der Einheit des Staats als ihrem einfachen Selbst ihre letzte Wurzel haben, macht die Souveränität des Staats aus."

[37] lā ʾilāha ʾillā llāhu, or there can be no God but God. The Shahadah, the first pillar of Islam, functions similarly to the basic norm, or rather, the basic norm functions similarly to the Shahadah. It is a profession of unity and of the singular source of normativity. As a result of the requirement of unity which flows from the concept of sovereignty, the logical structure of the law mirrors that of monotheism. If one has understood the concept of God as a unity and as omnipotent, then one must also understand that there cannot be two Gods. Of course, just as

By providing a source for the order perceived in the world, as with the Shahadah, the basic norm satisfies the same requirement for legal theorists as the *causa prima* did for the scholastics. If there is no order (or no need for order) in the world, then there is no need to posit a first cause or any other scientific ordering principle (e.g. evolution). Likewise, to the extent that commands of the sovereign are without order or random and to the extent that we accept them as such, the notion of the legal becomes superfluous.[38] (This question will be discussed in the following Chapter.)

However, legal science, indeed the legal profession itself, is premised on the analysis of norms as ordered, relating to each other and to human action. Kelsen, following upon Cohen's concept of *Grundlegung*, provides us with the basic norm as a foundational, constitutive principle. With this construction we have a crucial lens through which we can understand Rousseau's concept of the *volonté générale* and other affirmative conceptions of the state in general. While the authority resulting from the general will may be absolute as a matter of principle, this does not mean that the state's exercise of power is therefore absolute or that the content of state action is arbitrary.[39] Rather, the exercise of state power must

there may not be any one God at all, but rather many gods or no gods, it is also conceivable that there is not one source of authority, but rather many sources of authority existing simultaneously or perhaps no authority whatsoever. If there is no authority whatsoever, then there can be no law and thus no state (see below in Parts III and IV). If there are genuinely multiple, independent sources of authority existing in the same time and place, then it is impossible for legal science to comprehend them. In such a situation, each source would make conflicting demands on the allegiance of subjects and each subject would have to choose which source to obey, resulting in a situation akin to civil war. However, in most cases of multiple sources of authority, as with some polytheistic belief systems, there is some kind of hierarchy of authority similar to Mt. Olympus which, in the end, results in a unitary sovereign – this is the subject of the area of law known as "conflicts of law" which actually deals not with conflicts but with resolutions of apparent conflicts.

[38] Whereas the main problem that the legal reductivists have with the basic norm is that it fails to explain order (i.e. why one is obligated to follow the law), the main problem that the natural law theorists have with the basic norm is that it fails to explain disorder (i.e. why one is required to follow the law when it is unjust). This is the theodicy problem in other terms (as well as one of Constant's main concerns).

[39] While Bodin refers to the sovereign as that which possesses absolute power, it is not power, as a matter of fact, but rather authority, as a matter of normativity, which can be considered absolute. Power always permits the possibility of conflict; the principle of authority within a legal system does not. Compare Carl Schmitt, *Der Wert des Staates und die Bedeutung des Einzelnen*, p. 51,52: "Das Recht, das nur von der höchsten Gewalt ausgehen kann, setzt seinem Begriffe nach eine höchste Gewalt voraus. Was aber höchste Gewalt ist, bestimmt sich wiederum nicht nach einer Tatsache, sondern nach einer Bewertung, demnach entsprechend den Normen einer rechtlichen Betrachtung. Die höchste Gewalt, die den Staat ausmacht, ist ihrem Wesen nach eine Einheit, die nur durch wertende Kriterien gewonnen wird. Der Satz, das Recht

always be and always is in accordance with the authorization of the general will, whatever the content of that authorization may be: “Je conclus donc que comme le premier devoir du législateur est de conformer les lois a la *volonté générale*, la premier règle de la économie publique est que l’administration soit conforme aux lois.”[40] As a corollary to this statement and in the spirit of Kelsen, we would have to add that any apparent state action contrary to these laws or the general will is a mere usurpation and thus invalid.

If the *volonté générale* is conceived in Kelsenian terms as a first or constituting norm, then the actions of the sovereign must necessarily be derivable from its normative content. A primary function of Kelsen’s framework of a hierarchy of norms is to convert Constant’s problem of political legitimacy resolvable only by vague, factual appeals to the ‘will of the people’ into a problem of normative validity resolvable by legal analysis.

---

könne nur von der höchsten Gewalt ausgehen, kehrt sich daher gegen die Machttheorie um und erhält den Inhalt, dass höchste Gewalt nur das sein kann, was vom Rechte ausgeht. Das Recht ist nicht im Staat, sondern der Staat ist im Recht.”

40 Rousseau, *Discours sur l’economie politique*, p. 52.

Chapter III

Deus sive Civitas

The question regarding the relationship between the individual and the state (Chapter II) is at its heart a question based in the Enlightenment and Political Modernity where the issue is one regarding the individual's place in a political order based on liberty and reason. In contrast, the question regarding the existence of the state itself is very much a 20th century question following on the intellectual legwork accomplished in Europe in the 19th century and the political developments of the first half of the 20th century. To paraphrase the first sentence of Heidegger's *Einführung in die Metaphysik*, why is there a state and not nothing? This is not merely analogous to the ontological question, it is one and the same with it. With regard to political phenomena, the ontological question is a normative question, it is a political question: Why should there be a state at all? This is the case regardless of the outcome of the query. The positive response (there is a state, or, there is normatively binding law) requires making something the case that is not directly supported by the simplest empirical data. However, the negative response, i. e. that such things do not exist on the basis of not being directly supported by the simplest empirical data, equally constitutes a choice, a political preference of sorts. The concept of hypostasis plays a central role in such considerations. This chapter will attempt to show that Kelsen's use of the concept hypostasis (and thereby also the state) as a fiction unnecessarily degrades the concept into the realm of the purely subjective. This will be shown on the basis of the conceptual history of the term, which rather suggests that hypostasis entails realization, but also personification, also in the sense of Hobbes' analysis of πρόσωπον as person leading up to his conception of the Leviathan in Chapter 16 of *Leviathan*.

The title of this chapter refers to Spinoza, replacing the category of the natural with the category of the social. In keeping with one of the central themes of 'going back to the roots', it seems worth noting that the terms 'nature' and 'state' have each supplanted the term 'God' in their own ways in the modern mind. Anticipating Kelsen's admonitions against excessive hypostatization, Spinoza's usage of the formula qualifies the supposed transcendence of God with the immanence of nature. Likewise here with the immanence of the state, in which the operative term is neither the ahistorical 'status' nor the pre-formed and thereby tendentially transcendent 'respublica', but rather 'civitas' which evokes the thoroughly immanent condition of being a citizen (*civis*), the right of citizenship and then only by extension the city or even the state itself.

1. Jurisprudence and Theology

A recurring theme in the works of both Carl Schmitt and Hans Kelsen is that jurisprudence shares a remarkable similarity in method with theology.[1] Each is concerned with textually verifiable, authoritative prescriptions and each is also concerned with understanding these prescriptions within a rational framework.[2] In contrast with other fields that apply the faculty of reason to the facts of the world, neither jurisprudence nor theology is prima facie bound to an empirical reality. Thus, it does not seem to be obvious why we should bind ourselves to any external authority in developing our own normative precepts, whether they be legal or theological in nature.[3] Likewise, and equally in contrast with other sciences, both jurisprudence and theology nonetheless have recourse to an authority, which on each discipline's terms is absolute. Thus, on the other hand, it should also not be obvious why we should seek recourse in reason. Why even question the law when it issues from God, the all-knowing and all-powerful, or the sovereign, the absolute ruler. On the one hand, jurisprudence and theology

---

1 Of course, the treatment of jurisprudence and theology in parallel does not begin with Schmitt and Kelsen, but rather with an increased interest in synthesizing the systems of church and state beginning with the early scholastics, or even Augustine's *De Civitate Dei*, and extending most prominently into the works of Spinoza and Leibniz.

2 See Schmitt, Politische Theologie, p. 44. "Beide haben ein duplex principium, die ratio …. und die scriptura, das heisst ein Buch mit positiven Offenbarungen und Anordnungen."

3 One could argue that the external success condition in theology is the satisfaction of the will of God and that the condition in the case of jurisprudence is the satisfaction of the will of the sovereign. Just as the physician defines his profession in terms of helping the sick, the theologian is primarily obedient to God and the jurist to the state. However, such an objection begs the question (i) as to whether a supposedly authoritative text comprises the will of God / the state in the first place and (ii) whether the divine or political "will" is really something external, empirical in the same sense as the health of a patient in medicine or, to use another example, the movement of an object in physics. These issues revolve around the status of the words that are printed on the text in front of me. To hold that an authoritative text expresses a given will requires assuming that (a) the very words in question were written down through an empirically verifiable occurrence in the natural world (such as God etching the ten commandments in stone in the presence of Moses) and (b) the meaning of such words derives from a will which is completely external to that of the reader (such as when the absolute monarch proclaims "*l'etat c'est moi*"). It cannot behoove the serious theorist to make either such assumption, nor can we pretend that doing so actually serves the interests of a legitimate religion or state.

are enlightened by human reason, which is necessary, but in some sense subjective; on the other hand, they are determined by the revealed word (divine or sovereign), which is in some sense arbitrary, but absolute.

These similarities between theology and jurisprudence are not accidental. Whether our reference is to the all-powerful legislator of the *Torah*, the figure of Leviathan or a Western representative democracy, the fundamental question is the same: what is the relationship between the individual and the law which the individual is given to understand and act upon? One could say that there is no inherent relationship between the subject / believer and the law, that the law is necessarily heteronomic to the individual and therefore neither good nor bad, neither just nor unjust in any practically rational or normative way. It is certainly possible to belittle religion as a naive attempt on the part of believers to voluntarily submit themselves to the whims of a projected authority in exchange for a make-believe future recompense. Similarly, one could snicker at the loyal citizen who refuses to evade tax obligations or who voluntarily risks sacrificing his life in the battlefield. However, in each such circumstance, both for the believer and the citizen, the figure in question, be it God or the state, does serve as a real motivation for action. Moreover, this figure in each case is neither merely subjectively imagined nor something which can only be accounted for from a psychological perspective. Surely, both belief and obedience are internal to the respective subject in each case. However, in each case, at least in the case of *proper* religion and a *proper* state (marginal cases such as religious cults or fringe militias need not overly concern us here), the belief and / or obedience in question are cases of intentional states which are generally shared by a community, even a society, of others.[4] In both religion and the commonwealth, the constituting individuals are always *many*, but they are also necessarily in some sense *one*.

It is this shared intentionality which makes of many one that raises again the question posed above: what is the relationship between the individual and the religious / political law? A merely subjective, imaginary, intentional state requires no such relation at all. It is only when I seek to align my intentionality with others that I require a coordinate along which to align. If such a coordinate would not be known to exist independently of my intentionality, then I would have to

---

[4] Kelsen has a generally disfavorable view of such attitudes, see Kelsen, *Was ist Gerechtigkeit*, p. 21: "Dass viele Individuen in einem Werturteile übereinstimmen, ist keinerlei Beweis dafür, dass dieses Urteil richtig, d.h. in einem objektiven Sinne gültig ist. Gerade so wie die Tatsache, dass die meisten Menschen glauben, oder doch geglaubt haben, die Sonne drehe sich um die Erde, kein Beweis dafür ist oder war, dass dieser Glaube auf Wahrheit beruht." However, the relevance of shared belief in the legitimacy of the state or the existence of God is not that such belief would serve to prove the exterior reality, but rather that the belief itself in some way might actually create the reality.

create one. As a coordinate, the only required quality of this reference is that of unity. Kelsen pointed out this requirement in his 1913 treatise *Über Staatsunrecht*:

> Die Annahme, dass die Rechtsordnung der Wille einer einheitlichen Staatsperson sei, ist nur der Ausdruck für die logische Geschlossenheit, die innere Widerspruchslosigkeit eines Systems von Rechtsnormen. Bei der damit verbundenen Personifikation findet ein ähnliches Denkbedürfnis seine Befriedigung wie jenes, das den nur viel komplizierteren und auf zahlreichere Quellen zurückführenden Denkprozess in Bewegung setzt, der zum Gottesbegriff führt.[5]

Kelsen's core argument is a scholastic one. In any given realm, there can either be one will or many. If there are many wills, then either they are in conflict with one another in respect to the realm or they are at peace. If the wills are in conflict with one another, then it is the case that no one will is omnipotent. However, both the concept of God and the concept of the sovereign require some kind of omnipotence. Therefore, the wills, if they are many, cannot be in conflict with one another. However, if they are at peace with one another, then either all wills are subordinate to one will or all wills form a union together. Thus, even if there are many wills, both the concept of the sovereign, i. e. the head of the state and God, require that a single will be the origin of all that is willed, or all that becomes law, whether human or divine.

As discussed above with respect to the figure of Rex, the singular will can initially either be found in a single individual or in a single idea that unifies many individuals as if in one body, i. e. a *societas* or corporation. Likewise, the source of unity can also either be identified as a concrete object, such as a golden calf or physical king, or as a mere idea. In both Chapters I and II, I have suggested that the source of sovereignty cannot lie in physical qualities alone, but rather in an idea. That is, it is not the actual manifestation of a physical entity which counts, but rather the perception of the same on the part of the subject which is ultimately operative. And again, if we conceive of the state as a legal order, it is not the flesh and bones of the king, but rather the authority of the sovereign which is the source of order. Thus, even if we posit a physical king, or golden calf, as the source of unity, it is never the physical manifestation itself which counts, but rather the idea thereof, which through whichever means comes to be valid in the mind of the believer / citizen / official / lawyer / theorist. Here there is a further parallel between theology and jurisprudence: both God and the state exist only as (normative) ideas and, as such, both can only exist in the internal aspect.[6] I

[5] Kelsen, *Der soziologische und der juristische Staatsbegriff*, p. 221, citing Kelsen, *Über Staatsunrecht.*

[6] Internal aspect as a distinguishing feature of social rules, as opposed to habits, as described by Hart in his *The Concept of Law*, Chapter IV, "Sovereign and Subject".

hope to show in the coming sections that this is not a concession in the face of the realities of a scientific worldview, but rather entails a strong ontological claim regarding that of which we speak when we talk about the state, the law, and even ourselves.

2. State as Hypostasis

A multitude of men are made one person when they are by one man, or one person, represented; so that it be done with the consent of every one of that multitude in particular. For it is the unity of the representer, not the unity of the represented, that maketh the person one. And it is the representer that beareth the person, and but one person: and unity cannot otherwise be understood in multitude. *Leviathan, Chapter 16*

If the state would not be known to exist, then we would have to create one. This should not indicate that the state is an eternal form, but it also does not indicate that the state, with its legal order, is pure fiction. Searle suggests that institutional reality is ontologically subjective, but epistemically objective, in the sense that institutional reality does not exist as part of brute reality, but that it can be agreed upon and verified by a community of agents. However, in addition to the distinction between material reality and shared institutional reality, there must be a further distinction between that which is arbitrary and that which is not. In *Leviathan*, Hobbes makes the claim that the state is precisely not arbitrary, but rather necessarily existent. In a normal circumstance the state is known to exist, in which case there is a duty to respect its authority. However, even when the state's existence is called into question, as may have been the case during the English Civil War, then, and especially then, is it necessary for the state to exist. In the quote above, Hobbes claims that the function of such a state, or sovereign, is to unify the multitude into one person. Moreover, the unifying function is the essential function in Hobbes' account with the threat of sanction and the enforcement of order serving merely as means to the end of unity. Therefore, what is the state? It is essentially a unity.

Pure unities, however, do not exist in the material world, as also Kelsen was aware. Therefore, Kelsen uses the concept of 'hypostasis' to refer to the concepts of God and state as unifying *ideas*:

Um Gott als Einheit gegenüber der Vielheit der Welt zum Ausdruck zu bringen, fungiert die Personifikation als erkenntnistheoretisches Hilfsmittel. Sie wird allerdings in der Theologie zum Substrat einer Hypostasierung. Verzichtet man auf die Personifikation, dann verliert man eben die erste Voraussetzung für den transzendenten Gottesbegriff. Es ist im Verhältnis von Staat und Recht nicht anders.[7]

---

[7] Kelsen. *Der soziologische und der juristische Staatsbegriff*, p. 225. See also, p. 219.

The concept of hypostasis is an historically rich notion, which, as a central metaphysical term of late antiquity and the early Middle Ages, traverses the development of concepts such as individuality, objectivity and reality in the history of Western thought. While Heinrich Dörrie reports that Aristotle only used the term hypostasis to refer to the physical world, e.g. in *Meteorology* referring to sediment,[8] Aristotle used the functionally related term ὑποκείμενον (i.e. that which *underlies*, as opposed to hypostasis, that which *stands* beneath) to refer to a thing's underlying material individuality which he held to be its properly substantial aspect.[9] Accordingly, for Aristotle, the hypostasis / hypokeimenon is that which is real in a thing as opposed to its mere form which is general and non-instantiated. The term hypostasis itself takes on an ontological importance with the Stoics where it is used to reflect upon how something becomes real, or comes into existence.[10] The Neo-Platonists also thought of the hypostasis as that which is real in a thing. However, for the Neo-Platonists, the hypostasis, i.e. that which really underlies a thing or gives it its substance, is not a function of the thing's material individuality, but rather its ideality, the idea or form which manifests itself in the thing.[11] Throughout this history, the development of the notion of

---

[8] Dörrie, p. 46, FN 1.

[9] See Book Z, p. 3: "Wesen wird, wenn nicht in mehr, so doch in vier Hauptbedeutungen ausgesagt. Denn das Sosein, das Allgemeine und die Gattung werden für das Wesen eines jeden gehalten, und dazu viertens das Zugrundeliegende (ὑποκείμενον). Das Zugrundeliegende aber ist dasjenige, von dem das übrige ausgesagt wird, das selbst aber nicht wieder von einem anderen ausgesagt wird." See Seidl, Horst's Introduction to Aristoteles' Metaphysik, XXV: "ὑποκείμενον" meint wörtlich das 'Zugrundeliegende' und hat bei Aristoteles eine zweifache Bedeutung, nämlich als letztes Aussagen-'Subjekt' und als stoffliches "Sustrat". .... In der ersten Bedeutung dient ὑποκείμενον zur Bestimmung von οὐσία, 'Substanz', als dem, 'wovon alles übrige ausgesagt wird, während es selbst von nichts anderem mehr ausgesagt wird', d.h. als letztem Aussagen-Subjekt, dem Einzelding. Die zweite Bedeutung ergibt sich daraus, dass der Form- die Stoffursache 'zugrunde liegt', wobei nun die Erschließung des Einzeldings auf seine immanenten Ursachen hin erfolgt." Further, in his commentary to Book Z, Seidl continues: "Die vierte Bedeutung von Wesen als Zugrundeliegendem geht auf das Einzelding und sein stoffliches Substrat und entspricht einerseits die Auffassung von Vorsokratikern, andererseits, mit neuem Verständnis, auch der des Aristoteles."

[10] Dörrie, pp. 49 ff. "Wenn eine Flüssigkeit verdünstet und dabei ein Bodensatz sich niederschlägt, so tritt etwas zuvor Latentes in sinnfällige Erscheinung. Dazu muss gleich gesagt werden, dass ὑφίστασθαι stets doppelt gebraucht werden kann: Oft, und besonders in der älteren Stoa, bedeutet es, dass das ungeformte Sein vor den Einzeldingen besteht, vor ihnen da ist; zweitens bedeutet es, dass etwas durch die und die Voraussetzungen in die Existenz tritt, also real wird. ὑπόστασις, aber, hierin ganz Verbalsubstantiv, kommt im philosophischem Gebrauch fast nur im letzterem Sinne vor, bedeutet also Realisierung und Bestand."

[11] See Dörrie, pp. 64 ff. E. g. p. 64: "So kommt es in der Verwendung von ὑπόστασις in dem einen Punkte zu einer Umkehrung: im Platonismus wird kaum mehr gefragt, wieso sich das Einzelne realisiert, sondern vielmehr, wie das (zuvor latente) Allgemeine, d.h. Weltgeist und

hypostasis tracks the hylomorphic debate more generally regarding whether it is the ideality or rather the materiality of an entity that actually makes something real. These competing conceptions were to some extent held in tension by Thomas Aquinas and the middle scholastics. However, eventually nominalism came to hold that the forms or ideas, i.e. universals, which the Neo-Platonists thought to constitute the reality of a thing, i.e. to be a thing's hypostasis, are mere names that we give to the thing and that they have no reality independent of such conventionality. As such, hypostasis became synonymous with fiction in the derogative, Benthamian sense, i.e. a metaphysical holdover from a less enlightened period, that tends toward being instrumentalized sophistically within the public discourse. It is in this sense that Kelsen seems to be familiar with the term: The hypostasis, or that which is the subject of an '*Hypostasierung*', is that about which we make believe but which has no 'real' existence, which is to say that it cannot be empirically shown to exist in the material world.[12]

However, despite its ontological disputability in this regard, Kelsen still recognizes the important function of the hypostasis as a principle of unity. Continuing his comparison with the concept of God, Kelsen reasons:

"Wenn eine Analogie zwischen dem Mikrokosmos der Rechtsordnung und dem Makrokosmos der Ordnung des Universums zulässig ist – und sie ist keineswegs neu und schon dem primitiven Denken bewusst –, dann steckt in der grandiosen Personifikation aller das Universum beherrschenden Normen, dann steckt in dieser Idee eines persönlichen, einheitlichen Gottes die gleiche oder doch eine verwandte Oekonomie des Denkens wie in der juristischen Konstruk-

---

Weltseele, sinnfällig werden." Also p. 74, "das reine Sein manifestiert, hypostasiert sich im νοῦς und in der Weltseele." See also Perez Paoli, p. 7, in which he reflects on the ideality and reality of the soul as hypostasis: "Die Seele ist das zur Hypostase eines Anderen gegebene Leben. Dies erläutert Plotin am Beispiel des Feuers: eines ist die bei ihm seiende Wärme, ein anderes die Wärme, die es gewährt..." See also Halfwassen, p. 328: "Das, was aus der Überfülle des überseienden und übermächtigen Einen als die erste Manifestation des Absoluten hervorgeht, ist für Plotin das sich selbst denkende göttliche Nous, der sich selbst als Inbegriff und Fülle des wahren Seins weiß; er ist als die ὑπόστασις des Einen die eigentliche Wirklichkeit. Seine grundlegende Struktur ist die Einheit in der Zweiheit von Wissendem und Gewußtem, Denkendem und Gedachtem, Denken und Sein." Particularly conducive for our analysis is not only that Halfwassen uses proper reality (*die eigentliche Wirklichkeit*) as a synonym of ὑπόστασις, but also that Halfwassen describes the manner of being of this proper reality, Nous, in a self-constituting way: it is the unity of the duality of that which knows and that which is known, that which thinks and that which is thought, the faculty of thought and the being itself.

[12] See Kelsen, p. 252, citing Feuerbach: "'Gott erfüllt, was der Mensch wünscht; er ist ein den Wünschen des Menschen entsprechendes Wesen.' Im Wunder wirkt der supranaturale Gott die Erfüllung aller Wünsche, auf die Verzichten muss, der sich im Bereiche der Natur bescheidet. Mit dieser treffenden Psychologie des überweltlichen Gottesbegriffes ist zugleich der Schlüssel zu dem überrechtlichen Staatsbegriff gegeben."

tion eines einheitlichen, persönlichen Trägers der staatlichen Rechtsordnung, der Staatsperson, des persönlichen einheitlichen Staates."[13]

As Kelsen states above, the idea of God or state as a unity is an epistemological heuristic, or in Kelsen's words, an *erkenntnistheoretisches Hilfsmittel,* an *Oekonomie des Denkens*, perhaps even a *Denkbedürfnis.*[14] Once we understand that it is *our* intentionality by which the idea heuristically becomes the basis of unity, it becomes quite superfluous to know whether the source of unity is an *actual* object in the physical world that is idealized or a *mere* idea without an objective reference in the physical world. For Kelsen, the idea of God or state does not result from the existence of an object to which such an idea would correspond. Rather, 'God' and 'state' correspond to the ideas which we have of them and these ideas exist because of the necessity of understanding the phenomena in our world as part of a unified order. For this reason it is irrelevant whether the unifying will in a realm is in one individual or in many individuals and it also irrelevant whether the worshipped God is an actual object (such as the Golden Calf) or an idea (as in the Logos), the mental activity involved in recognizing the highest will, whether in theology or jurisprudence, always presupposes a unity and it is *this* category which shapes the respective idea and determines the concept. Even if there would be a golden calf that is magically omnipotent in the physical world, it would be nothing but a golden calf unless it constituted the unity of an order. However, unities, whether God or state, do not exist in the physical world – at least, they can never be so perceived. No sense impression in and of itself could ever exhibit the one God or true sovereign. As a result of the practicality of understanding the universe and the realm of the state as one order, we use the category of unity to apperceive both God and state as 'necessary' personifications.

3. The Problem of Many, of No Gods

This same process which leads to a monotheistic conception of God as well as the preconception of the sovereign as a unity could well be dismissed as an historical accident merely arising from this Abrahamic religious tradition and / or those political structures of the early modern state that so influenced Bodin, Hobbes, Spinoza, but also the early Kelsen under the k.u.k. monarchy and shortly thereafter when writing *Der soziologische und juristische Staatsbegriff*. For ex-

[13] Kelsen, *Der soziologische und der juristische Staatsbegriff*, pp. 221, 222, citing Kelsen, *Über Staatsunrecht.*

[14] See Vaihinger's operative notion of fictions of which Kelsen was throughly aware, also as analyzed in Bouriou, *supra*.

ample, Dreyfus and Kelly convincingly argue in *All Things Shining* that indeed polytheistic structures have at times in the past prevailed even in Western society and that a polytheistic model could well provide a fruitful frame for thriving in the post-modern world today.[15] Kelsen's argument, however, is not based on historical precedent but rather on the logical structure of ordered systems, and the law of non-contradiction (or regarding conflicts of laws) which they entail. Even with the existence of a polytheistic society in which many gods predominate and even in the face of political liberalism in which individuals and groups are free to imbue themselves with meaning from a myriad of sources, there can be no *rational* order in such constellations unless some gods (or sources of meaning) are given priority over others. To insist on a lack of any priority is to accept its counterpart: irrationality and the anarchy which pertains to it. However, to accept some prioritization for the sake of rational order is, in the end, to accept one single source for all order, to posit the unity of the state and of God.

Nonetheless, the problem for the category of unity posed by Dreyfus and Kelly with the example of polytheism is not fully resolved by simply pointing to the unity presupposed by theological and legal orders. The argument of those who emphasize a plurality of values and interests in contemporary society acknowledges the formal requirement of unity in a rationally ordered system. The problem seems to be much more that, at least in contemporary Western society, there has come to be much less of an ordered system in the first place. Without a common religious faith, so Böckenförde's dilemma, the values of a society will tend to erode until the very civic fabric comes apart.[16] At least for Western Judeo-Christian society, a unified system of value has devolved over the last centuries into local sources of meaning (families, businesses, groups of friends) without any inherent connection to each other.

Prior to the Enlightenment, we can assume that the issue of a common faith simply did not present itself in the same manner, not because peoples were necessarily more ethnically homogenous, but rather because the respective hypostasis was considered to be much more real. Not only were states, together with a co-opted Church, much more inclined to use the police power to enforce social mores, there was often also a common conception of God as a punisher and redeemer in this world and in the next. Furthermore, we imagine that in the European Middle Ages, it was imminently clear who this God was and in which physical and cultural manifestations God was made present, i. e. the Bible, the Mass, the Church and the King, not to mention the multitude of commonly accepted

---

[15] Dreyfus, Hubert L, and Kelly, Sean. *All Things Shining: Reading the Western Classics to find Meaning in a Secular Age*. Free Press: New York 2011.

[16] Böckenförde, Ernst-Wolfgang. *Staat, Gesellschaft, Freiheit*. 1976.

miracles which formed a canon of medieval belief. In the modern era, all of this changed. In the 21st century, this mélange of meaning now almost appears to us as an alien civilization, which makes Böckenförde's insights all the more pressing.

The criticism of religion as a source of value, and therewith also of a certain kind of natural law, goes hand in hand with the modern understanding that even if God cannot be proven to not exist, God certainly also cannot be proven to exist, with the result that it is impossible to identify any one god as the source of order. Even if we would grant a divine status to the Golden Calf, the fact that any other contingency can claim the existence and moral order of any other rivaling deity (the existence of which can equally not be dismissed) means that no god can be taken as the objective source of order.[17]

Framed positively, this agnostic stalemate expresses itself in the language of tolerance, as Kelsen asserts:

> Das moralische Prinzip, das einer relativistischen Wertlehre zugrunde liegt oder aus ihr gefolgert werden kann, ist das Prinzip der Toleranz, das ist die Forderung, die religiöse oder politische Anschauung anderer wohlwollend zu verstehen, auch wenn man sie nicht teilt, und daher ihre friedlichen Äußerungen nicht zu verhindern.[18]

Negatively, however, the language of tolerance with its accommodation of diverging viewpoints requires a dismissal of all affected truth claims, with only a backhanded appreciation of that which is different or outside the mainstream discourse. In this paradigm, diverse 'views' are valued not because of any values contained in the ideas themselves, but rather because they originate in individuals to whom we owe respect, a respect, however, that is exhausted in the form of accommodation. Kelsen fully embraces this brand of liberalism by dismissing religious belief as a psychological[19] or emotional[20] need on the part of those unwilling or unable to accept the logic of value relativism.

---

[17] For example, as argued in Rawls' *Political Liberalism*. Our time is characterized not so much by Atheism, a lack of belief in the divine, as it is by 'Atheology', i.e. a rationalization of a lack of recourse to any divine sources in the social realm or, in other words, the rationalization of disorder which, depending on the interpretation, can be found inchoately with Friedrich Hayek in his *Law, Legislation and Liberty* and perhaps more pronouncedly with Milton Friedman, *Capitalism and Freedom* and Ayn Rand, for example *Atlas Shrugged*.

[18] See Kelsen, *Was ist Gerechtigkeit*. 50.

[19] See above, *Staatsbegriff* 252.

[20] Kelsen, *Was ist Gerechtigkeit*, p. 26–27: "Aber das Bedürfnis nach absoluter Rechtfertigung scheint stärker zu sein als alle rationale Erwägung. Daher wendet sich der Mensch zur Religion und Metaphysik, um hier diese Rechtfertigung, d.h. die absolute Gerechtigkeit, zu finden….Der Mensch muss an die Existenz Gottes, und das heisst an die Existenz einer absoluten Gerechtigkeit glauben, aber er ist unfähig, sie zu begreifen, das heisst se begrifflich zu bestimmen. Jene, die eine solch metaphysische Lösung des Problems der Gerechtigkeit nicht

As described above, the hypostases, God and state, each satisfy the need of identifying a source of unity for the respective order. However, as the satisfaction of a psychological or emotional need on the part of some to believe in a value greater than themselves, the very hypostasis which logically serves to create unity comes to function de facto as a superfluous or even alternate source of order. For example, in the natural world, God can be understood as an hypostasis in the form of a first cause which enables a unified scientific view of the world. However, when God is understood as the *efficient* cause for everything which occurs in the world, the belief in God permits the possibility of an alternate universe in which events occur not according to the laws of nature but rather according to the will of God. Likewise with the political realm, the state as hypostasis can be understood as the unifying source of political order. However, the state as a source of unifying order becomes pernicious, especially in Kelsen's view, when it is viewed distinctly from the legal order, resulting in placing the state above the law or allowing the state itself to make the law by fiat or decision.[21]

Therefore, Kelsen advocates ridding ourselves not of the logical presupposition of a unity, but rather of the hypostasis as personification, whether this be God or state, which humans have traditionally, though in Kelsen's view pre-critically and thus incorrectly, used as a heuristic for understanding the world around them. The hypostasis as personification is a mere projection, a façade to which any ascription of actual existence apart from the system with which it is associated (i.e. the natural world or legal order) entails a serious categorical error threatening the actual unity of the order.[22] For Kelsen, the state in this sense is a redundancy, to be conceived as an unnecessary hypostasis of the legal system, just as God has come to be seen as an unnecessary hypostasis of the natural world.

---

annehmen können, dennoch aber die Idea absoluter Werte aufrecht erhalten, in der Hoffnung, sie rational wissenschaftlich bestimmen zu können, täuschen sich selbst mit der Illusion, dass es möglich sei, in der menschlichen Vernunft gewisse Grundprinzipien zu finden, die jene absoluten Werte konstituieren – die aber in Wahrheit von den emotionalen Elementen ihres Bewusstseins konstituiert werden."

[21] This is at the heart of the constitutional guardian debates between Kelsen and Schmitt. See Vinx, L. *The Guardian of the Constitution: Hans Kelsen and Carl Schmitt on the Limits of Constitutional Law.* Cambridge: Cambridge University Press.

[22] Kelsen. *Der soziologische und der juristische Staatsbegriff*, p. 252. "Die Fernhaltung aller Politik ist zwar eine heute allgemein anerkannte Forderung der positivistischen Rechtswissenschaft. Allein erfüllt kann sie nur werden, wenn auf den Begriff eines metarechtlichen Staates verzichtet wird. Und dieser Verzicht ist, weil er das operieren mit zwei beziehungslosen Erkenntnissystemen aufhebt, nicht nur eine logisch-erkenntnistheoretische, er ist auch eine ethische Notwendigkeit. An Stelle der theologischen Methode der 'doppelten' Wahrheit tritt mit der Systemeinheit das dem logischen Ideal der einen Wahrheit immanente Ideal der Wahrhaftigkeit."

4. "Absolute Positivism"

As described above in Chapter II, Lars Vinx argued that the void of validity created by the purely formal postulate of the basic norm can be filled-in within the Kelsenian conceptual structure by Kelsen's strong commitment to the role of social democratic institutions in providing the basis and content of the law. However, an equally convincing and instructive interpretation of Kelsen's work is the above cited article "Absolute Positivism" by Christoph Kletzer. In it, Kletzer argues that Kelsen's legal theory is indeed a purer, more consequential theory than either that of his Neo-Kantian predecessors or Anglo-American successors. Whereas Kelsen's predecessors sought to explain a complex relationship between the state (or society) and the law[23], and his successor Hart and the succeeding analytical jurisprudence have largely sought to ground the concept of law in the social fact of participants in the legal order acting according to a Rule of Recognition, Kelsen did not hesitate to let the legal system stand isolated on its own terms. For Kelsen, there is nothing outside of the legal order by which it is, or could ever be, justified: neither God, nor state, nor social fact. Rather, the legal order is something which, if justified at all, is justified (or validated) on its own terms. Kletzer characterizes this approach in the following as a Kantian turn:

> As long as we stick with our realist common sense, i. e., the idea that what is actual are the things and that the relation between these things is only contingent, secondary and external to them, then we should not be surprised that our relation to these things also turns out to be contingent and ultimately external to these things. It is thus our realist ontological commitments tacitly implicit in our common sense, which lead to the epistemological impasse of the impossibility of knowing anything. Consequently, it is in the name of having a promising epistemology, i. e., in the name of being able to know anything at all, that we have to criticize, rethink and ultimately change our ontological commitments. Ultimately, this means that we have to take the relation to be the actually existing entity and the 'thing' to be the secondary entity. This is what the Kantian reformulation of the object from being a 'thing in itself' to being a 'phenomenon' or, which is the same, a 'thing for us' actually means.[24]

Laws can only ever be understood as laws for us. Even if there would be a law 'in itself' existing independent of humans and its relation to them, it would again only be relevant as an object of human knowledge in its phenomenal aspect, insofar as it is a law for the subject. Laws are always only relevant to relations between agents as they can only ever be perceived and understood through language. Kelsen was not the first or only Neo-Kantian legal theorist and it seems that indeed most theorists in the generation prior to Kelsen would have largely

---

[23] For examples, see Jellinek's Zwei-Seiten Theorie in his *Allgemeine Staatslehre* or von Gierke's *Das deutsche Genossenschaftsrecht.*

[24] Kletzer (2013).

agreed on this characterization of the "phenomenal", i.e. agential aspect of laws. According to Kletzer, however, what is revolutionary about Kelsen's theory is that he creates a system of understanding legal norms, complete with the formal postulate of the basic norm, in which a participant in the legal system need not seek recourse to any other source of authority outside of the legal system itself. With the postulate of the basic norm, each law becomes a law for me (i.e. it is valid for me) and there is no need to dig any deeper in order to find a 'real' source of validity of the laws. Indeed, to do so would be to seriously misunderstand the function and meaning (or lack thereof) of a legal system as well as the essence of normativity itself – the is-ought distinction which is so central to Kelsen's work represents the impossibility of a law having any relation whatsoever with a reference in the world, whether we attempt to locate this reference in a really existent state or a really existent God.

Kletzer continues:

> If there is to be law then it is by necessity. Put differently: viewed from the point of view of the law, the law exists necessarily and the validity of the law leaves open no meaningful questions to be answered by legal philosophy. Viewed from the point of view of philosophy, however, there can be no positive law and no legal validity.[25]

Kletzer argues that Kelsen's "absolute positivism" envisions a closed system of norms in which the validity of each norm is dependent solely on the validity of the system as a whole, the validity of the system as a whole though is presupposed, as evidenced by the purely formal criterion of the basic norm. However, this absolute validity only makes a claim to being valid within the legal system itself and only with respect to individuals as legal theorists (legal philosophers), lawyers, or legal subjects. Neither particular norms nor the legal system itself, insofar as it is pure and absolute, are able to refer to anything outside of the legal system. For this reason, while its validity is perfect for itself, it is invisible, non-existent to the external observer, i.e. in the external aspect. The philosopher who understands the law as part of a moral philosophy, i.e. as making reference to something outside of itself, must shake his head at such claims to positive validity. However, the legal theorist need not take such a broad perspective and thus can embrace this view of the law as *perfect* with respect to validity, even if it is *nihilistic* with respect to value.[26]

---

25 Ibid.

26 Kletzer (2013): "Absolute positivism is thus aware that it is a philosophical doctrine about philosophy, about the limits of philosophy. As such a philosophical doctrine about the limits and incompetence of philosophy, absolute positivism to a certain extent has to be both a reflexive and also an anti-philosophical doctrine."

The most compelling aspect of Kletzer's Kelsen interpretation is that Kletzer paints Kelsen as a theorist who laid the intellectual foundation for a value-less legal theory, to which the sociological aspects of Hart's *The Concept of Law* and the more reductivist positions within legal positivism today owe much.

A true positivism thus has to be able to bear these anti-philosophical tendencies within it. Positivism cannot be itself without at the same time being a doctrine about the end of philosophy, about the outpour of philosophy into the world. Insofar as the loss of God has meant that philosophy was promoted from the maidservant (ancilla) to the vicar of theology, we can say that only an absolute positivism can free itself from a mode of thinking that was formed by the paradigms of theology. For the problem with the loss of God is not only that we lose the firm foundations of the divine rules and the secular rules based on these divine rules. Rather the problem is that the loss of God has changed the paradigm of the validity of rules itself. Without God rules hold and apply differently, they are valid in a different manner and sense. And whereas relative positivism privily awaits the revelation of a final validity, awaits and lacks the absolute, absolute positivism has learned the full lesson of the absolute immanence of validity: the world does not lack legitimacy. Neither does the law.[27]

Kletzer seems to use the term 'philosophy' synonymously with what can more generally be considered moral philosophy or ethics, i. e. the study of value. Kletzer implies with his argument that objective, 'philosophical' values are derived from religious or cultic beliefs and that a moral philosophy without God can only represent a transitional period between a theocentric value system and the end of philosophy, i. e. a world entirely devoid of value. Whereas "relative positivism" is inconsequent in its search for values or principles on which to base law's validity, "absolute positivism" has learned that in a world without God there is no basis or principle of validity in the first place.

5. Value Nihilism

Stanley Paulson, as mentioned in the Introduction, accords with Kletzer in attributing to Kelsen a purely formal concept of validity, a concept of validity that is 'fictional' in the common, derogative sense, i. e. as something divorced from the actuality of the world and of human conduct and thus to be eliminated. However, the concept of fiction as found with Vaihinger and of hypothesis as found with Cohen do not necessarily require such a nihilistic interpretation. Certainly for Vaihinger and Cohen on whom Kelsen relies, these concepts are not merely superfluous constructs, but rather integrally tied to, even constitutive of, human action. At least in one passage of the *Allgemeine Theorie der Normen* (pp. 206–

27 Ibid.

207)[28], Kelsen is ambiguous as to whether he views the basic norm and legal normativity in general as a merely formal or as a substantive construct. On the one hand, Kelsen says that the basic norm is merely thought and is fictive, as opposed to something which is actually willed. Moreover, the basic norm is self-contradictory. On the other hand, Kelsen states that the basic norm serves as the foundation of the positive norms which constitute the legal order and that this results in an objective meaning which can be ascribed to the legal order. If merely formal, the basic norm would be a postulate which we *pretend* to be the basis of validity for the legal system; if it is a substantive construct, the basic norm would be the first in a hierarchy of norms that are actually action guiding. The question is whether Kelsen's legal theory is a theory for understanding the legal system in the absence of value or whether it constitutes a pure theory of value in the neo-Kantian tradition.

Where Kelsen leaves room for doubt on this question in the *Allgemeine Theorie der Normen*, the posthumously published *Secular Religion* (2012) clarifies Kelsen's position in this regard. Subtitled 'A Polemic against the Misinterpretation of Modern Social Philosophy, Science and Politics as "New Religions", *Secular Religion* is an essay against the tendency of concepts, relating to God, religion and most generally value, creeping into social, political and scientific discourse: "Science can only describe and explain, it cannot justify reality."[29]

Secular Religion began in 1954 as a response to Eric Voegelin's 1952 work *The New Science of Politics*. In 1958, the University of California Press accepted the text for publication under the title *Defense of Modern Times*, but it remained unpublished. Then, in following years, publication still pending, the text was

---

[28] The passage states: "Die Grundnorm einer positiven Moral- oder Rechtsordnung ist – wie aus dem Vorhergehenden ersichtlich – keine positive, sondern eine bloß gedachte, und das heißt eine fingierte Norm, der Sinn nicht eines realen, sondern eines bloß fingierten Willensaktes. Als solche ist sie eine echte oder 'eigentliche' Fiktion im Sinne der Vaihingerischen Philosophie des Als-Ob, die dadurch gekennzeichnet ist, dass sie nicht nur der Wirklichkeit widerspricht, sondern auch in sich selbst widerspruchsvoll ist. Denn die Annahme einer Grundnorm – wie etwa die Grundnorm einer religiösen Moralordnung: 'Man soll den Geboten Gottes gehorchen' oder die Grundnorm einer Rechtsordnung: 'Man soll sich so verhalten, wie die historisch erste Verfassung bestimmt' – widerspricht nicht nur der Wirklichkeit, da keine solche Norm als Sinn eines wirklichen Willensaktes vorhanden ist, sie ist auch in sich selbst widerspruchsvoll, da sie die Ermächtigung einer höchsten Moral- oder Rechtsautorität darstellt, und damit von einer noch über dieser Autorität stehenden – allerdings nur fingierten – Autorität ausgeht….Der Denkzweck der Grundnorm ist: die Begründung der Geltung der eine positive Moral- oder Rechtsordnung bildenden Normen, das ist die Deutung des subjektiven Sinnes der diese Normen setzenden Akte als deren objektiven Sinn, das heißt aber als gültige Normen, und der betreffende Akte als norm-setzende Akte. Dieses Ziel ist nur im Wege einer Fiktion zu erreichen…."

[29] Kelsen, *Secular Religion*, p. 271.

referred to as *Religion without God?* and *Theology without God?*. Kelsen ultimately withdrew the manuscript (then under the title *Secular Religion*) from publication in 1964 and it lay in storage until the Hans Kelsen Institute posthumously published it in 2012.[30]

In the introductory remarks to *Secular Religion*, Richard Potz summarizes Voegelin's thesis, against which Kelsen's work is directed: "If the transcendent principle of order is lost, the result is what he (Voegelin) calls a Gnostic immanentism, which leads to the divination of man as the basic malady of modern times and finally culminates in the quasi-religious totalitarisms of the 20th century."[31] Voegelin's argument is that the evils of the 20th century can be traced to the 'false' religions which filled the void of transcendence in the wake of the Enlightenment's rejection of the 'true' Judeo-Christian Religion of the 'one true God'. Kelsen vehemently rejects this characterization by his former pupil and instead argues that the Enlightenment philosophers broadly conceived, including Hobbes, Hume, Kant, Saint-Simon, Proudhon, Comte, Marx and Nietzsche, were not religious at all.

In *Secular Religion*, Kelsen argues that no social science can be based on a "transcendent authority beyond any possible human experience" (271), that it is a fundamental mistake to see theological tendencies in the thoughts of men who largely sought to "emancipate human thinking from the bondage of theology" (3), that the "development of modern science is the result of its emancipation from religion and theology" (4), and that the science of modern times is differentiated from that of the Middle Ages by objectivity and independence (ibid.). Kelsen reflects that Hobbes considered religion to be the fear of invisible power, "feigned by the mind, or imagined from tales publicly allowed" (87, citing *Leviathan* Ch. VI) and Kelsen claims that secular morality cannot constitute a religion because a religion without God is a contradiction in terms (100). Kelsen states that a revelation is a "conveyance of a divine truth by a supernatural, superrational act of God" (103) and that the "essence of a religious experience is to ask metaphysical questions and to find the answers in the wishful imagination that is the specific product of this experience" (149).

It is of no relevance here to discuss the nature of God or Kelsen's atheism generally. The relevant question, as stated above, regards the relationship between the individual and the collective as mediated through norms. In particular, if (i) we accept along with Hobbes, Spinoza, Leibniz, Kelsen and Schmitt that there is an inherent relationship between authority, revelation, textual interpretation and the general normative relationship between the many and the one as

---

[30] Id. at p. xi–xv.

[31] Id. at p. vii.

these present themselves in the spheres of theology and jurisprudence and if (ii) we follow (at least the late) Kelsen as seen through Kletzer that modern science has made redundant the hypostases of God and state which made possible theology and jurisprudence in the first place, then we must be very careful to clarify and explicate the nature and being of that which is now redundant. The claim with which we are faced is that, on the one hand, our advances in knowledge following the Enlightenment have made the acceptance of both 'God' and 'state' irrational or super-rational, and on the other hand, more explicity with Kletzer and more implicitly with Kelsen, the rules of validity have thus changed such as to allow only for a relative validity of norms – the absolute validity of God and state as typified by earlier centuries is no longer viable.

The assumption which connects these two claims is that the absolute validity of the past was dependent on an omnipotent God. However, it seems that this assumption becomes baseless upon closer consideration. If there is validity at all, it is not now nor has it ever been a function of an omnipotent God, but rather of an individual's practical rationality. It is difficult to find this Kantian point in the writings of Kelsen. For example, in *Secular Religion* Kelsen criticizes Cassirer, who asserts that religious conviction is maintained by man himself, by stating: "But true religious conviction is belief in the existence of a supernatural being, which, in its relation to man, has such an overpowering authority that man can only be seized and overwhelmed; and it is this supernatural power and especially divine grace which – according to true religion – produces religious conviction."[32] However, religious conviction, just as with adherence to a legal code, is not in the first instance a result of being overwhelmed by an all-powerful existence. Even if we were to assume such an omnipotent authority, religious conviction could then at most arise *secondarily* in the face of a supernatural being resulting from an individual deciding for himself that the most desirable course of action is to adhere to a religious or legal code, just as an individual could most rationally decide to obey a tyrant as a means of avoiding death or enjoying its favor.

Without ignoring legitimate criticisms according to which at least the Christian Church, sometimes benevolently and sometimes malevolently, has often instrumentalized just such a belief system, religion can hardly be reduced to the mere expectation of rewards and punishments. Heinrich Heine describes the absurdity of such motivations with reference to a conversation with Hegel:

> Eines schönen hellgestirnten Abends standen wir beide neben einander am Fenster, und ich, ein zweyundzwanzigjähriger junger Mensch, ich hatte eben gut gegessen und Kaffee getrunken, und ich sprach mit Schwärmerey von den Sternen, und nannte sie den Aufenthalt der Seligen. Der Meister aber brümmelte vor sich hin: 'Die Sterne, hum! hum! die Sterne sind nur ein

[32] Kelsen. *Secular Religion*. 92.

leuchtender Aussatz am Himmel.' Um Gotteswillen – rief ich – es giebt also droben kein glückliches Lokal, um dort die Tugend nach dem Tode zu belohnen? Jener aber, indem er mich mit seinen bleichen Augen stier ansah, sagte schneidend: 'Sie wollen also noch ein Trinkgeld dafür haben, dass Sie Ihre kranke Mutter gepflegt und Ihren Herrn Bruder nicht vergiftet haben?'[33]

The point of Heine's anecdote is to illustrate that the reward for a good action is in performing the action itself. This applies equally to the non-believer and the believer as well as to the two possible worlds in which God, as a 'supernatural and superrational' being exists and does not exist. For both believers and non-believers, and for citizens everywhere, whether in classical Rome, Medieval Europe or Post-Modernity, reasons for action always lie in the agent, not in an external force.

Indeed, the notion of belief itself as used by Kelsen is problematic. In his criticism of Cassirer above, Kelsen states that 'true *conviction* is the *belief* in a *supernatural being* that has an *overpowering authority'*. Here, there are two competing categories: first, there is the belief in a supernatural being that overpowers, which is a characterization in terms of brute force; second, however, there is the conviction of authority, which is a description of normativity. The belief in something which over*powers* is a belief in a material object which stands in the way of my material objectivity. The conviction of something which has authority over me, on the other hand, pertains to my own practical rationality, and relates to my obligation to act, i. e. on my own volition. Far from allowing the question of the relationship between the individual and the collective in the context of an actual hypostasis, Kelsen instead prejudices this relationship by framing the individual as wholly subservient to the omnipotent divine.

6. Kelsen's Golden Calf

Wie der Staat, so ist Gott als Persönlichkeit: Wille. Gott ist persönlicher Geist oder geistige Persönlichkeit – so lautet in der christlichen Gotteserkenntnis die nähere Bestimmung des Satzes vom geistigen Wesen Gottes. Sie bedeutet die Überordnung des geistig-persönlichen Willens über das Denken und Erkennen. "Die Frage, die dadurch entschieden wird, ist die, ob wir mit Aristoteles das geistige Wesen Gottes in das Denken seiner selbst (eauton noein) zu setzen und dementsprechend die dianoetische Tugend als die eigentliche Bestimmung des Menschen zu erkennen haben, oder ob Gott die höchste Energie des persönlichen Willens ist und die praktische Tugend der dianoetischen übergeordnet werden muss. Der christliche Glaube entscheidet in letzterem Sinne." (citing Kaftan in *Dogmatik*, p. 188). Dementsprechend ist der Gehorsam gegen seinen (Gottes) Willen der eigentliche und wahre Gottesdienst so wie ja auch der Gehorsam gegen den Willen des Staates der eigentliche Staatsdienst ist.[34]

---

33 Heine, Heinrich. "Fatale Eyer", in: *Gestaendnisse*. (1854).

34 Kelsen. *Der soziologische und juristische Staatsbegriff*, p. 225–226.

Here we are not discussing Kelsen's theological commitments. Instead, we seek to understand how and why legal positivism develops under Kelsen to embrace the strictly relativistic position suggested by Kletzer. In this sense, the quote above provides a useful key for understanding Kelsen's approach to normativity, purely volitional from the perspective of the legal system itself, relative from the outside.

Kelsen states in the last sentence of the quote above that obedience to the will of God (as opposed to the reason of God) is the true form of worship just as obedience to the will of the state is the true form of *Staatsdienst* (perhaps to be translated as civil service, patriotism or subjugation). As is evident from the discussion of *Secular Religion*, Kelsen clearly dismisses any notion of an objective God just as, in *Der soziologische und juristische Staatsbegriff*, he ultimately dismisses the notion of the state as an unnecessary hypostasis. However, while Kelsen also dismisses the idea of obedience to the divine will (i.e. as 'wishful imagination'), the entirety of Kelsen's Pure Theory nonetheless upholds the idea of obedience to the 'will' of the legal order, grounded on the basic norm, *as if it were* a state. As such, Kelsen succeeds in dismissing the materialistic idea of the omnipotent, overpowering state just as he succeeds in dismissing the idea of the omnipotent, overpowering God. These refutations on the part of Kelsen, however, do not extend to the notion of obedience itself, at least within the frame of the legal order, which Kelsen maintains in rather mechanistic form, *as if* God or state were still there coercing its subjects into submission.

While a person's subjective reasons for following the law can vary significantly for Kelsen,[35] the objective reason for following the law in Kelsen's Pure Theory in its mature form nonetheless flows directly from the hierarchy of norms ending in the basic norm.[36] Kletzer is correct in pointing out that this validity is merely relative viewed from outside of the legal order; seen from within the legal order though, each norm enjoys absolute validity, is absolutely binding upon the subject. There is no room for rationalization on the part of the subject when encountering the legal norm. Rather, each subject must strictly follow the will which the norm expresses. The relation between sovereign and subject which the norm represents is here a direct manifestation of the sovereign will.

---

[35] For example, see Kelsen, *Allgemeine Staatslehre,* p. 10: "Der Staat sei ein Herrschaftsverhältnis, d.h. ein Verhältnis, in dem der Wille des einen zum Motiv für das Verhalten des anderen wird, auf das der erste Wille gerichtet ist, oder ein – irgendwie qualifizierter – Herrscher selbst, dessen Willen die ihm untertanen (oder zugleich ihn bildenden?) Individuen bindet, im Sinne von: motiviert. Für eine Wirklichkeitsbetrachtung gibt es nur eine Vielheit von solchen Motivationsverhältnissen, und die Einheit des Herrschenden ist realiter ebensowenig gegeben, wie die der Beherrschten."

[36] See Kelsen, *Reine Rechtslehre*, p. 67: "In der Grundnorm wurzelt letztlich die normative Bedeutung aller die Rechtsordnung konstituierenden Tatbestände."

The overpowering sovereign, just like the overpowering God, can coerce me to act according to its will out of sheer force. In this scenario, the 'norm' is merely the communication of the will of the tyrant (or God) along with the explicit or implicit threat of punishment in the event of non-compliance. However, just as the state cannot be encapsulated in the physical presence of one individual tyrant, God cannot be encapsulated as an object whatsoever. Kelsen is aware of this in the passage above in which he refers to God as a spiritual (*geistig*) entity and Kelsen even addresses this topic at length in the political context in the *Hauptprobleme* when he develops his theory of norms as connecting points of attribution, in which the state does not consist of an actual will at all but is rather constructed.[37] Despite the clear rejection of the possibility of both a divine and a political will, Kelsen nonetheless maintains in the Pure Theory a notion of norms according to which the sovereign, or the legal order, wills and the subjects obey – basically a normative veneer that Kelsen places over the naked reality of power and violence characteristic of factual reality.[38]

I submit that this voluntarist view of legal norms can be traced through Kelsen's voluntaristic view of God. The ultimate *Gretchenfrage* is not whether or not one believes in God (whatever that might mean), or what one believes God to be, but rather how one perceives one's own agency, whether individualistically or communally, whether instrumentally, voluntaristically or rationalistically determined. Though Kelsen suggests above in citing to Kaftan that God's will is clearly prior to God's reason, this relationship has not always been seen in this way. Thomas Aquinas[39] and Suarez favored a more rationalistic interpretation of God[40] and, more relevantly for modern legal theory, Montesquieu considered God's rationalistic relation to its own laws to be a paradigm for understanding human laws:

> Les lois, dans la signification plus étendue, sont les rapports nécessaires qui dérivent de la nature des choses; et, dans ce sens, tous les êtres ont leurs lois, la divinité a ses lois, le monde matériel a ses lois, les intelligences supérieurs a l'homme ont leurs lois, les bêtes ont leurs lois, l'homme a ses lois […] Dieu a du rapport avec l'univers, comme créateur et comme conservateur: les lois selon lesquelles il a créé sont celles selon lesquelles il conserve. Il agit selon ces règles, parce qu'il les connait; il les connait parce qu'il les a faites; il les a fait, parce qu'elles ont du rapport avec sa sagesse et sa puissance.[41]

The concept of obedience put forth by Kelsen is that that which the sovereign wills must be followed absolutely without recourse on the part of the subject to

[37] Kelsen, *Hauptprobleme*, pp. 176ff.

[38] See Kelsen, *Reine Rechtslehre*, p. 34.

[39] Spade and Panaccio (2016).

[40] See Shields and Schwartz (2016).

[41] Montesquieu. *De l'Esprit des Lois*, Book I, Ch. 1.

comprehension or critical evaluation of the command. This is the case of a God with an omnipotent will capable of issuing any norm without any qualification. However, if instead of seeing God primarily as will, we see God primarily as reason, then the proper form of worship is not obedience, but rather understanding: we obey not by following the norm but by understanding it.

Kelsen errs in presuming that religion is about subjective propositional belief in a supernatural, super-rational entity and that, even in the absence of the divine presumption, legal obedience must follow a similar path. Of course, such a blind and misguided belief in this kind of hypostastic form cannot but inform a blind and misguided obedience. Kelsen's mistake here is not that he believed in the Golden Calf, but that he did not believe in the Golden Calf. By presuming that religion is about a false god and in not making an effort to understand it, Kelsen is left with a false sense of obedience in the religious realm and therefore generally of normativity in the political. Had Kelsen instead espoused the idea of a thoroughly rational God, whose worship consists in understanding, then Kelsen's sense of normativity *sans* God would have been significantly different.

For the issue of normativity, the question of divine existence itself is completely inconsequential. Indeed, one could even say that religion is much more about commitment to or faith in a normative system then it is about subjective belief in any given proposition.[42] Religion cannot primarily be interested in the defense of a mythology naively understood. Rather, religion is about a stance in the world, it is normative. It is in this sense that Cohen asserts that proper theology must be ethico-theology,[43] or in other words, political theology.

7. Spunk

"'Denkt bloß', sagte Pippi träumerisch, 'denkt bloß, dass ich das gefunden habe! Gerade ich und niemand anders!'
'Was hast Du gefunden?' fragten Thomas und Annika.
'Ein neues Wort', sagte Pippi…, 'Ein funkelnagelneues Wort!.'
'Was für ein Wort?' fragte Thomas………
'Spunk!', sagte Pippi triumphierend.
'Spunk?' fragte Thomas. 'Was bedeutet das?'
'Wenn ich das bloß wüsste!' sagte Pippi."

---

42 In referring to the faith on which Comte bases his vision of a positivistic society (*Secular Religion*, p. 158), Kelsen states that "'faith' by its nature refers to the supernatural, and a 'faith' which refers to something natural and is demonstrable is no faith in the proper sense of the word."

43 Cohen, p. 21.

Until it is possible to reach a consensus regarding what is meant by the concept 'God', 'spunk' or even 'state', it is senseless to ask someone else whether they believe in such an entity. If religion were about belief in a merely subjective propositional content, it would make no more sense for one to believe in God than for Pippi Longstocking to have discovered a word which no one else understands and for which she herself does not know the meaning. A key purpose of establishing a canon of written texts, whether these are considered themselves to be divine revelation, legal codes or merely commentaries thereon, is to embed a given concept within a (textually represented) normative framework. For example, it is senseless to believe in a personal God only accessible to oneself and it is very impractical to believe in a God who literally moves the heavens and the earth. However, it is neither senseless nor impractical to believe in a normative framework, to have faith therein, to commit oneself to norms whether divine or political.

The challenge underlying *Secular Religion* and the reason why Kelsen insists that both social and natural sciences (including legal science) must be purely descriptive and without any recourse to value is that Kelsen believes that there is no objectively normative source of unity for the collective reality. The Enlightenment having thrown off the yoke of the Church with its mythologies and personified explanations of the natural and social world, Kelsen sees any insertion of evaluative or normative terms as a necessarily subjective endeavor, such as if Pippi would attempt to base a legal theory on the principle of Spunk. The argument against value in the social sciences for Kelsen is ultimately an argument against the possibility of private language. When Kelsen hears people speak of God or State, all that he can hear is 'Spunk' and spunks clearly do not exist. Here, it seems that Kelsen's imagination is too narrow and his program too reductivist. The ancient problem of naming abstract or non-material entities is that the name can always hypostasize and become a reality unto itself. This is why it is so important in religious traditions to have scripture which embeds the meaning of any given god in a tradition of writings reflecting cultural norms that extend across generations, which contributes significantly to solidifying a core meaning within the tradition and avoids the danger of 'spunkifying' the center of cultural meaning, i. e. attributing private meaning to a common good. A similar danger in the political realm is that of propaganda or even doublespeak, for example after the September 11, 2001 attacks in the United States when 'Freedom' became a justification for all kinds of questionable, at times illegal and, in hindsight, oppressive and unpatriotic actions. However, the danger of 'spunks' arising without a community of meaning does not entail that a community of meaning does not or should not exist in the first place. Indeed, the very function of the spunk story from Anstrid Lindgren is to show that Pippi is rebellious or perhaps simply orphaned in a society that is very strongly imbued with meaning.

Was thaten wir, als wir diese Erde von ihrer Sonne losketteten? Wohin bewegt sie sich nun? Wohin bewegen wir uns? Fort von allen Sonnen? Stürzen wir nicht fortwährend? Und rückwärts, seitwärts, vorwärts, nach allen Seiten? Giebt es noch ein Oben und ein Unten? Irren wir nicht wie durch ein unendliches Nichts? Haucht uns nicht der leere Raum an? Ist es nicht kälter geworden? Kommt nicht immerfort die Nacht und mehr Nacht?

Nietzsche's madman ends his tirade by exclaiming that he has come too early, that the people in the town square have not realized what they have done. When Kelsen criticizes Cassirer and Voegelin for their attempts at re-inserting a concept of value into our understanding of society, he is akin to the people in the town square who laugh at the madman for searching for God. It is quite possible that Kelsen, like the townspeople, did not understand the full significance of God's death, for Kelsen seems to believe that empirical science can replace the faith that was once had in God.[44] However, faith in science is also a normative stance and scientific 'progress' is of course driven by value. How we discover the world and what we do with our scientific discoveries are always embedded in value. "Wer im Mythos lebt, weiß das nicht."[45]

8. The Tyranny of Necessity

Before that time, as I said at the start, the gods behaved dreadfully under the tyranny of Necessity. But with the birth of Love and the love of beauty came all good things for gods and men.[46]

In giving his account of institutional reality, John Searle has often used the example of a stone wall in the British countryside. When this wall was built centuries ago, it may have been meant to physically separate one town from another or to mark a property line. Initially, the wall may have been controversial, functioning only on account of its sheer mass and height. However, as time went on and one generation gave way to another, the townspeople may have begun to recognize not just the brute force of the wall (that they could not climb or bust through), but

44 See Kelsen, *Secular Religion*, p. 98: The philosophers' assumption that moral and political principles can be found in human reason is certainly an illusion, for these values have their ultimate source in the emotional, not in the rational, component of the human mind. The philosophers' illusion was the result of their overestimation of the faculties of human reason.

45 Attributed to Jürgen Mittelstraß by Hogrebe (2005).

46 Plato's *Symposium*, para. 197b, Agathon's speech, p. 44. In the same paragraph, Agathon states that Love "is such a wise and gifted poet that he can even make poets of others, for everyone becomes a poet when he falls in love, however deaf to the muses before […] And it is not only poets that [Love's] wisdom (here Sharon says that wisdom has the meaning of skill) engenders, the genius of Love also generates all human life, making all mankind." Also, consider the similarity between the 'tyranny of necessity' and the world of desire dependent reasons for action depicted in Chapter II.

its normativity. The wall may have become not just a hindrance, but a property line or an administrative boundary. If this has occurred, then the demarcation which the wall once represented could well persist long after the actual stones have fallen away. Now, assuming that this has occurred and the normativity of the property line or administrative boundary has persisted, one could imagine that an iconoclastic townsman of the future could come along, long after the last stone has disappeared, and demand to know why it is the case that he and his fellow townspeople are not allowed to cross the line. In previous times, the response would come quite naturally that, even if others would want to cross the line, they simply would not be able to do so. Now, they *could* quite easily do so, but *should* they? The iconoclast would say yes, as a matter of course. However, Chesterton reminds us that if you happen to come across a fence in the countryside and you do not know what function it serves, before you tear it down, you should first figure out what function it might have served in the past. You should tear down the fence only if the fence's past functionality is no longer relevant today.[47]

Austin might say to the iconoclast that even if it is possible to cross the line, he still should not do so, so as to avoid the sanction associated with the iconoclast's breach of the norm. Hart would maintain that the iconoclast should not cross the line because the rule forbidding the crossing thereof is duly enacted by the county government and there exists as a matter of social fact a Rule of Recognition according to which the county government has the authority to decide upon boundary lines. Kelsen would say that both the likelihood of a sanction and the existence of social recognition of the normative framework are irrelevant to whether the iconoclast should cross the line. Rather, the iconoclast should refrain from crossing the line because the county government has issued a relevant norm forbidding such conduct and the county government has been authorized to issue such a norm as a result of a hierarchy of norms ending in a basic norm.[48]

---

[47] Chesterton, The Thing, Ch. 4: "In the matter of reforming things, as distinct from deforming them, there is one plain and simple principle; a principle which will probably be called a paradox. There exists in such a case a certain institution or law; let us say, for the sake of simplicity, a fence or gate erected across a road. The more modern type of reformer goes gaily up to it and says, "I don't see the use of this; let us clear it away." To which the more intelligent type of reformer will do well to answer: "If you don't see the use of it, I certainly won't let you clear it away. Go away and think. Then, when you can come back and tell me that you do see the use of it, I may allow you to destroy it."

[48] Technically, to stay true to Kelsen's view of the legal norm as a hypothetical norm, we would have to say that the Kelsenian norm is not directed to the iconoclast at all, but rather to the policeman who asks himself why he should arrest the iconoclast for crossing, or attempting to cross, the line.

Of course, Kelsen explicitly states about the basic norm that this is a logical prerequisite of the legal system resulting from the is-ought distinction. Indeed, it is the case that if the legal system is a system of norms, then a first norm is required in order to avoid the problem of infinite regress. However, this logical prerequisite of the basic norm does not yet settle the question of the content of the basic norm. While the *Reine Rechtslehre* does not explicitly state that the basic norm is empty of content amounting to the prescription: 'you ought to follow the norms of this constitution / legal system', this is nonetheless the predominant reading of the basic norm's meaning and this reading is fully supported by Kelsen's other works including *Der soziologische und juristische Staatsbegriff*, *Allgemeine Theorie der Normen*, *Was ist Gerechtigkeit?*, and *Secular Religion*. Especially in *Secular Religion*, Kelsen's reasoning in support of an empty basic norm is evident. The basic norm must be empty because (a) there is no divine normative source and (b) any substantive value, e. g. the golden rule, is ultimately subjective. As Kletzer says, the rules of validity change following the "death of God". However, what Kletzer's dictum actually means and what becomes evident from Kelsen's *Secular Religion* is that the Pure Theory is written for a world in which validity in the sense of binding normativity no longer exists. The Pure Theory is merely a theory for assisting lawyers and others who are already committed to following the law in the mundane (and wholly uninteresting) task of identifying which norms are actually applicable. The question of why a subject would actually want to follow the law becomes either a speculative question of moral philosophy or an irrelevant musing likely to impede the value-free, objective endeavor of scientific discovery – the question of the 'bindingness' of the law is entirely formal for Kelsen and does not permit the possibility of the substance of normativity.

This solution, however, is too easy. Instead of creating the pre-requisite for a legal science, Kelsen's "absolute positivism" destroys its very need. If there is no value inherent in a legal norm, then there is no possibility of interpreting its meaning in its application. The semantics of a rule become non-existent and the only job left for the lawyer is to apply the rule according to its syntax. Why follow the basic norm? Well, it is required for the legal system to exist. But why should the legal system exist? Well, without the legal system, there can be no political order, no state. But why should there be a state in the first place?

A legal system without value is a legal system without meaning and is tantamount to the absence of legal order in the first place – a return to the desire dependent circumstance of the natural state. Kelsen succeeded in bringing modern legal theory full circle to its post-theological, pre-Hobbesian roots. It should be understood as the ultimate de-constructivist project, stripping man of its bond to society and subjugating it to the tyranny of necessity.

Il y aura toujours une grande différence entre soumettre une multitude et régir une société. Que des hommes épars soient successivement asservis à un seul, en quelque nombre qu'ils puissent être, je ne vois là qu'un maître et des esclaves, je n'y vois point un peuple et son chef: c'est, si l'on veut, une agrégation, mais non pas une association; il n'y a là ni bien public, ni corps politique. Cet homme, eût-il asservi la moitié du monde, n'est toujours qu'un particulier; son intérêt, séparé de celui des autres, n'est toujours qu'un intérêt privé.[49]

Kelsen sought to preserve individual autonomy by developing a system in which there is no ultimate source of normativity, and therefore no risk of heteronomic control by authority outside of the legal order. The price of this purely formal approach though, as Rousseau points out in the quote above, is that once there is no longer a unity in the society, once the legal order is of form only and the individual norms are simply projections of power, then the society becomes a mere multitude enslaved by the state and the state, no longer identical with the legal order, becomes the only thing which really exists vis-à-vis its former citizens who are no longer even subjects, but servants. This is the tyranny of servitude which Rousseau describes above and which we might imagine to exist in various dictatorships across the world. However, this is in some ways only a prelude to the tyranny of necessity to which Plato alludes to in the *Symposium*: it is the heteronomy of the material in the absence of value, in which that which guides human conduct is not the choice of acting in a certain way, but rather the requirement of acting only according to material needs.

9. A First Convention

Avant donc que d'examiner l'acte par lequel un peuple élit un roi, il seroit bon d'examiner l'acte par lequel un peuple est un peuple; car cet acte, étant nécessairement antérieur à l'autre, est le vrai fondement de la société.[50]

If there is not to be a tyranny of necessity, a freedom of the most naïve variety, then there must be some kind of a rule of order. However, this is not just any kind of arbitrary order in the way that Hobbes' Leviathan is sometimes understood. As Rousseau points out above, it is not a matter of simply instituting a king to save us from ourselves. Rather, the modern understanding requires that sovereignty derives from the people and that in order to understand the order of sovereignty, i.e. the order of that which issues the commands, it is necessary to understand the order which comprises a people. Even now, over two centuries since the French Revolution and the Declaration of Independence, and as reflected in Kelsen's *Stufenbau* ending in the basic norm, as well as Hart's Rule of Recognition, the

[49] Rousseau. *Du contrat social*. Ch. 1.5.

[50] Ibid.

default paradigm is of an order which comes from the top-down, even though popular sovereignty is almost universally acknowledged. While constitutional / political theory has become thoroughly modern reflecting notions of popular sovereignty, our notions of governance (i. e. the exercise / implementation of that popular sovereignty / power) and most importantly our notions of order (i. e. the expression and validity of laws) remain but mere adaptations of the *ancien regime*. Indeed, Hayek remains here the exception in a paradigm dominated by a thetic approach to social order. However, we need not begin with Hayek's presumptions in order to arrive at a conception of order that eschews the hierarchical. Historically and conceptually, the road to popular sovereignty is also paved *ex negativo*.

In the religious context, God is most commonly perceived as both omnipotent and personal in the sense of having a personal relationship with the believer. This proves to be a very motivating conception on the part of believers (e. g. "faith can move mountains"). Very often though, this particular kind of religious motivation which combines a belief in divine omnipotence with a belief in the personal divine intervention by God in worldly affairs is limited to personal or at most communal contexts. For example, I may believe that God will intervene to cure my illness or I might believe that I am acting on God's behalf in supporting my family, village or church community. While such behavior can manifest itself oppressively at the communal level, the risks of the belief in the absolute omnipotence of God combined with a belief of a personal relationship can threaten to become exponentially more dangerous at the societal level. At its most dangerous, the terms 'state' and 'God' become interchangeable and the personal relationship with God is replaced by the personal cult of a political leader with catastrophic consequences.[51] We often do a great job of diagnosing such characteristics as fascist or totalitarian when attributed to the state. However, the normative structure in the case of religion is no different. This structure in each case involves the naturalistic fallacy by which normative importance is attributed to facts in the natural order.

If we dismiss the question of whether God factually created the heavens and the earth (thus making all people subservient to God as first and final cause) or actually formed the nation of Israel (thus bestowing rights of sovereignty) or actually bestowed political and civic privileges upon its people (thus resulting in the rights of life, liberty and the pursuit of happiness), then ultimately such rights and obligations are rights and obligations that are, in some way, constituted by us for ourselves.

---

[51] Cf. the personal aspects of the communal and the anonymous aspects of the societal in Toennies, *Gemeinschaft und Gesellschaft*.

Acknowledging in Moore's naturalistic fallacy that God's past actions in the world are technically irrelevant for our future course of action, we are left with the realization that we are on our own to determine our normative course, to judge upon that which is right and wrong. It is only in this, post-Nietzschean, context that Kelsen's parallel between the state and God becomes especially interesting. Only once God is dead is there a renewed need to consider a hypostasis, a first norm, as the source of the normative order.

10. The Social Construction of the State

Ἔστιν δὲ πίστις ἐλπιζομένων ὑπόστασις, πραγμάτων ἔλεγχος οὐ βλεπομένων.[52]

The discussion with respect to the nature of hypostasis, and the nature of the state, does not primarily revolve around an issue of epistemology, i. e. how we come to know or perceive things, but rather of ontology, i. e. what there is to know. Is there something or is there nothing? Does the state exist or does it not exist; is there a basic norm, i. e. is there a normative order, or, upon further reflection, is there actually no basic norm, no normative order? Is it all just a matter of our perception, our belief, or is there really something to it all?

In the first section of this chapter, Jurisprudence and Theology, I point out that both jurisprudence and theology have two things in common: first, each discipline is dependent on a normative code, usually written in some form, that imposes duties based on an external authority. Second, this authority hypostasizes in an idea, the objective existence of which is dependent on adopting an internal perspective. In the next section, State as Hypostasis, I discuss how Kelsen, in concordance with Hobbes, conceives of the state as a unifying idea and how Kelsen refers to this idea as an hypostasis, the historical background of which I sketch. The upshot of the sketch and of Kelsen's own view is that the hypostasis of the state has come to be seen as pure fiction, or make believe. This leads to the Problem of Many and of No Gods: the late 20th century was characterized by a political liberalism which espouses a plurality of sources of value, which, in turn, leads to a degradation of the role of value and meaning altogether, at least in the objective sense. The solution to this, so Kletzer in his Absolute Positivism, is to fully embrace Kelsen's view of the absolute validity of the legal order, which is

---

52 Hebrews 11.1. Relevant translations are from the New American Bible: "Faith is the realization of what is hoped for and evidence of things not seen."; the King James Bible: "Now faith is the substance of things hoped for, the evidence of things not seen." Zürcher Bibel: "Der Glaube aber ist die Grundlegung dessen, was man erhofft, der Beweis für Dinge, die man nicht sieht." Luther Bibel: "Es ist aber der Glaube eine feste Zuversicht dessen, was man hofft, und ein Nichtzweifeln an dem, was man nicht sieht."

a validity from the internal perspective only, entailing a complete relativism from the 'outside' perspective of practical philosophy. The question is whether this is a valid move to make in the conceptualization of the legal order. Is it possible, for example for the lawyer, to bifurcate his intentionality between the absolute validity of the system of laws in which she operates and the society in which she lives? Is the absolute validity of the Kelsenian legal order not then actually just an absolute validity in name only and is it not in reality a thoroughly relativistic affair, like the rules of a soccer game? Kelsen seems to think that there is no alternative to such Value Nihilism and in his posthumously published *Secular Religion* shows why this is the case: without an omnipotent, supernatural, super-rational God there is simply no longer any source of objective value. To presume otherwise is to simply subject oneself to a make-believe world. Depending how this late position is to be understood, one could think that Kelsen had it right earlier in his career when he referred to the necessity of conceiving of the state, and of God, as a unity, and that omnipotence, whether evidenced within the sanctioning state or the punishing God, is always a secondary quality, subservient to the essential requirement of unity. In the following section, Kelsen's Golden Calf, I show how Kelsen nonetheless remains tied to the voluntaristic worldview of omnipotence in creating his hierarchy of norms which entail absolute authority / validity of substantive norms within the legal order. In Spunk I suggested that Kelsen's reservation with respect to a source of value existing in society is that Kelsen sees this source of value to require a kind of private language being imposed upon the collective. I suggest that Kelsen's reservation is misplaced to the extent that social meaning, both in religious and legal contexts, derives not from private attributions, but from extended cultural traditions, often concretized in written form. In the preceding two sections I then try to show that conceiving of the legal order without a substantive basis for its validity is tantamount to envisioning the lack of political order itself and reconceiving a kind of Hobbesian state of nature, a Tyranny of Necessity, and that the resolution of this development must lie, not in a return to the supernatural or super-rational, but rather to understanding the deeper meaning of conventionality.

With Rousseau, this deeper meaning of conventionality is taken to be that the existence of a state, or with Kelsen, a legal order, is not dependent on something exterior to the state such as a sovereign king, but rather is internal to the state itself. The state develops from within itself, i.e. from the convention of itself. Formulated from the individualistic perspective, the state develops out of the conventionality of its citizens.

"Now faith is confidence in what we hope for and assurance about what we do not see. This is what the ancients were commended for."[53] In this New Testament passage, this precise formulation of which has its roots in Luther's 1545 translation and which provides a key definition for the concept of faith / belief / Glaube / fides / πίστις, we see a foretelling not just of the path of modern Christianity, but of modern ontology and political / legal theory. We saw above that Kelsen dismisses characteristic Christian belief, and therewith belief in any political reality which transcends the formalistic structure of Kelsen's Pure Theory, as a kind of psychological therapy which transcends rationality: "Im Wunder wirkt der supranaturale Gott die Erfüllung aller Wünsche, auf die Verzichten muss, der sich im Bereiche der Natur bescheidet. Mit dieser treffenden Psychologie des überweltlichen Gottesbegriffes ist zugleich der Schlüssel zu dem überrechtlichen Staatsbegriff gegeben." (as quoted above at FN 12). Above in 'Empiricism or Positivism', we saw a similar sentiment with respect to ontological truth claims on the part of the Vienna Circle:

> ...Zu der einen 'von zwei Arten von Aussagen' gehören die Aussagen, wie sie in der empirischen Wissenschaft gemacht werden; ihr Sinn läßt sich feststellen durch logische Analyse, genauer: durch Rückführung auf einfachste Aussagen über empirisch Gegebenes. Die anderen Aussagen, zu denen die vorhin genannten gehören, erweisen sich als völlig bedeutungsleer, wenn man sie so nimmt, wie der Metaphysiker sie meint. Man kann sie freilich häufig in empirische Aussagen umdeuten; dann verlieren sie aber den Gefühlsgehalt, der dem Metaphysiker meist gerade wesentlich ist.[54]

Faith is belief, according to the Oxford Dictionary (5th edition). It is confidence, reliance, belief, especially in the absence of evidence or proof; it is belief based on testimony or authority. Likewise, the Oxford Dictionary tells us that *belief*, for its part, besides faith and confidence, is trust, also in God, acceptance of received theology, and mental acceptance of a statement, fact or doctrine as true or existing. 'Glaube', says Duden, is also a feeling of (religious) conviction or certainty, especially of the kind that is independent of proof or facts. As such, faith, belief and 'Glaube' all represent a mental state which is in some way inferior to the mental state of knowledge, to the extent that we value knowledge over ignorance (which we do). It is thus no wonder that Kelsen dismisses belief (in miracles, or in the otherworldly conception of God, or in the extra-legal conception of state) as irrelevant for legal science. Equally unsurprising is the Vienna Circle's insistence that all beliefs (or statements) regarding metaphysical entities be submitted to the crucible of empirical reality. What point is there in having assurance in something which does not exist? What is also interesting here, is that for Kelsen

53 Hebrews 11:1–2, New International Version.

54 "Wissenschaftliche Weltauffassung: Der Wiener Kreis", in: *Ausgewählte Texte*, as quoted above under III. 'Empiricism or Positivism'.

faith is belief (in German both faith and belief are usually translated as *Glaube*) and belief is a mental assurance of something which does not exist; equally for the Vienna Circle, metaphysical terms do not represent any kind of shared reality but instead are the product of subjective mental states, also corresponding to the definition above, all of which flows from an understanding of mental states corresponding to the Luther Bible's translation of Hebrews 11,1: "Es ist aber der Glaube eine feste Zuversicht dessen, was man hofft, und ein Nichtzweifeln an dem, was man nicht sieht."

However, the Oxford Dictionary also has a second definition for faith, which is: fidelity; a pledge, a solemn promise; the duty of fulfilling a trust or promise; allegiance, obligation. Whereas the first definition describes a mental state with a mind-to-world direction of fit, i. e. a belief which may or may not be true, the second definition describes a mental state with a world-to-mind direction of fit, i. e. fidelity which keeps one committed to a person, a pledge, promise or obligation to act in a certain way, an allegiance to a cause, or country. In this understanding, Kelsen, in his dismissal of the hypostatization of the state, would be seen to dismiss not a hypostatic conception of state as an assertion of fact which does not exist in reality, but rather a hypostatic conception of state as a potential kind of existence which is dependent on the collective mental states of its citizens. These two conceptions comprise a significant difference. But this is not just a peculiarity of the Oxford Dictionary.

Rather, this reflects a fundamental tension inherent in post-Scholastic thought which Dörrie pointed out well in his article on Hypostasis.[55] Dörrie, whom Halfwassen cites extensively in his *Hegel und der Spätantike Neuplatonismus*, provided a comprehensive study of the historical development of the concept of Hypostasis from its classical Greek roots up through the Scholastic period ending with Luther's gloss of hypostasis as *Zuversicht*, which was based, in Dörrie's view, on a philological mistake on the part of Melanchthon. In contrast to *Zuversicht*, which corresponds to the first Oxford definition of a mental confidence / assurance with respect to a propositional content (in this case, the confidence of something to come, i. e. today understood as the putative second coming of Jesus and salvation of the world), Dörrie shows that, prior to Luther, hypostasis was never understood as a mental propositional state, but rather as an ontological realization of something else, as the νοῦς is the realization of the ἓν in Neo-Platonic thought.[56]

[55] Dörrie, p. 46 ff.

[56] Id. at p. 74: "Das Eine ist mehr als ὑπόστασις, da es sich über das Sein erhebt; das reine Sein manifestiert, hypostasiert sich im νοῦς und in der Weltseele."

So wird nunmehr die Gleichsetzung von *substantia* mit ὑπόστασις auch vom neuplatonischen Sinne her verständlich. Da alles, was besteht, den Grund seines Bestehens außer sich hat, ist ein jedes die ὑπόστασις seines Grundes. Mithin ist jedes Sein ὑπόστασις, denn in jeder Realisierung drückt sich die Wirkungskraft eines Grundes aus. Einzig das höchste Eine *ist* nicht, kann also nicht Hypostase von irgendetwas sein.[57]

Instead of being a confidence or assurance, ὑπόστασις is a substance, reality or realization, which corresponds much more closely to the non-Luther translations (even that of *Grundlegung* (i. e. foundation)) of Hebrews 11:1 cited above. However, to say that faith is substance is still a far cry from saying that faith is fidelity, allegiance or duty as the Oxford Dictionary would have it. Here we do not need to engage biblical scholarship, nor is there a primary philological interest in the conceptual history of ὑπόστασις. However, as Kletzer points out, just under the surface of Kelsen's denial of the extra-legal character of the state, along with his identification (as we will see in the next chapter) of the legal order with the strictly formal hierarchy of norms, lies an ontological claim that nothing exists, or at least that no scientifically minded person can hold that there are things that exist, beyond the realm of empirically verifiable data. Phrased in this way, Kelsen's premise indeed seems plausible. Nor, at first glance, does Hebrews 11:1, neither in the Luther nor in the NIV translation, offer much of a counter-argument: "*Es ist aber der Glaube eine feste Zuversicht dessen, was man hofft, und ein Nichtzweifeln an dem, was man nicht sieht.*" And: "Now faith is confidence in what we hope for and assurance about what we do not see." As definitions of faith, these passages are also definitions of delusion: faith is confidence in what we hope to be the case in the absence of any supporting evidence. This strongly resembles the kind of pre-critical, pre-scientific worldview that Kelsen objects to in the passages above. Even the King James Version, which much more closely mirrors Dörrie's historical contextualization of ὑπόστασις as substance, remains ambiguous: "Now faith is the substance of things hoped for, the evidence of things not seen." Here, faith is no longer the blind confidence in the impossible, but rather the substance, i. e. reality of what is hoped for. Does this mean that what is hoped for, the evidence of things not seen, is essentially faith? Is faith then essentially an end in itself? Perhaps.[58] However, for our analysis of Kelsen's use of the term ὑπόστασις, as well as the somewhat more important inquiry into the ontological status of the state, ὑπόστασις as substance may not seem to be of particular relevance: regardless of what ὑπόστασις might have meant prior to Luther or Melanchthon, in the time between Luther and Kelsen ὑπόστασις had

[57] Id. at pp. 69–70.

[58] Id. at p. 88, discussing Thomas: "Neben der kausalen Erklärung ist fides aber auch essentialiter zu verstehen: als substantia ist fides zugleich essentia rerum sperandarum."

taken on the meaning of make believe and it was this counter factual notion of the state which Kelsen sought to eliminate from legal theory.

The conceptual framework is more complicated than that, though, for ὑπόστασις as *substantia* reflects an ontological commitment of the scholastic period which Dörrie contends is itself problematic given the origins of the term in late antiquity. *Substantia* was always the Latin translation of the neo-platonic term ὑπόστασις. However, in contrast to the logical category and attic term of οὐσία for which *substantia* also serves as the standard Latin term, *substantia* as ὑπόστασις derives from a differing ontological paradigm.[59] In the neo-platonic conception, to say that something is a substance (ὑπόστασις) is not necessarily or only to say that the something cannot be predicated of another, but rather, quite distinctly from the category of οὐσία, a ὑπόστασις actually receives its being from another. As such, substance as ὑπόστασις is not so much a static reality, characterized by its lack of being able to be predicated of other subjects or its persistence through time, but rather a dynamic realization, something which occurs thanks to an action (ἐνέργεια) via another being.[60] A prior being may hypostasize itself into a 'lower' being as a matter of course resulting from an overexuberance of its own existence.[61] That which is hypostasized, i. e. the hypostasis, is then inferior to that which hypostasized, i. e. the particular source of the hypostasis' existence, such that the respective hypostasis is dependent upon its source, but not vice versa.[62] Dörrie even says that ultimately the term ὑπόστασις comes to mean merely an act, as opposed to a state, and thus it is a realization, as opposed to reality / substance, it is a manifestation and even πρόσωπον / perso-

59 For example, Dörrie discusses the distinction of the two uses of *substantia* by Thomas: "[Das Wort *substantia*] war ja für das Gebiet der Logik terminologisch genau fixiert worden und bedeutete die erste Kategorie; man wußte, dass es Übersetzung von οὐσία in diesem aristotelischem Sinne ist. Thomas wußte aber auch, dass *substantia* als Übersetzung von ὑπόστασις anders zu bestimmen ist, und drückte das so aus: *substantia non sumitur hic secundum quod est genus generalissimum contra alia genera divisum* (d. h. als die erste Kategorie) *sed secundum quod in quolibet genere invenitur quaedam similitudo substantiae*. Es soll etwas davon ausgedrückt werden, dass substantia – ὑπόστασις die Grundlage der Realisierung ausdrücken kann." Id. at pp. 88–89.

60 See id. at p. 72. In discussing the innovations of Plotin's theory relative to the earlier schools: "Die Realisierung der unteren Stufe geschieht durch die aus der oberen ausströmenden ἐνέργειαι."

61 Id. at p. 71: "Denn in dieser Notwendigkeit drückt sich nicht etwa ein Zwang aus, den das hypostasierte Objekt ausübt, sondern vielmehr der Überschwang jener Kraft, die der hypostasierende Seinsgrund ausstrahlt."

62 Ibid.: "Das Eine als Seinsgrund senkt in Geist wie Seele die Notwendigkeit ein, sich immer auf das Eine zu beziehen und somit das Folgende durch Emanation von ἐνέργειαι anzuregen, sich aber von ihm fernzuhalten."

na / person or mask.[63] Dörrie gives an account of Origen's description of the hypostasis of Christ even as a *representation* or *expression* of God, which allows to be seen that which is beyond comprehension.[64]

In contrast to ὑπόστασις as confidence or assurance, we see that ὑπόστασις in the Neoplatonic conception has a very different shape, one which has the potential of fundamentally altering not only the meaning of Hebrews 11:1, but also, with respect to Kelsen's consideration of the state as hypostasis, the way by which we can conceive of that which has existence beyond the realm of physically verifiable facts. The hypostasis is that which is realized by the action of another. It is neither that which is believed to have an independent reality nor that which actually has independent reality. Accordingly, faith as the realization of things hoped for (or promised), evidence of things not seen, as the New American Bible translates Hebrews 11:1, can be understood as not just a core definition of what the author of Hebrews considers to be faith, but also the program of social ontology: by virtue of a commitment, an allegiance, the acceptance of a duty or an obligation, i. e. by virtue of a certain normative stance, it is possible to realize that which is not seen, i. e. an institutional reality, if done so in community.

With this alternative, historically contextualized conception of ὑπόστασις, it is possible to counter Kelsen's position that the state as a hypostasis cannot be merely believed into existence. A hypostasis, whether it be the state or some other kind of being, is indeed not merely wished into existence, but is rather the necessary result of a kind of action on the part of another being / other beings. This adds a significant amount of context against which to evaluate / criticize Kelsen's analysis of the possibility of the existence of the state as an extra-legal entity.

However, it should still be recalled that Kelsen's real problem with the state as hypostasis, i. e. the extra-legal state, was not just that such a conception was extra-rational, but rather that if the state stands apart from the law, it is no longer possible for the legal system to constitute a unity and that there could then no longer be a legal science as such.[65] As can be seen whenever and wherever the

---

[63] Id. at pp. 82, 83: "Das Wort ὑπόστασις kann geduldet, ja beibehalten werden, wenn es jeden Anklang an eine Pluralität göttlichen Seins veliert, sondern *nur* Ausformung bedeutet; es hört auf, 'Realität' zu bedeuten; es bedeutet nur mehr 'Realisierung', Manifestation. Und so wird verständlich, dass das Wort in dieser letzten Phase mit πρόσωπον nahezu gleichbedeutend wird."

[64] Id. at p. 76: "Gott gleicht einer Figur, die so riesig ist, dass niemand sie ganz ins Auge fassen kann. Christus ist ein genaues Abbild – χαρακτήρ – dieses Riesenbildes, nur in solchen Maßen, dass man es überschauen und betrachten kann: nur durch ihn kommt man zur Erkenntnis des Vaters."

[65] See *Der soziologische und der juristische Staatsbegriff*, p. 138: "Nichtsdestoweniger behält der Terminus des Staates etwas von seiner ursprünglichen rechtsfeindlichen Bedeutung

'rule of law' is called into question, if there is an entity outside of the law which is capable of and which actually does interfere with the functioning of the legal system, then there is *de facto* not much of a legal order at all. The problem is that, if there are two independent beings, with no relation to one another (*beziehungslos* as Kelsen states in the footnote above), then neither one can be sovereign; and if the state as an independent entity is the sovereign independent of the legal order, then the legal order is ultimately of no consequence.

Again here, the crucial difference would seem to be the kind of entity which is supposed to be hypostasized as state. Conceiving the state as a fiction unique to each and every individual's wishes, i. e. that which Kelsen above describes as serving the function of satisfying the psychological needs of certain people, results in an uncontrollable phantom, according to which any particular or collective projection of state power might be partially or wholly at odds with the actual legal order, a situation which would place any legal order at risk of populist manipulation, let alone extra-rational influence. At the same time, conceiving the state as an independent reality, an independent substance in the Scholastic understanding of ὑπόστασις, results in a legal order which is always subject to manipulation by a contravening political order. As characterized by Schmitt's sovereign that manifests itself in the state of emergency, such a reality would make a farce of legal science to the extent that any systematization of the positive law could be rendered meaningless by a single contradictory edict of the sovereign.

---

bei. Sein historischer Ursprung macht ihn immer wieder zu einem Ausdruck für gewisse, gegen die positive Rechtsordnung gerichtete politische Postulate, die sich dennoch den Schein geltenden Rechts geben wollen. Denn eine allzu gefällige Theorie deckt manche Rechtswidrigkeit der Machthaber mit Hilfe ihres Doppelstaatsrechts, womit sie sich ein wissenschaftliches Instrument geschaffen hat, das eine verteufelte Ähnlichkeit mit dem Zylinder des Taschenspielers zeigt: es hat nämlich einen doppelten Boden, und man kann aus ihm immer herauszaubern, was den jeweiligen politischen Bedürfnissen der 'obersten Organe' entspricht. Das ist es, was der Staatsrechtslehre den Charakter der Unaufrichtigkeit aufprägt: Ihr System, das sich als ein System des positiven Rechts und als solches freilich von jeder Politik verschieden und unabhängig erklärt, hat eine Hintertüre, die sich diese 'Wissenschaft' sorgfältig offenhält, um durch sie eben jene 'Politik' wieder hereinzulassen." Later, in the chapter entitled *Der übernatürliche Gottesbegriff und der überrechtliche Staatsbegriff als Hypostasierung gewisser, den Natur- bzw. Rechtsgesetzen widersprechender Postulate*, Kelsen continues regarding the extra-legal concept of state: "Er ist ein Ausdruck bestimmter, in der Rechtsordung nicht anerkannter politischer Postulate, er soll die Befriedigung von politischen Interessen ermöglichen, die die Rechtsordnung nicht gelten lässt, die im Widerspruch zur Rechtsordnung stehen [...] Die Fernhaltung aller Politik ist zwar eine heute allgemein anerkannte Forderung der positivistische Rechtswissenschaft. Allein erfüllt kann sie nur werden, wenn auf den Begriff eines metarechtlichen Staates verzichtet wird. Und dieser Verzicht ist, weil er das Operieren mit zwei beziehungslosen Erkenntnissystemen aufhebt, nicht nur eine logisch-erkenntnistheoretische, er ist auch eine ethische Notwendigkeit.

As such Kelsen's rejection of an hypostasized state seems well founded. However, these variations do not reflect the ontological paradigm which Dörrie describes above, in which the hypostasis is neither substance (οὐσία) nor make believe (*Zuversicht*), but rather the act of realization, manifestation or even personification. Nor do Kelsen's bogeymen of conceiving the state as supernatural existence or fiction exhaust the significant positivistic ways of conceiving of the law and state during his time[66] or even within the long arc of positivistic conceptions of the law.

Particularly Hobbes, in *Leviathan*'s 16th Chapter, conducts an extended analysis of that which, beginning in the 17th Chapter, will become the state, or Leviathan. The 16th Chapter is a discussion of personhood and the authority that artificial persons can wield on behalf of those whom the artificial persons impersonate. Hobbes explicitly shows the etymology of the term *persona* coming out of the term πρόσωπον / mask.[67] For Hobbes, the feared Leviathan is not a supernatural, heteronomic being, but rather the personification (with Dörrie – realization, manifestation) of the multitude which Hobbes describes as creating the state / commonwealth in the 17th Chapter. Schmitt even refers to this aspect of the realization of Leviathan in the constitution of the commonwealth when he begins his discussion of Hobbes' figure of the Leviathan by describing the famous title picture of 1651 which shows a man composed of many individual persons.[68] In this picture, the personification, or hypostasis, of the state, is not something fictional or extra, but rather the culmination of the individuals gathered together in the commonwealth. The state is precisely required because, as a result of its authority, it is able to bring the disparate interests of the individuals together as one, something which cannot attain without the notions of personification and authority.

---

[66] Two prime examples being the characterization of law and state set forth in Hermann *Cohen's Ethik des reinen Willens* and Felix Somlo's *Juristische Grundlehre*.

[67] See Hobbes, *Leviathan*, Ch. 16: "The word Person is latine: insteed whereof the Greeks have πρόσωπον, which signifies the Face, as Persona in latine signifies the disguise, or outward appearance of a man, counterfeited on the Stage; and sometimes more particularly that part of it, which disguiseth the face, as a Mask or Visard: And from the Stage, hath been translated to any Representer of speech and action, as well in Tribunals, as Theaters."

[68] Schmitt. *Der Leviathan*, p. 25: "Auf der Titelseite der ersten englischen Ausgabe des *Leviathan* von 1651 ist ein Kupferstich angebracht, der, zusammen mit dem Titel 'Leviathan' und dem Motto aus dem Buche Hiob 41, 24 (non est potestas super terram quae comperetur ei), dem Werk Hobbes schon auf den ersten Blick einen ganz ungewöhnlichen Eindruck sichert: ein riesenhafter großer Mann, der aus zahllosen kleinen Menschen zusammengesetzt ist, hält mit dem rechten Arm ein Schwert, mit dem linken einen Bischofsstab schützend über einer friedlichen Stadt."

Chapter IV

Legal Norms as Plurale Tantum

"Wir haben die Sprache und sie hat uns."
Franz Mon

Following the rejection of traditionalist conceptions of God and state with Kelsen, we shall find an alternative to the personal conception of the sovereign in Somlo's conception of legal norms as *plurale tantum*.

1. Validity and the Collective

From the perspective of legal theory, the concepts of God, state and, as we will see in this chapter, validity are ultimately interesting insofar as they require us to determine the relationship between the individual and the collective. In turn, the commonality among theology and jurisprudence is that the relation between the collective and the individual is mediated through normative language, often in the form of a *written* normative language. Even if this relation is mediated through an oral tradition and even if the tradition uses mythology to communicate a story of the divine in superficially descriptive terms (e.g. 'I am the God who created the heavens and the earth'), it is nonetheless incumbent upon the jurist to understand this described relation between man and God, which is to say the individual and the collective, not in the light of factual description, but rather in the light of normativity.

Though Kelsen's state is superfluous, the law yet remains. Christoph Kletzer seeks to lay the final straw by contending, with Kelsen, that in the absence of a generalized belief in God, absolute validity no longer exists. Yet the law continues in its existence and it will persist, not because of its issuance from a divine will or a sovereign state, and also not because of the postulate of the basic norm, but rather because it expresses a necessary relation between the individual and the collective. As long as the relation between the individual and collective exists, as long as we as individuals continue to live in a society, the collective must be able to lay a claim to the agency of individuals. To deny this is to conjure the Hobbesian natural state, which also means to deny individual agency and to reject the possibility of human rationality.

The law's claim to validity is both much stronger and much weaker than it may traditionally seem. No tyrant's death can release us from our bondage to each other and we cannot expect that by merely replacing one set of codes with another we could make an unlawful society lawful (or a lawful society unlawful). It is not just a sociological curiosity that the ties that bind us are very persistent throughout time. Rather, the endurance of legal norms within a system through time is one of law's most defining features. A legal theory must not merely allow for such a feature, it should build itself around it. Nonetheless, in doing so, legal theory must account for a relation between the collective and the individual that is not one-sided. The law's claim to validity on this view is weaker, though, because there is no omnipotent entity that overwhelms its subjects with its might. Rather, sovereigns rule with the simple artifice of authority, ultimately a figure of the imagination, based on norms that live and die in individual minds. This relation is not circular but constitutive. Validity can be predicated of the law because it is constituted by us. It is a part of our institutional reality. The content of the law, though, is an open question, one which for Kelsen does not present itself within the line of legal theoretical inquiry.

Kelsen eschews the view that the validity of a specific legal norm obtains in the particular relation between sovereign and subject. Indeed, Kelsen holds that legal norms lack a categorically valid character at all and instead merely hold hypothetically. It is not the case that subjects should refrain from murder, but rather that if someone does commit murder, then he or she should be punished in such and such a way. Each hypothetical norm (or hypothetical judgment) in turn is valid only if it occurs within a hierarchy of norms. The 'bindingness' of the law, on the part of the sovereign's representative (i. e. the official) and the individual subject, is either presupposed as a matter of systemic validity (with respect to the official) or considered irrelevant as a matter of motivation for the strict application of the law to the subject.

2. Modernity and the Law

In substantive concurrence with Kletzer, Horst Dreier sees Kelsen's stance towards validity as a function of his understanding of the relationship between law and the natural world.[1] Dreier explains that in his work, *Vergeltung und Kausalität*, Kelsen points to classical Greek and Roman society as successful instances of breaking away from a mythological model of the world in which natural phenomena were viewed as inherently connected to a moral order. For the Greeks

[1] Dreier (2017).

and Romans, breaking away from the mythological meant understanding that nature is part of a causal order and not the result of divine powers and, conversely, that humans, not gods, are responsible for their own actions and social order.[2] Kelsen sees the tendency toward natural law theories that ensues in the post-classical period as a regress towards a mythological framework characteristic of more primitive societies and that this regress is only (finally) overcome through the Enlightenment's focus on the "powers of understanding," "the ideal of objectivity," the "emphasis on logic" and the "tendency toward relativism."[3] Kelsen sees this enlightenment process ending in a complete positivisation (*Vollpositivierung*) of the law[4] in which the law is "essentially structured in an endlessly changing manner adapting to dynamic relations as they change in space and time."[5] Dreier summarizes:

> Herausragendes Merkmal ist die Veränderbarkeit des Rechts. In der Moderne wird Recht disponibel, wird zum künstlichen Produkt eines sich autonom setzenden Willens, welche Gestalt auch immer er annimmt. Die diesem Autonomisierungsprozess adäquate wissenschaftliche Betrachtung bildet Kelsens Reine Rechtslehre.[6]

For Kelsen, the retreat from mythology in the social realm entails a natural progression towards relativism. Abandoning the framework of the eternally divine pre-ordination characteristic of primitive mythology (e.g. pre-Homer) and post-primitive theocracy (e.g. post-Constantine), Kelsen develops his Pure Theory to focus on a concept of law as ever changing, determined solely by the immediate preferences of a legal order's constituent members. As such, the *Reine Rechtslehre* can be seen as having the goal of capturing disparate administrative acts as they occur across space and time within a single normative framework. Since the law is inherently mutable, normativity within the system does not attach to individual norms, but rather to official acts within the legal system, which are respectively permitted, required or forbidden as the legislation, administration, execution or adjudication of particular legal norms.[7] Kelsen's theory is one

---

[2] Id. at p. 6: "Auf der einen Seite erscheint die Natur nicht laenger als von goettlichen maechten gelenkt, sondern unterliegt dem Kausalitaetsprinzip, also prinzipiell erforschbaren Zusammenhaengen von Ursache und Wirkung – bis hin zu vollstaendiger technischer Weltbemaechtigung. Und auf der anderen Seite kann der Mensch sich jedenfalls prinzipiell als schoepferischer Gestalter wie Ordner seiner eigenen Sozialwelt begreifen, sich Regeln und Normen selbst schaffen."

[3] Ibid., citing to Kelsen's "Was ist die Reine Rechtslehre?" 1953.

[4] Dreier uses Luhmann's term: "Vollpositivierung des Rechts".

[5] Id. at p. 7. Dreier citing Kelsen from *Die philosophischen Grundlagen der Naturrechtslehre und des Rechtspositivismus* (1p. 928).

[6] Id. at pp. 7–8.

[7] See Kelsen. *Reine Rechtslehre*, § 12: "[Die Reine Rechtslehre] lässt die im Rechtssatz [als hypothetisches Urteil formuliert] an eine bestimmte Bedingung geknüpfte Folge den staatli-

of administrative normativity grounding out in a basic norm which primarily predicates validity of all official actions within the legal system. Kelsen's theory purposefully and explicitly denies the possibility of validity for individual norms considered independent of their administrative context, such as the norm forbidding theft or, in Kelsen's terms, the hypothetical imperative which attaches a certain sanction to the act of theft.[8] Again, for Kelsen, all such norms are relative to the legislative will and therefore inherently mutable.

Dreier, along with Kelsen, allows that such a theory can be overburdening with respect to its value relativism.[9] However, such is the burden which must be born as a result of living in a demythologized, modern and rational society. While Kelsen disparages this sense of 'burden' on the part of many when faced with this consequent value relativism as a weakness or inability to let go of childish sentiment in the face of reason, it is nonetheless quite rational to take seriously those who instinctively sense the wrongness of the assertion that anything can be right, or even that there is no 'rightness' to the legal order in the first place. The objection against Kelsen's relativism is not that individuals should not be expected to individually evaluate the propriety of their state's laws and their own related actions within that legal framework, for this is always the case. Rather, the objection to Kelsen's relativism is that a legal system divorced from all value is lacking in certain essential respects.[10] The concept of law does require a claim

---

chen Zwangsakt, das ist die Strafe und die zivile oder administrative Zwangsvollstreckung sein, wodurch allein der bedingende Tatbestand als Unrecht, der bedingte als Unrechtsfolge qualifiziert wird. Nicht irgendeine immanente Qualität und auch nicht irgendeine Beziehung zu einer metarechtlichen Norm, einem moralischen, das heißt aber dem positiven Recht transzendenten Wert macht, dass ein bestimmtes menschliches Verhalten als rechtswidrig, als Delikt – im weitesten Sinne des Wortes – zu gelten habe; sondern ausschließlich und allein: dass es im Rechtssatz als Bedingung einer spezifischen Folge gesetzt ist, dass die positive Rechtsordnung auf dieses Verhalten mit einem Zwangsakt reagiert."

[8] Kelsen's motivation for phrasing all legal norms in the hypothetical form and for denying any normative relation to the individual subject lies in his experience of the tendency on the part of many theorists to attribute value to legal norms. See *Reine Rechtslehre*, p. 21: "Sie von ihm [i.e. the ideological aspect] zu befreien, ist das Bemühen der Reinen Rechtslehre, die den Begriff der Rechtsnorm von dem der Moralnorm, aus dem er hervorgegangen, völlig loslöst und die Eigengesetzlichkeit des Rechts auch gegenüber dem Sittengesetz sicherstellt. Dies in der Weise, dass die Rechtsnorm nicht, wie es von der traditionellen Lehre zumeist geschieht, so wie die Moralnorm als Imperativ, sondern als hypothetisches Urteil verstanden wird…"

[9] Id. at p. 16ff.

[10] Compare *In Defense of Legal Positivism* in which Matthew Kramer makes the opposite claim that it is perfectly possible to imagine a legal system in which there is no value. While it is possible to imagine that a dictator can issue commands to others in a way as to satisfy certain minimal requirements of sovereignty traditionally understood, Kramer's contention only begs the question as to whether such a circumstance consists of a state and of law within the modern understanding. Our concept of law necessarily requires the question of whether value has any

to being right,[11] whether this is phrased in terms of a claim to justice, legitimacy or validity. Though Kelsen does acknowledge this aspect by embedding official actions and the legal norms on which they are based within a hierarchy of norms based on a principle of validity (i. e. the basic norm), the positioning of this principle as a purely formal construct, and solely with respect to official actions, belies this central purpose. Kelsen characterizes modern legal theory as being based on understanding, objectivity, logic and relativism. However, in focusing on relativism and a certain narrow view of logic[12], Kelsen thereby sacrifices the complementary aspects of understanding and objectivity which the project of positivism is presumed to represent.

3. Objectivity and its Propositional Content

This conflict within Kelsen's work can be brought into closer focus if we examine in the *Allgemeine Staatslehre* and *Reine Rechtslehre (1934)* the relative emphases which Kelsen places on normativity, objectivity and relativism. In the *Allgemeine Staatslehre*, Kelsen draws a connection between the meaning of official acts and their context within a valid hierarchy of norms by focusing on the mental, and normative, nature of the law and state. First, he points out that all facts, acts and processes normally associated with the concept of state can be reduced to mental states.[13] The essence of the state, and thus the legal order, is not in the outer, physical processes, such as a proclamation of a law or its execution, but rather in mental states which are transformed by individuals into physically manifested, outer conduct.[14] These states are not merely psychological though, such as could be sufficiently captured by the natural sciences. Rather, there is a particular content to the mental states, which can be an object of understanding:

So wie das Denken mathematischer oder logischer Gesetze ein psychischer Akt, darum aber der Gegenstand der Mathematik oder der Logik – das Gedachte – kein Psychisches, keine mathe-

---

inherent connection to law. Prior to addressing this issue, hypotheticals presuming an outcome one way or the other are of no use. Compare also, Kramer's *Objectivity and the Rule of Law*.

[11] It is a matter of course that Recht and Recht are not separate homophonous words, but one and the same. Hegel's is a philosophy of law, not a philosophy of right.

[12] As discussed in the first chapter, Kelsen repeatedly proceeds on the assumption that the logic of 'ought' judgments requires denying a cognitivist view of norms.

[13] Kelsen, *Allgemeine Staatslehre*, § 4, p. 13.

[14] Id. at p. 14: "Indes kommt es für eine auf das Wesen des Staates gerichtete Betrachtung nicht auf die in der Welt des natürlichen Seins und sohin nach kausaler Gesetzlichkeit ablaufenden seelisch-körperlichen Prozesse, sondern auf den geistigen Inhalt an, den diese Prozesse 'tragen'."

matische oder logische "Seele", sondern ein spezifischer geistiger Sachgehalt ist, weil die Mathematik und Logik von dem psychologischen Faktum des Denkens solchen Inhaltes abstrahiert: So ist der Staat, als Gegenstand einer spezifischen, von der Psychologie verschiedenen Betrachtung, ein spezifischer geistiger Gehalt, nicht aber das Faktum des Denkens und Wollens solchen Inhaltes, ist er eine ideele Ordnung, ein spezifisches Normensystem, nicht aber das Denken und Wollen dieser Normen.[15]

If legal norms can function as an object of understanding, then mental states relating to such norms must have an aboutness, a propositional content and must thus be intentional. Here Kelsen contends that there is a mental substance to the state (and to the legal order with which the state is synonymous) that is independent of the psychological state of thinking or wanting. The state exists as a system of norms that is separate from any actual thinking or wanting of such norms. This normative order is something that we can gain access to through our thought and volition, but it cannot be reduced to such thought and volition itself. That which remains if we abstract the individual mental states is *das Gedachte* or *Gewollte*, that aboutness which we think, act on, or enact when we think about or will a legal norm. It is the legal norm's propositional content which transforms the particular norm and the legal order / state generally from a mere psychological or sociological state into a normative order and which thereby allows it to become an object of study and theory. Thought and volition are necessary for understanding the legal order, but we cannot sufficiently understand the legal order if we only analyze individual (psychological) thoughts and volitions – for this we need the concept of normativity as an objective order of that which is thought and willed, i. e. propositions. The Kelsen of the *Staatslehre* summarizes:

So die immer wiederkehrende und in den verschiedensten Wendungen auftretende Behauptung seiner [des Staates] objektiven, d. h. von der subjektiven Willkür der den Staat bildenden Menschen unabhängigen Existenz; sie wäre völlig unmöglich, wenn der Staat, der Staatswille oder die Staatsseele sich nur als Summation subjektiver Willensakte darstellen würde.[16]

Propositions, i. e. mental content (*Gehalt*) as opposed to mere mental states (*Zustände*), are required in order for the legal order to be an object of study independent of psychology or sociology. However, one would be remiss to assume that Kelsen locates the propositional content of legal norms in the minds of legal

---

[15] Ibid. "…Der Eigengesetzlichkeit, des Eigensinns, jenes besonderen Gegenstandes, den wir 'Staat' nennen und zum Objekt einer eigenen Wissenschaft gemacht haben, können wir uns nicht bemächtigen, wenn wir unsere Betrachtung auf irgendwelche seelische Prozesse des Denkens und Wollens, sondern nur, wenn wir unsere Erkenntnis auf ein spezifisch Gedachtes und Gewolltes richten, für das die seelischen Akte des Denkens und Wollens gleichsam eine *condition sine qua non*, nicht aber die *conditio per quam* sind. Nicht im Reiche der Natur – der physisch-psychischen Beziehungen – sondern im Reiche des Geistes steht der Staat."

[16] Ibid.

subjects, i.e. in the subjective law (*subjektives Recht*). Kelsen's theory does not presume an individual subject that understands or assents to the objectively valid legal norms, but rather requires only that these objectively valid norms exist in principle as an object of understanding.[17] The position which Kelsen takes on this point proves consequential for his transition from an emphasis on understanding and objectivity toward an emphasis on relativism.

4. Subjectivity and Interpretation

There is a question of general effectiveness, recognized by Kelsen, which presents itself when the norms of a legal order are not known or recognized by a sufficient degree of subjects. However, if we negate the importance of individuals within the state participating in its propositional content, a completely separate and much more fundamental question is thereby raised about the relationship between the subject and the state within the legal order as it is mediated through legal norms considered as propositions. In other words, if propositional content is required in order for a legal system to maintain normativity and not be reduced to a succession of mental states, what does it mean for the theoretical reconstruction of the legal system if we say that intentionality on the part of individuals is irrelevant for the legal theoretical consideration?

If (i) we consider the state and the individual purely as extra-legal empirical facts, then the relation between the two becomes one of causal necessity – legal theory and legal science hence lose their objects of inquiry and legal 'norms' themselves become merely instruments for the exercise of brute force. If (ii) we consider the state as a normative order but the individual still as extra-legal, then legal norms take on a meaning within the normative order, legal science as a discipline for ordering such norms gains its object of inquiry, but legal theory as the study of the conflict of the normative order of the state *cum* individual still does not attain. Problems and therewith an object of study only arise for legal theory if (iii) we cast the state as a normative order and the individual as an autonomous agent (i.e. agent or person) within that order. Only then can the relationship between the individual and collective be arbitered.

Kelsen hints at such a distinction, only to then commit himself to the second, but also largely to the first, of these positions:

[17] See Kelsen, *Allgemeine Staatslehre*, p. 18. Kelsen allows that a certain minimal understanding of the objectively valid norms is required from the perspective of effectiveness of the law. However, this is a distinct consideration from that of the validity of the objective propositions. See also *Hauptprobleme*, p. 44ff.

Ein Gegensatz zwischen Individuum und Staat, ein Problem kann hier nur gegeben sein, sofern der Staat als Norm vorausgesetzt wird, deren Sollen mit dem Sein des individuellen Wollens und Handelns in Konflikt, in jenen tragischen Konflikt gerät, der das Kernproblem aller sozialen Theorie und Praxis ist. Sofern es sich in der Antinomie darstellt, dass das Individuum einerseits nur Teil eines Ganzen, des Staates, andererseits aber doch selbst Ganzes sei, verliert diese Antinomie den Charakter eines logischen Widerspruchs, wenn man bedenkt, dass die Individuen, richtiger die individuellen Wollungen und Handlungen, nur als Inhalte der die staatliche Ordnung bildende Normen, des Sollens also, integrierende Bestandteile eines Systemganzen sind, während der zum Ganzen des Staates in Widerspruch geratende Akt des tatsächlichen individuellen Wollens und Handelns in der Seinsebene verläuft.[18]

There is only a conflict between the state and the individual if we consider each to be independently normative and to be acting on the same plane within the same system. For Kelsen, however, the individual, insofar as it is of interest for the legal order, exists only as an entity acting completely within this order. All other thoughts, desires or wishes are irrelevant for Kelsen's normative theory since such manifestations are phenomena within the non-normative sphere. Since the legal order does not recognize any normativity outside of itself, any thoughts or volitions of an individual that are at odds with the legal order are necessarily just at the factual level and thus of no consequence for the legal order. Moreover, the individual for Kelsen is not relevant as an agent, but rather as a source for conduct which then becomes an input for the calculus of the legal system. We can imagine that a legal norm states: if one man kills another, then he shall be punished with death. In Kelsen's system, such a norm is not addressed primarily to the putative killer, but rather to the prosecutor or sentencing judge. The individual's act of killing is relevant for the legal system only to the extent that it acts as an input for subsumption within the legal order. No conflict can arise in this scenario because even if the killer thought himself to be acting in the right, e. g. in defense of the life of another, if this norm is not reflected in the legal order, then it is irrelevant for the subsumption of the offense. Unless a legal norm explicitly requires a judge or administrator to inquire into the mental state of a subject, that subject's intentionality, i. e. the propositional content behind the subject's actions, is irrelevant for the legal consideration.

With this background, it is easier to understand the even stronger relativistic tendencies of the *Reine Rechtslehre (1934)*. Since the norms of a legal order are completely relative to the will of the legislator, without contextualization of any kind, all written norms can only be taken at face value. Because of this, the scope of legal knowledge necessarily ends whenever there is a gap in the normative framework. Whereas jurisprudential method would otherwise suggest a process for 'finding' the appropriate norm in such a case, Kelsen's position is that the

[18] Id. at p. 15.

underlying process is actually not one of understanding norms, but rather of willing political outcomes.

> Die Frage, welche der im Rahmen einer Norm gegebenen Möglichkeiten die 'richtige' ist, ist – voraussetzungsgemäß – überhaupt keine Frage der auf das positive Recht gerichteten Erkenntnis, ist kein rechtstheoretisches, sondern ein rechtspolitisches Problem.[19]

Although Kelsen here discusses the difficulty of, and his own stance towards, addressing gaps in the normative framework, it is very reminiscent of, and indeed exposes the same fundamental issue involved with, Carl Schmitt's criticism of the legal positivist method at the constitutional level when he accuses legal positivists of abdicating their duties as jurists precisely then when their services would be most needed.[20] As Schmitt maintains in the first chapter of *Politische Theologie*, one can only know the essence of something by studying it at its margins, whether it be the state of emergency (*Ausnahmezustand*) for constitutional law, or gaps in normal jurisprudence. Legal theory cannot be silent in the face of uncertainty or ambiguity, but rather must insist that such cases are central. As Schmitt states in quoting a 19th century theologian:

> Die Ausnahme erklärt das Allgemeine und sich selbst. Und wenn man das Allgemeine richtig studieren will, braucht man sich nur nach einer wirklichen Ausnahme umzusehen. Sie legt alles viel deutlicher an den Tag als das Allgemeine selbst….Kann man [die Ausnahme] nicht erklären, so kann man auch das Allgemeine nicht erklären. Gewöhnlich merkt man die Schwierigkeit nicht, weil man das Allgemeine nicht einmal mit Leidenschaft, sondern mit einer bequemen Oberflächlichkeit denkt. Die Ausnahme dagegen denkt das Allgemeine mit energischer Leidenschaft.[21]

The exception is more important than the rule because the exception proves the rule, the rule flows from the exception. The exception is an expression of reality, the rule a reflection of normality.[22] Kelsen would say that the exception, as an expression of reality, has no place in a normative system, that legal norms can only reflect the normal case and that everything else is outside the realm of legal analysis. Kelsen would warn that legal theory should not overextend itself into

---

19 *Reine Rechtslehre*, § 38, p. 98.

20 See *Politische Theologie*, Vorbemerkung zur zweiten Ausgabe, p. 8–9: "Diese letzte Epoche der deutschen Staatsrechtswissenschaft ist dadurch gekennzeichnet, dass sie die staatsrechtliche Antwort auf den entscheidenden Fall, nämlich die Antwort auf den preußischen Verfassungskonflikt mit Bismarck und infolgedessen auch die Antwort auf alle weiteren entscheidenden Fälle schuldig geblieben ist. Um der Entscheidung auszuweichen, prägte sie für solche Fälle einen Satz, der auf sie selbst zurückgefallen ist und den sie nunmehr selbst als Motto trägt: 'Das Staatsrecht hört hier auf'." This phrase, 'das Staatsrecht hört hier auf', is attributed by Schmitt to Anschütz.

21 Id. at p. 21.

22 Id. at pp. 20–21.

questions of social fact or the political. Even if we would allow that there is a 'political' outside of the 'legal' (recall that Kelsen identifies the political order with the legal order), we would at least have to expect of a legal theory that it sufficiently explains the legal. This itself, though, is suspect for Kelsen.

The telling sign with respect to Kelsen is not that he cannot explain normative gaps, but rather that he does explain them as opportunities for political activism, as a matter of political fact. However, if the exception proves or exposes the rule, then the rule itself is nothing but political fact. Normativity, even the law itself, becomes nothing but a façade which Kelsen imposes upon raw force. Kelsen himself seems to affirm this:

[…] die Norm oder das Sollen, in dem sich das Recht selbst darstellt und von der Jurisprudenz dargestellt wird, erscheint – auch in seiner von der Reinen Rechtslehre geläuterten, von allen moralisch-absoluten Wert befreiten Bedeutung – als bloße 'Ideologie'.[23]

And then:

Spricht man der 'Norm' oder dem 'Sollen' jeden Sinn ab, dann hat es keinen Sinn zu behaupten: dies sei rechtlich erlaubt, jenes rechtlich verboten, dies gehört mir, jenes dir, X sei dazu berechtigt, Y dazu verpflichtet, u. s. w. Kurz, all die Tausende von Aussagen, in denen das Rechtsleben sich täglich äußert, haben ihre Bedeutung verloren.[24]

And finally:

Ist der normative Sinn des Rechts nur eine 'Ideologie', dann ist eine Rechtslehre, die den immanenten Sinn des Rechts erfassen will, das Recht, so wie es sich den rechtserzeugenden und rechtsanwendenden Organen, dem rechtsuchenden Publikum darstellt, auf die Eigensetzlichkeit einer Ideologie gerichtet… Des ist sich gerade die Reine Rechtslehre voll bewusst.[25]

Kelsen justifies his normative relativism (or, with Kletzer, nihilism) by framing his work as a public service that exposes the law for what it is, i. e. an ideology, while nevertheless maintaining a framework for as-if normativity for tradition's sake and for satisfying the intellectual needs of lawyers.[26]

---

[23] *Reine Rechtslehre.*, § 15, p. 34.

[24] Kelsen, *Reine Rechtslehre.*, § 16, p. 35.

[25] Id. at p. 36.

[26] Id. at p. 37: "Die Möglichkeit und Erforderlichkeit solcher Theorie ist schon durch das jahrtausendalte Faktum der Rechtswissenschaft erwiesen, die – solange es ein Recht gibt – als dogmatische Jurisprudenz den intellektuellen Bedürfnissen der mit dem Recht Befassten dient. Es liegt kein Grund vor, diese durchaus legitimen Bedürfnisse unbefriedigt zu lassen und auf solche Rechtswissenschaft zu verzichten."

5. The Structure of Law

Kelsen asserts: (i) the Kantian categorical imperative is an 'empty formula'; (ii) any attempt to objectify an 'ought' results in subjecting to logic a category which is illogical; (iii) the only object of rational thought in the social realm are interests and conflicts of interest which can only be solved through ordering the interests one against the other; and (iv) if there would already exist societal order on the basis of reason, then it would be foolish to develop a theory of legal positivism.[27]

Each of these four positions which Kelsen describes in quick succession in the *Reine Rechtslehre (1934)* has, with or without Kelsen's influence, become a core assumption underlying much of modern legal positivism: ad (i), since all categorical imperatives, whether the Kantian or some other version such as 'seek the good', are ultimately void of normative content, it is not possible to use any such norm as a basis for 'finding' norms that are objectively valid independent of the positive law; ad (ii), even if it would be possible to identify norms that are objectively valid independent of the positive law, it would not follow that such norms should become the basis of a legal order – this would entail a category mistake by applying a logic of existence to normativity; ad (iii), because of (i) and (ii), all legal norms merely reflect social interests and, since all such interests are completely relative to social inputs which by their nature are mutable, the proper object of legal theory is not the interests themselves but rather an ordering of these interests through a system of secondary norms;[28] ad (iv) legal positivism

---

[27] Kelsen. *Reine Rechtslehre*, pp. 14, 15: (i) "Alle derartigen Versuche haben bisher immer nur zu völlig leeren Formeln geführt, wie: 'Tue das Gute und meide das Böse', 'Jedem das Seine', 'Halte die richtige Mitte', u. dgl. Auch der kategorische Imperativ ist ganz inhaltslos."; (ii) "Die Gerechtigkeit, ein Ideal des Wollens und Handelns, muss sich, zum Gegenstand der Erkenntnis gemacht, unversehens in die Idee der Wahrheit verwandeln, die ihren – negativen – Ausdruck im Identitätssatz findet. Diese Denaturierung des Problems ist die unvermeidliche Folge der Logifizierung eines von vornherein logosfremden Objekts."; (iii) "Vom Standpunkt rationaler Erkenntnis aus gesehen, gibt es nur Interessen und damit Interessenkonflikte, deren Lösung durch eine Interessenordnung erfolgt, die entweder das eine Interesse gegen das andere, auf Kosten des anderen befriedigt oder aber einen Ausgleich, ein Kompromiß zwischen den gegensätzlichen Interessen stiftet."; (iv) "Angesichts eines Vorhandenseins einer absolut guten, sich schon aus der Natur, der Vernunft, oder dem göttlichen Willen ergebenden gesellschaftlichen Ordnung wäre die Tätigkeit des staatlichen Gesetzgebers der törichte Versuch einer künstlichen Beleuchtung bei hellstem Sonnenlicht."

[28] I use here the Hartian terminology of secondary norms as hierarchical norms. The terminology is confusing because Kelsen considers the primary function of legal norms to lie in their hierarchical function, i. e. as directives on which officials are to act. Accordingly, Kelsen allows that norms could be considered to have a secondary aspect as being directed to affect the behaviour of individual subjects. See Kelsen, *Reine Rechtslehre*, p. 30. Somlo's terminology is again

is justified *ex negativo* – other forms of legal theory, e.g. natural legal theories, could be justifiable (and would be preferable) were it not for positions (i)–(iii), positions (i)–(iii) being the case, however, legal positivism is the only viable theory.

Upon closer examination, positions (i) and (iii), together with the conclusion (iv) orbit around the central proposition (ii) that a logic of norms entails predicating truth of value and that such an undertaking is impossible, violating the is-ought distinction. I believe that the theory of legal norms which Felix Somlo develops in his *Juristische Grundlehre* attacks the heart of this position by attempting to demonstrate that which Kelsen deemed impossible. Namely, Somlo shows (a) the viability of categorically imperative order, (b) the logical relation of objective norms with each other, (c) that legal norms cannot be reduced to mere reflections of immediate social interests, and, importantly, (d) the project of legal positivism is nonetheless crucial for our understanding of legal order even if (a) through (c) hold.

6. The Starting Position

"Es ist doch sonderbar bestellt, sprach Hänschen Schlau zu Vetter Fritzen, dass nur die Reichen in der Welt das meiste Geld besitzen."[29]

---

different, according to which primary rules (or sources of law) are those which come directly from the sovereign (*Rechtsmacht*) and secondary rules (or sources of law) are those that come from a political body (*Staatsorgan*), see also Somlo, *Juristische Grundlehre*, § 100.

[29] Somlo, *Juristische Grundlehre*, § 29, p. 94. Somlo provides Lessing's rhyme as the solution to the question of why people normally follow the law: "F. Klein bezeichnet es als eine staunenswerte Tatsache, dass "die Menschen immer und überall tun und unterlassen, was das Recht anbefiehlt oder verbietet, das Gegenteil ist immer und überall nur im geringen Umfange zu beobachten, so dass es den Charakter einer Ausnahme kaum je verliert." Die Erklärung dieser erstaunlichen Tatsache liegt aber einfach darin, dass nur diejenigen Normen rechtliche sind, die von einer Macht herkommen, welcher der Gehorsam nur ausnahmsweise verweigert wird." As such, and as to be discussed below, the law may be derivative of sovereignty, but sovereignty is derivative of habitual obedience. This dependency of the sovereign on obedience is the same dependency as described in Chapter 3 in which the state is dependent on the collective which provides the state its personhood and authority. Hart, much like Hänschen Schlau, might be said to presume that people follow the law because there is a rule of recognition which establishes the criteria of validity for primary legal norms. As will be indicated below, Hart mistakes the priority of the phenomenon: people do not follow the law because of a rule of recognition, but rather the rule of recognition indicates the legal norms that people will follow. The question to be addressed is not how the rule of recognition relates to the legal system – this is tautological. Rather, one must address why people follow some norms and not others.

To best realize the importance of Somlo's work today for the proposed interpretation of legal theory, it is perhaps best to start with the framework adopted by H.L.A. Hart. In *The Concept of Law*, Hart claims that law can most adequately be defined as the union of primary and secondary rules.[30] Primary rules he defines as those under which "human beings are required to do or abstain from certain actions." Secondary rules are those according to which "human beings may by doing or saying certain things introduce new rules of the primary type."[31] According to Hart, primary rules directly concern human actions whereas secondary rules provide for operations according to which duties or obligations to act are created or modified. The two conceptions of rules are essential for Hart because he claims that a legal system precisely consists of certain primary rules which obtain their validity and legal character from other secondary rules. Thus, a certain primary rule such as 'you should not steal' would be a law if there was a corresponding secondary rule to the effect of 'the legislature or other law-making body has the authority to impose the duty that you should not steal." Hart claims that a top-down ordering of the law, i. e. the existence of in-themselves normatively binding secondary rules, is necessary to ensure that the corresponding legal order is endowed with certainty, efficiency and dynamism.

By conceiving of the law within this top-down framework, Hart seems to develop his theory within the most straightforward context possible, i. e. it is part and parcel of individual legal norms that they exist within a hierarchical structure of norms. One of the constants of legal theory is typically that the sovereign has the power to enact laws independent of the subject's consent, as a master over a servant. This framing of the law within a hierarchically normative framework of course also fits well within Kelsen's basic view and, on Hart's characterization, Austin's as well. Despite the fact that Hart argues primarily against Austin's conception in *The Concept of Law*, Hart's basic argument is that the necessary complement to Austin's theory of sovereignty, the habit of obedience and commands backed by threats, is the unification of primary and secondary rules through a rule recognizing the hierarchical structure of the legal order. While Hart's Rule of Recognition reduces the legal order to a question of social fact and therefore fundamentally opposes the normative stance of Kelsen's *Grundnorm*, both Hart and Kelsen are united in their opposition to the possibility of validity actually inhering within a legal order. Despite their many differences, for the present purposes Hart and Kelsen are both the heroes of current mainstream legal theory (characterized by (i) through (iii) above) and the main antagonists of (the following interpretation of) Somlo's conception of law.

30 Hart. *The Concept of Law*, p. 79.

31 Ibid.

The opposition of both Hart and Kelsen to an inherent validity of the law is hardly surprising given the shared premise that the legal system consists of a hierarchy of arbitrary norms cascading from sovereign to subject. If Rex's laws would be endowed with inherent validity, this would lead to a form of totalitarianism. Therefore, the validity of Rex's laws must either be fictional (i. e. Kelsen's ultimate position) or come from the factual recognition of Rex's role in providing secondary norms for the legal system as such (i. e. Hart's position). Given a liberal democratic predilection, Hart and Kelsen cannot but adopt one or another of these positions. Nonetheless, each of the above scenarios presumes a certain kind of sovereignty which actually raises an even more fundamental question regarding the source of the law. By rejecting all three of the options, Somlo's theory opens a path towards a new frontier of legal analysis altogether.

7. The Flux of Sovereignty

The elephant in the room for both Kelsen's and Hart's theories is the concept of sovereignty. While Kelsen clearly sees the sovereign (or state) as a legal construct and Hart sees it being closely tied to factual recognition of a hierarchical system, neither are able to successfully answer the question of why it exists in the first place. In the moral aspect, we ask why *we should* follow the law, in the sociological aspect, we ask why do individuals almost universally group themselves together into collectives, and in the legal aspect, the inquiry must seek to understand what is the nature of sovereign relations such that some individuals command and others (must) follow. Even if we should dismiss these first two (moral and sociological) aspects as being irrelevant for a legal theoretical investigation, they are bound to nonetheless be present when conducting the 'strictly' legal analysis.

The issue of sovereignty is one of the most perplexing issues of the modern state and indeed addressing it, for example in the classical cases of Schmitt or also Leo Strauss, has at times suffered from a taint of traditionalism or even totalitarianism. Where sovereignty was once thought to adhere to God or to God's representatives on earth, the absolute power concept of sovereignty as it has existed since Bodin and, on some interpretations, Hobbes is hardly but a secular equivalent of the same. Nonetheless, I would posit that it is hardly surprising that in failing to address the nature of sovereignty, why and how it exists, Kelsen and Hart also fail to give satisfactory accounts of value and validity in the law. Presupposing the existence of an absolute sovereign, Hart and Kelsen presuppose the hierarchical tendency of norms within legal systems and therefore have to start from an assumption which I will argue to be misleading.

In contrast to his better received counterparts,[32] Somlo is able to free himself from these preconceptions of sovereignty and instead proceeds in his investigation in the *Juristische Grundlehre* not by asking how legal norms are related to the sovereign, but rather how sovereignty is related to legal norms. Thus, the first chapter of the *Juristische Grundlehre* addresses the concept and kinds of norms generally, with special focus on norms of convention. Only after this preliminary treatment, and in differentiation to the previously treated norms, does Somlo come to define the legal norm toward the end of the first chapter (§ 26) as a normative expression (*Willenssatzung*) of a sovereign:

Die Rechtsnormen sind demnach Willenssatzungen, und zwar in Gegensatz sowohl zu den unmaßgeblichen Kollektivnormen, als auch zu den unmaßgeblichen Individualnormen – maßgebliche; sodann sind sie zum Unterschied sowohl von den Konventionalnormen wie auch von den befolgten Individualnormen solche, die von der noch näher zu bestimmenden 'höchsten Macht' herrühren, auf deren Begriff der ganze Rechtsbegriff abgestellt ist und auf deren Bestimmung nun mehr alles weitere ankommt.[33]

Somlo states that the problem for legal theory is not so much a lack of agreement regarding the definition or nature of the law, but rather a detailed analysis of what this definition or nature entails.[34] This is what we see with the definition above: Somlo adheres to the traditional conception of the legal norm as an expression of the will of the highest power (i. e. the sovereign). However, for Somlo, the crux of the matter is only exposed when the analysis of the details begins, which here entails the closer analysis of understanding wherein the highest power consists.

Somlo considers that the essence of each norm, regardless of its kind, is that it 'wants' to be valid. In other words, the nature of all prescriptions and directives,

---

32 An inescapable circumstance of the interbellum period in German speaking Europe and the Manichean approach to thought and culture typified by the National Socialist regime is that the legal theorists of the time became classified into pro and contra camps, with those tending to support the regime becoming villains and those tending to oppose the regime becoming heros. Thus, Schmitt became taboo but thereby also guaranteed the posterity of his ideas and the social democrat Hermann Heller is remembered for standing in opposition and dying in exile, but then providing a framework for post-war political reconstruction in Germany. While Kelsen was certainly a star in Central Europe in the 20's and 30's, his ideas only were received in the English-speaking world once he immigrated to the United States. Somlo died too young (1920) to enjoy either of these fates and so, outside of Hungary, has primarily lived on in the footnotes of Kelsen's earlier works.

33 Somlo, *Juristische Grundlehre*, § 26, p. 86.

34 Id. at § 17, p. 54: "Es wird sich zeigen, dass der Jurisprudenz eigentlich nicht so sehr eine Einigung über das Wesen des Rechts fehlt, als eine in die Einzelheiten gehende Herausarbeitung ihres zugrunde gelegten Begriffes. Damit ist unsere Aufgabe gekennzeichnet. Sie besteht nicht im Ergrübeln irgend eines neuen Rechtsbegriffes, sondern nur in einer Zergliederung und sorgfältigen Erklärung dieses vorhandenen Rechtsbegriffes der Juristen."

in short all 'oughts', is that their internal logic is to be followed.[35] Of course, we do not typically follow all norms that are addressed to us or that we perhaps happen to come upon. Rather, we only follow those which we deem significant in one way or another. For this reason, each of us is constantly ordering or systematizing a system of norms, discarding or relegating some norms as out of fashion or antiquated, and prioritizing others as of particular relevance. In a moment of national crisis, we might emphasize norms of patriotism. As society develops and traditions are lost, we might choose to disregard the norms of our grandparents, such as removing one's hat upon entering a church. In this pack of norms, each of which is fighting for superiority,[36] some gain the highest status of being the law. On Somlo's definition, these are the norms which issue from the highest power, or sovereign. As such, the initial function of sovereignty is simply that it marks the *differentia specifica* of *legal* norms in contrast with all other norms.

Any time there is a collective, e.g. a church community, a country club, a criminal gang, a professional or industry association, a league of nations, the collective must necessarily issue norms that are heteronomous to its individual members as a means of organizing behavior for the good, or integrity, of the organization. Since the norms are heteronomous to my own will, it will not always be convenient or desirable for me to act accordingly. In such a situation, even though there is a general habit of obedience on my part and that of others, I may choose to leave the collective, as long as the collective (e.g. the country club) is only a relative power. As long as it is an option for me to switch to a different country club or to quit playing golf altogether, the by-laws of my own country club do not in themselves enjoy the force of law. A country club only applies to a particular set of individuals and membership is voluntary. Since there is no general habit of obedience on the part of everyone (i.e. non-members) and since

[35] For example, see id. at § 28, p. 90 ff: "Da es zum Begriffe der Norm gehört, die Verwirklichung einer Forderung zu verlangen, so ist jedes durch einen besonderen Urheber von den übrigen Arten abgegrenzte System von Normen von diesen übrigen Arten vollkommen unabhängig. Jedes vermag zu fordern ohne Rücksicht auf die anderen Normarten, jedes System von Normen bestimmt dementsprechend seine eigenen Grenzen selbst. Sie stoßen nicht wie die Körper aneinander, sondern das Gebiet, das die eine Normart bevölkert, ist für die andere ein leerer Raum."

[36] See id. at § 28, p. 91: "Wir kommen also zu dem Ergebnis, dass jede Normart den übrigen gegenüber Selbstherrlich ist, und folglich die übrigen auch verletzen kann, wenn sie will." The slightly more metaphorical phrasing can be found in Somlo, *Gedanken zu einer ersten Philosophie*: "Begriffe sind harmlose, weder streitsüchtige, noch herrschsüchtige Bedeutungen, es sind friedlich, neben einander stehende Lämmchen in den Gefilden der lauteren Bedeutungen; sie tun sich gegenseitig nichts Zuleide. Anders die Sätze. Jeder von Ihnen hat die Mitbedeutung der unbedingten Geltung, der Richtigkeit. In jedem besonderen Satzsinne ist der Sinn mit Inbegriffen, dass es ein unbedingt gültiger Satz sei. Es ist ein Geschlecht von kampflustigen, herrschsüchtigen, sich befehdenden oder sich gegen andere verbündenden Bedeutungen."

even those for whom there is a general habit of obedience may at any time exit the collective, a country club is an unlikely candidate for sovereignty. However, there are other collectives of a much more general nature, the rules of which apply to everyone and from which there is no exit clause – and those from whom such norms arise are the highest powers, the sovereigns. That such sovereigns exist is not an empirical matter of fact, but, as with Kelsen's *Grundnorm*, a legal *a priori* resulting from the necessity of the jurist to understand and order the social world as a normative unity.

Somlo's definition of law quite clearly follows Austin's conception of law as the commands of a sovereign which enjoys a habit of obedience. However, whereas this Austinian framework is typically interpreted as 'imperial'[37] or hierarchical in nature, Somlo gives the Austinian frame a decidedly non-imperial, non-hierarchical flavor. For Somlo, order is not a function of sovereignty, but rather sovereignty is a function of the order (as expressed through legal norms) which results from collectives. If there is no order as a matter of fact, then there is no sovereign and thus there are no legal norms – a scenario of the Hobbesian state of war.[38] However, if an order does exist, then there must be a principally unifying factor which Somlo calls the highest power (*höchste Macht*) or sovereign.[39] That there is a sovereign though, does not establish wherein, or with whom in particular, sovereignty lies. Actually locating this highest power for a given society at a given time can be arduous.[40] Nonetheless, the fact that one sovereign exists for any ordered society is a matter of certainty resulting from the

---

[37] See Bix (2018).

[38] See Somlo, *Juristische Grundlehre*, § 31, p. 99: "Alle Zeiten, in denen diese bestimmt geartete oberste Macht in Bezug auf bestimmte Menschenkreise nicht zustande kommt, sind rechtlose. Wenn z. B. ein Bürgerkrieg lange und unentschieden wütet, wenn allgemeiner Aufruhr an Stelle der Ordnung tritt, wenn eine äußere Macht die bestehende Staatsgewalt niederwirft, sich aber nicht behaupten kann und auch sonst keine Macht zustande kommt, deren Normen allgemein befolgt werden, so besteht eben zu solchen Zeiten kein Recht. Allerdings wird sich ein solcher Zustand nicht lange erhalten. Die allgemeine Zügellosigkeit und Unordnung würde den betreffenden Kreis bald vernichten. Denn, und das sei besonders betont, nur allgemeine Zügellosigkeit und Aufruhr kann Platz greifen, wenn das Recht aufhört zu sein. Es muss kein Recht geben, aber die Alternative lautet: entweder rechtlich geregelter Zustand oder jener bellum omnium contra omnes des Hobbes."

[39] See ibid. ff: "Wenn die Menschen die im Übereinkommen gesetzten Normen befolgen, so ist ja auch wiederum jene höchste Macht in Gedanken mitgesetzt, die wir als Rechtsmacht bezeichneten und deren Merkmal es gerade ist, dass die von ihr herrührenden Normen gewöhnlich und mehr als irgendwelche anderen befolgt werden."

[40] See, for example, id. at § 32, p. 102: "Freilich kann eine Rechtsmacht auch aus labileren Elementen bestehen, deren Vorhandensein die ohnedies nicht leichte Feststellung dessen, wo in einem gegebenen Kreise von Menschen die Rechtsmacht sei, noch mehr erschwert."

fact that every society is a collective and every collective in some necessary way exerts normativity over its individuals.

There is a certain circularity in Somlo's logic. The legal norms issue from the sovereign which is present if and only if there is a legal order, presumably a collection of legal norms that are present if and only if there is a sovereign. Which comes first the sovereign or the law? This question of priority or genesis does not present itself with the classical imperial, hierarchical or monarchical picture in which God or king rescues lost souls from a state of disorder. In contrast to this classical view, Somlo's conception opens a pandora's box of unknowns and questions, which have no universal answers. Somlo says that any jurisprudential analysis of constitutional law requires as its foundation an historical and sociological investigation of the particular qualities of sovereignty in that state.[41] He states that to say that the author of a legal norm is a sovereign is only to refer to such author's ability to generally realize (succeed with) his norms or, in other words, to cause them to be followed.[42] Further, Somlo says that there is a close mental connection between the habit of obedience and all other factors of societal and political culture, thus giving the notion of obedience an inexhaustible nuance.[43] Finally, he qualifies that a sovereign may be the sovereign as long as it issues law in a particular way. As soon as the sovereign goes against certain beliefs or other norms though, it may cease to be the sovereign.[44] The one constant for Somlo is that, in order to have the requisite persistence through time, the sovereignty must be of an institutional nature.[45] Sovereignty can be embodied in an individual (e. g. a monarch) or a multitude of individuals (e. g. a people itself). However, if such an individual or collective fails to represent an institutional form, then whatever power may exist at any given time will not have the prospect of lasting.

---

[41] Somlo, *Juristische Grundlehre*, § 95, p. 314: "Jede juristische Behandlung eines gegebenen Staatsrechts erfordert als Grundlage eine historisch-soziale Untersuchung über die Beschaffenheit der Rechtsmacht in jenem Staate."

[42] Id. at § 36, pp. 108, 109: "Die Bezeichnung des Urhebers von Rechtsnormen als einer Macht bedeutet weiter nichts, als seine Fähigkeit zum gewöhnlichen Verwirklichen seiner Normen, mit anderen Worten: zur Verursachung ihrer Befolgung."

[43] Id. at § 37, p. 111, citing F. Klein: "Der Rechtsgehorsam ist mit allen Faktoren der Gesellschaftskultur und des Staatslebens in engem geistigen Zusammenhang, und das gibt ihm seine unerschöpflichen Nuancen."

[44] Id. at § 40, p. 119: "Solange ein Machthaber in einer bestimmten Weise Recht schafft, mag er als Rechtsmacht gelten. Sobald er aber gewisse Überzeugungen verletzt, hört er auf, Rechtsmacht zu sein." For the alternative conception, i. e. in which law remains law on account of its source, regardless of its coherence within a general frame of reason, see Alexander (2009).

[45] Id. at § 32, p. 103.

Whereas Kelsen, Hart and most of mainstream legal positivism establish clear rules for recognizing legal authority within a territory, Somlo's theory is almost created as if to establish the greatest degree of uncertainty (and therewith flexibility) possible. Most, even natural law, theorists acknowledge the importance of clear rules establishing a line of authority from the highest legislator to the lowest administrator. Somlo, on the other hand, would hold that a line of authority can only be of use on the assumption that the highest legislator identified by such rules is actually the sovereign in the territory and that such sovereign has actually issued a corresponding system of secondary norms. However, if the legal norms are really the commands of a sovereign which enjoys a habit of obedience, then there can certainly be norms that exist outside of the standard hierarchical framework of legislator, administrator, judge. Since no sovereign can be bound by a clean 'scientific' (hierarchical) ordering of norms, it is always possible for a sovereign to contradict such a system through the express or implied issuance of law. As such, immediate legislation (i.e. legislation coming directly from the sovereign, which Somlo calls a primary source of law) always trumps mediate legislation (in Somlo's terminology – secondary sources).[46] If you add to this openness with respect to the sources of law the additional factor that both mediate and immediate sources of law can issue both express and implied norms, then the determination of the content of the law goes from a fairly dry, clerical activity of deducing one paragraph from another to a seemingly open-ended task of divining the content of any one norm from a nearly infinite universe of meaning. Somlo thereby succeeds in accounting for a much more generalized concept of law, i.e. one which aligns much more closely with law's principle condition – sovereignty. In doing so, Somlo seems to destroy much of the foundation which theorists have used in attempting to develop a 'scientific' theory of law.[47]

---

46 See Id. at §§ 100, 101.

47 Of relevance here is Tönnies' distinction between society and community, where society is based on the merely instrumental reasoning amidst structures which are in some sense optional, and community is based on the agency of norms held in common with others. A corporation, for example, is defined by a framework of artificial rules which define the rights and duties of its shareholders and officers. The corporate 'legal' framework is thoroughly objective in the sense of being empirically evident and is thus dry, clerical, even boring – and it is also thoroughly optional. The normativity of a village community, though, presents itself precisely not in a dry and clerical manner, but is messy and complex. The objectivity of such a community lies not in its communal by-laws, but rather in the very real interactions of its members. Membership in such a community is also in a real sense not optional, since to extract oneself from community for the purpose of existing solely at the societal level is to live solely on the basis of the instrumental, hypothetical imperative and to thus ultimately deprive oneself of the possibility of agency.

However, if we consider the emptiness of the scientific program which Kelsen develops, we see that it is actually Somlo who makes the more serious attempt at laying the foundation for legal science. Only in inverting the norm of sovereignty as Somlo seeks to do, is it possible for the legal theorist to actually look at the world to determine the source and content of the legal norms.

8. Plurale Tantum

Aus dem hier entwickelten Begriff der Rechtsmacht folgt zugleich, dass es eine Rechtsnorm als isolierte Einheit, ohne dass sie zugleich einer Vielheit von Schwestern angehörte, nicht geben kann.[48]

If we can postulate the institution of sovereignty, there is no guarantee that the norms of any one governmental body (i. e. a secondary source) actually reflect the will of the sovereign and therefore are to be counted as law – and even if they do reflect the sovereign's will today, there is no guarantee that they will do so tomorrow. However, if the sovereign is that entity or person which enjoys a generalized habit of obedience on the part of subjects and if legal norms are those norms which issue from a sovereign, it must follow that legal norms are those that are generally and habitually obeyed. Somlo insists that this 'generalized' quality of the law, i. e. that a sovereign and therefore also a legal system can only exist if it encompasses a sufficiently broad scope of human conduct, results in the fact that no one legal norm can be understood or conceptualized as an isolated entity. The legal norm can only be understood as a plurale tantum,[49] i. e. in the plural form or, as Somlo says, as one within a brotherhood of other norms.[50] If

---

[48] Id. at § 30, p. 98.

[49] Ibid.: "Darin, dass eine Macht ein weites Gebiet von Lebensverhältnissen normativ ergreifen muss, um zu einer Rechtsmacht werden zu können, ist bereits die Erkenntnis enthalten, dass es eine Rechtsnorm für sich gar nicht geben kann, sondern dass solche in der Wirklichkeit immer nur als ein begriffliches plurale oder besser gesagt multum tantum vorkommen können. Es ist damit zugleich der Wahrheit Ausdruck verliehen, dass dasjenige, was wir bisher als Rechtsnorm bezeichnet und zum Ausgangspunkt unserer Untersuchung gemacht haben, nur als Teil eines Ganzes gedacht werden kann. Der Begriff einer Rechtsnorm weist über sich selbst hinaus auf das Ganze einer von einem einheitlichen Urheber getragenen Vielheit von Rechtsnormen. Dieses Ganze nennen wir Rechtsordnung." See also § 112: "Jeder Rechtssatz gilt und bindet nur in notwendiger Wechselwirkung mit einer unbegrenzten Zahl anderer Normen, die ihn näher bestimmen, einschränken, oder in näherer oder entfernterer Beziehung ergänzen…. Es gibt gar keine einzelne Rechtsnorm für sich – die einzelne Rechtsnorm ist nur eine künstliche Isolierung –, es gibt nur Rechtsnormen, die in ihrem Zusammenhange gelten; es gibt nur eine Rechtsordnung, und nur dadurch, dass eine Norm dieser angehört, wird sie zu einer Rechtsnorm."

[50] Somlo. *Gedanken zu einer ersten Philosophie*, p. 44.

this is the case, then the task of understanding the law can be nothing but understanding law in its entirety, which is to say understanding the relation between the willing sovereign and the willing subject. The task of legal science is not so much to identify particular legal norms or to identify a particular sovereign. Rather, it is to understand the nature of the legal order itself, this plurale tantum that governs the relation between us as individuals and us as a collective.

Somlo insists that his is no longer an epistemological theory of law, but rather an axiological, or value-based theory.[51] This certainly does not mean that Somlo advocates for an ideological approach to law in which one value, e. g. patriotism or religion, determines the science of law. Rather, Somlo's position is that proper jurisprudential activity lies in weighing norms, or value propositions, against each other. For Kelsen, the normativity of the law only persists within the sphere of secondary rules (governmental bodies). There can very seldom be true conflicts of law and jurisprudential activity is therefore limited to the epistemological task of ordering administrative actions within the context of the legal system. Since conflicts rarely arise and, when they do, they can normally be finally resolved by following the hierarchical rules of the legal system, the Kelsenian jurist need never decide upon a question of value. For Somlo, on the other hand, juridical inquiry can *only* be a question of value and, since all norms (moral, aesthetic, grammatical, etc.) can be seen as coming to us unfiltered, it is the jurist's first task to determine which of the multitude of norms are actually legal norms and which of the legal norms supersede each other in a system of norms. The method which Somlo must employ in theorizing such a system of jurisprudence is thus neither solely axiological nor solely epistemological, but rather necessarily both axiological and epistemological.

Somlo follows his Neo-Kantian peers by insisting that legal science is a normative science in that its object clearly entails a system of norms. However, in contrast to at least Kelsen, Somlo does not hesitate at all in acknowledging the importance of fact for legal science.[52] A legal system can only be understood from the legal perspective as a system of norms, i. e. ought-sentences that seek to guide human conduct. However, much of any actual system of norms remains incomprehensible if considered within a factual vacuum. As a matter of principle, legal norms themselves issue from a sovereign. This sovereignty itself, though, depends

[51] Id. at § 28, p. 92: "Zu einer Hierarchie der Normen können wir uns erst erheben, wenn wir nach ihrem Werte fragen. Und dabei ist es von vornherein nicht nur nicht ausgeschlossen, dass uns die Verfolgung des Wertgesichtspunktes zu einer besonderen Art von Normen führen wird, sondern, da der Wert ein normativer Gehalt ist, ist es gar nicht anders möglich. Damit hätten wir aber den hier zu verfolgenden rein erkenntniskritischen Standpunkt verlassen und den axiologischen betreten, dem wir in einer besonderen Untersuchung gerecht werden wollen."

[52] Id. at § 43, p. 127.

on the fact of a general habit of obedience. More importantly, as quoted from Somlo above, legal norms want, demand, to be followed *in fact*. Somlo's personification of norms is poetic. However, what he really means is that the sovereign, who immediately or mediately issues a legal norm, does so wanting the norm to be obeyed. If the issuance itself is expressed, then it is a communicative act. Even if it is not express, the issuance in any case creates a normative relation between the sovereign and subject as they exist in fact. Whether as a communicative act or a mere normative relation, the legal norm cannot be understood as it exists in the legal system without taking into account the factual circumstance of the issuer who utters or implies the norm, nor of the addressee whose conduct the issuer seeks to direct. While as a strictly theoretical matter it is possible to view the legal norm outside of any such factual context, to do so ignores that that with which the law is actually concerned is the volition of individuals, whether sovereigns, subjects or administrative officials. This volition is incomprehensible without addressing the interplay of norm and fact in the intentionality of human beings.[53]

If every norm only exists as part of a whole – the plurale tantum, then the relation in question is not one between the individual and a particular norm seeking to guide his conduct, but rather one between an individual and the entirety of the normative order itself. The connection between the two is a function of the logical sentence.

9. The Logical Sentence

Much of the *Juristische Grundlehre*, including most of the considerations which are outlined above, consists more of questions of sovereignty, state and collectives then of the analysis of the strict functioning of a system of norms. The postulate of norms as *plurale tantum* suggests that questions of law presuppose questions of state and a general theory of law requires a preliminary investigation of the theory of state. This approach is validated when Somlo turns to analyzing legal norms proper at the beginning of the second part of the *Juristische Grundlehre*.

---

[53] Note that for John Searle, institutional reality always consists in a status function, that is a norm, to which he attributes the variable 'y' as it exists in the (factual) context 'c'. Normativity can only be understood within its appropriate factual context. Outside of such context, as Kelsen's project attests, normativity loses all meaning. For an alternative theory of institutional reality, and perhaps the prevailing one with respect to legal institutional reality, see MacCormick and Weinberger's *Grundlagen des institutionalistischen Rechtspositivismus*. A particularly interesting volume which brings Weinberger, Searle, Gilbert and Tuomela together is Eerik Lagerspetz (ed.), *On the Nature of Social and Institutional Reality*.

The most important passages for the present reconstruction can be found in the Sixth Chapter, "Legal Norm and Legal Text", as well as the 11th and 12th Chapters, "Sources of Law" and "Legal Interpretation (and Application)" and, importantly, Somlo's posthumously published, uncompleted manuscript on a theory of validity and truth, *Gedanken zu einer ersten Philosophie* (1926). In these passages, Somlo makes the first steps toward a theory of sentences, norms and meaning which capitalize on his innovative insights regarding norms and sovereignty discussed above. As we will see, it is ultimately Somlo's theory of language, likely influenced by Bolzano,[54] that is the key to understanding his theory of sovereignty and normativity.

In the first paragraph, § 60, of the Second Part of the *Juristische Grundlehre*, Somlo makes a relatively innocuous observation in distinguishing the logical from the grammatical sense of the general sentence:

> Wir wollen uns nunmehr vor allem zum Oberbegriff des Rechts zurückwenden und sogar noch einen Schritt nach oben hin über ihn hinaus tun. Wir unterscheiden zu diesem Zweck den Begriff des logischen oder des Bedeutungssatzes vom Begriff des grammatischen oder des Sprachsatzes.[55]

For Somlo, every sentence has a logical and a grammatical aspect. The grammatical aspect is that which is spoken (or written) at face value. The logical aspect is the meaning that is contained in the spoken sentence. Every normal (i. e. communicative) sentence must have a logical content (i. e. a meaning) and, at least within the realm of a verbal language, every meaning must be expressed within a grammatical form. Any given meaning could be expressed in a multitude of 'grammatical' sentences and any (normal) grammatical sentence presents a multitude of possible interpretations, i. e. possible meanings. This distinction itself is not unique to Somlo. He, himself, indicates in the footnotes to §§ 60 and 61 several predecessors and contemporaries who have made similar distinctions, including Kelsen[56] as well as Windelband and Wundt, the latter of whom gave the name judgment (*Urteil*) to that which Somlo calls 'logical sense' or 'meaning'.[57]

---

[54] See Somlo. *Gedanken zu einer ersten Philosophie*, p. 13.

[55] Somlo, *Juristische Grundlehre*, § 60, p. 179.

[56] See Kelsen, *Hauptprobleme*, p. 238, FN 1: "Es wäre ein arger Irrtum, wollte man den Rechtssatz, der erst aus den konkreten Gesetzen herauskonstruiert werden muss, mit einem der Sätze im grammatischen Sinne identifizieren, aus denen die konkreten Gesetzen aufgebaut werden. Es ist selbstverständlich, dass aus rein ästhetisch-stilistischen und auch aus anderen gesetztechnischen Gründen die eine Rechtspflicht statuierende ideale Norm mit allen ihren wesentlichen Bestandteilen tatsächlich auch im konkreten Gesetze nicht in einem einzigen Satz stilisiert wird, sondern hier in zahlreiche Sätze verschiedenster Struktur aufgelöst, ja sogar häufig auf zwei oder mehrere Gesetze verteilt erscheint. Sache der juristischen Konstruktion ist es, die ideale Norm aus diesen Teilen zusammenzusetzen."

[57] Also Kantorowicz in "Some Rationalism about Realism" (1934) makes a similar distinc-

What is interesting about this distinction for Somlo is that it seems to lead him to a theory of legal norms quite unlike other theories held by his Neo-Kantian contemporaries and unlike any other legal theorists since, but which, at the same time, predicts a significant strand of the philosophy of language in the 20th century, perhaps best exemplified by Wittgenstein's treatment of language, use and meaning in the *Philosophical Investigations*. Of direct relevance here is that, in developing a theory of norms as a theory of normative meaning connecting sovereign and subject, Somlo is able to develop a robust alternative to the Kelsenian theory, an alternative that is at once value-laden, because of the role of meaning inherent in the contextualization of sentences, and positivistic, as a result of such meanings being created by us.

Somlo states in § 60 that the grammatical (spoken) sentence can be considered as an isolated sentence (*isolierter Satz*) whereas the logical sentence can be considered as the sentence in context (*Satz im Zusammenhang*). The typical method for understanding the grammatical, or formal, sentence lies in understanding the normal meaning of its constitutive words together with the grammatical relations expressed in the sentence. The logical sentence, on the other hand, cannot be determined exclusively by its grammatical form. While the grammatical form is one element in determining the meaning of a logical sentence, there are many other circumstances which serve to fully contextualize it and thereby disambiguate its meaning.[58]

In a way, Kelsen also draws the same basic distinction. However, his distinction is much more formalistic in nature. Kelsen rightly points out that the grammatical sentence – 'Murder shall be punished with ten years' imprisonment' – cannot be understood as a legal norm (*Rechtssatz*) without taking into account other complementary grammatical sentences such as: 'Murder is the unlawful killing of another human without justification', 'Imprisonment is the forced confinement by the state to an institution', etc. Kelsen would make the unobjectionable claim that a single sentence written in a legal code is itself rarely if ever a sufficient basis for understanding the actual legal norm which it is meant to express. Instead, in order to properly identify the applicable norm, one would have to first set out all other relevant textual evidence, e. g. the applicable constitutional, legislative, and administrative provisions. Only upon considering this evidence would it be possible to make a proper judgment about the legal norm un-

---

tion at p. 1245: "…it is erroneous to believe that the law is the wording of the Law, still more erroneous to believe that it is the printed document. This prejudice overlooks the fact that only *meaning* of the Law counts in the decision."

[58] Somlo, *Juristische Grundlehre*, § 60, p. 181. For 21st century applications of this basic and profound idea, see the analysis of Kolman in "Wittgenstein and die Meistersinger" as well as of Rödl in "The Idea of Practice".

derlying the given text. What Kelsen does not seem to advocate is that the jurist would need to consult extra textual sources or sources without direct bearing on the norm in question. Kelsen's proposed method is one of rule formalism, or rule empiricism. For Kelsen, once the jurist's consideration extends beyond the admissible textual sources, the jurist then ceases trying to understand the legal norm as it exists and instead himself becomes involved in legislation.[59] Such activity would no longer involve knowing, but rather willing.[60] Kelsen's caution in the face of politicizing the judiciary is well-placed and his position with respect to textual interpretation largely reflects contemporary jurisprudential orthodoxy as a practical matter. Nonetheless, Kelsen's empirical approach to interpretation reflects his empirical and relativistic approach to the concept of law in general which, upon closer examination of Somlo's insights, should be rejected.

Somlo's main points applying the distinction between the grammatical and logical sentence are insightful in this regard, indicating the limitation of an overly formalistic concept of law and the naïve understanding of sovereignty and meaning which it entails. On the one hand, Somlo states that there are limitations regarding how the sovereign can change existing law. For example, it could be the case that legislation is issued which, despite its compliant grammatical 'ought' form and formal compliance with legislative procedure, actually does not contain a normative meaning or contains a normative meaning which adds no normative content to the existing system (i. e. is redundant) or is incomprehensible within the system.[61] Even if legislation is enacted which does succeed in expressing a normative meaning, or shifting the normative framework, such a

---

59 Kelsen, *Reine Rechtslehre*, § 39, p. 99: "Sofern bei der Gesetzesanwendung über die dabei nötige Feststellung des Rahmens, innerhalb dessen sich der zu setzende Akt zu halten hat, hinaus noch eine Erkenntnistätigkeit Platz greifen kann, ist es nicht eine Erkenntnis des positiven Rechts, sondern anderer Normen, die hier in den Prozess der Rechtserzeugung einmünden können; Normen der Moral, der Gerechtigkeit, soziale Werturteile, die man mit den Schlagworten Volkswohl, Staatsinteresse, Fortschritt, u. s. w. zu bezeichnen pflegt. Über deren Geltung und Feststellbarkeit lässt sich vom Standpunkt des positiven Rechts nichts aussagen."

60 Id. at § 39, p. 99: "[Die Reine Rechtslehre] zerstört die Meinung, dass im Wege der Erkenntnis Normen neu geschaffen werden könnten; eine Meinung die letztlich dem Bedürfnis entspringt, sich das Recht als eine feste Ordnung vorzustellen, die das menschliche Verhalten, insbesondere aber die Tätigkeit der Rechtsanwendenden Organe, der Gerichte vor allem allseits bestimmt; so dass deren Funktion und sohin auch die Interpretation nur als das Finden schon vorhandener und daher nur in einem besonderen Verfahren aufzudeckender Normen anzusehen ist."

61 Somlo, *Juristische Grundlehre*, § 62, p. 185: "Ob nun in irgendwelchen von der Rechtsmacht ausgehenden Sätzen überhaupt Normen enthalten sind oder nicht, ist eine Tatsachenfrage. Findet sich in einem Gesetz z. B. eine Einteilung, die zu seinem Verständnis überhaupt nichts beiträgt und die auch vom Gesichtspunkt des Wortgebrauchs des Gesetzgebers gänzlich unerheblich ist, so ist sie keine Norm.

norm must and can only be understood within the context of the entirety of the legal system.[62] A legal definition, but also a legal norm, is not any less binding than any other norm issuing from the sovereign. However, it is also not any more binding.[63] Somlo concludes his discussion on this point by stating:

> [Jurisprudenz] hat den Norminhalt wiederzugeben, aber sie braucht es weder mit den Worten zu tun, die der Gesetzgeber dazu verwendet hat, noch mit denselben Begriffen; ja es ist eben eine ihrer vornehmsten Aufgaben, den ermittelten Norminhalt in entsprechendere Begriffe umzuleeren.[64]

This particular discussion in §§ 60–62 as well as §§ 110–115 applies directly to the interpretation of written texts. However, Somlo's scope, and the importance of the general distinction between logical and grammatical sentences, extends far beyond textual interpretation. Legal formalism acknowledges that any written law can be ambiguous, but establishes rules for resolving any ambiguity in favor of 'sticking to' the text. Somlo's theory presents quite the opposite approach. For Somlo, that which is real and valid about a norm has no inherent connection to that which is written down (although the written text is certainly one piece of evidence among many). For Somlo, the logical sentence exists independently of any expressed form and is conditioned only by all other logical sentences with which it co-exists.[65]

Most jurists would readily acknowledge that the structure of law involves at its core the use of force by a state against individuals and that, at least in a fairly developed legal system, the means by which such force is carried out is through the written word. This is certainly also true for Somlo. And yet, I believe that Somlo was beginning to realize something much more fundamental in the *Juristische Grundlehre* with his concept of sovereignty as variable, the legal norm as plurale tantum and the distinction between logical and grammatical sentence. Somlo was working on a general theory of the collective as expressed in the law.

[62] Somlo, *Juristische Grundlehre*, § 62, p. 186: "Sie [legal definitions] dürfen, wie die Sätze der Rechtsmacht überhaupt, nicht aus ihrem Zusammenhang herausgerissen für sich und auch nicht rein ihrer grammatischen Form nach beurteilt werden, sondern sind mit den übrigen [i. e. definitions and other legal norms] in Zusammenhang zu bringen. Wenn dies gelingt, so gewinnen sie Anteil an der logischen Struktur der übrigen Sätze und erweisen sich dadurch als Normen."

[63] Id. at § 62, p. 186: "Die in der Form einer Legaldefinition ausgedrückte Norm ist also einerseits um nichts weniger verbindlich als andere Normen der Rechtsmacht; sie ist aber andererseits natürlich auch um nichts verbindlicher."

[64] Id. at § 62, p. 187.

[65] See also Kantorowicz, *supra*: "To the jurist the Law is the objective meaning of statute or opinion, that which the legislator or the judge would have meant if he had been able to fit his meaning into the whole body of the Law." As this touches closely upon the issue of interpretation, see also Marijan Pavčnik, *Juristisches Verstehen und Entscheiden*.

10. Absolute Validity

In the section above entitled "Subjectivity and Interpretation", I outlined three prisms available for understanding the relationship between the individual and the state: (i) conceiving both the individual and the state as factual entities entailing a relation of causal necessity; (ii) conceiving the individual as a factual entity and the state as a removed, normative entity, thereby ultimately denying the possibility of any such relation; and (iii) conceiving both the individual (subject) and the state as normative entities, thereby creating the possibility of conflict – and thus an object of study – within the law. Kelsen, as we have seen, chooses the second option. Meanwhile, a choice of the third option would result in enveloping both the individual (subject) and the state in a unifying normative framework that reeks of the myriad difficulties of natural law: which unifying order shall it be and what if the subject and the state pertain to differing orders? Kelsen's choice of a relative validity that pertains solely to the state as legal order indeed saves him from having to adopt a relative validity that also binds the individual (subject), i. e. Kelsen's choice saves him from having to openly adopt an ideology. In this way, while the individual as a point of attribution within the legal order can never escape the law (which may be either just or unjust), the individual as it exists (as a real person) remains unaffected. Nonetheless, the Kelsenian paradigm, as he himself admits in the *Reine Rechtslehre* (1934, *supra*) remains artificially bound in its validity by the contingency of social / political fact. Only by opening up the paradigm to social fact as it constitutes the legal order can an absolute validity be attained. In other words, only by (iv) recognizing the individual (as a real individual in fact), but as constituting and as an essential part of the state / legal order as a normative entity can we approach a notion of validity in the law that attains without reservation. In a sense, both (ii) and (iii) above are ultimately correct. Only by recognizing the normative relevance of the individual in fact can legal theory avoid Kelsen's compartmentalization while nonetheless grounding the normativity of the law in the reality of social fact.

With Somlo, legal norms should be understood as a plurale tantum. That which connects expressions of law to each other, resulting in the form of plurale tantum, is the fact that they derive from a logical form. Somlo says that that which we initially perceive is nothing but evidence or perhaps intuition and that these raw impressions of the world must first be formed into thoughts, sentences, before any consideration of validity or correctness can be undertaken.[66] What holds of

[66] See Somlo, *Gedanken zu einer ersten Philosophie*, p. 42: "Das zu Messende, das Material der unbedingten Richtigkeit war und ist etwas Psychologisches. Dieses Psychologische führt den Namen Evidenz oder auch Intuition. Alles Evidente oder Intuitive ist uns daher nur eine

mere perception, is also true of communication.[67] All that exists in nature are individuals faced with each other. In order to communicate, or to issue a directive, one individual must be able to formulate in language that which he wills internally and the other, on the basis of such formulation, together with all other evidence and intuition, must try to understand not just that which was expressed as the outer manifestation of the will, but also that which exists within the other, i. e. the will itself. Grammatical sentences are all that we can ever perceive. Yet, the grammatical sentence as mere fact is useless. It is only the sentence as thought or meaning, the logical sentence, which serves as the normative glue that binds us to one another.[68]

The meeting place of the factual and the normative is the human mind. Validity can never attach to the factual itself, but rather requires the formulation of a sentence, a thought in which a predicate is brought into connection with a subject. Bolzano holds that prescriptive statements also determine states of affairs such that truth and validity could be predicated of such statements:

> Der Satz: ich wünschte, dass Cajus ein ehrlicher Mann wäre, läßt freilich das Verhältnis, das zwischen Cajus und Ehrlichkeit obwaltet, unbestimmt, Cajus und Ehrlichkeit sind aber auch nicht Subject und Prädicat in diesem Satz; sondern das eigentliche Subject desselben ist der Sprechende, und das Prädicat, der Wunsch, daß Cajus ein ehrlicher Mann wäre.[69]

A speaker himself is neither valid or invalid; Caius himself is neither valid nor invalid; honest men themselves are neither valid nor invalid – each of these alone are merely facts or putative facts and facts are always conditional, that is, they do not exist necessarily, but are conditioned by their givenness in the world. The only thing which is not so conditioned is a meaning. Though arising in the world (of fact), meaning itself is not dependent on the contingency of fact, but rather on the thought of a speaker. Yet, per Somlo, meanings themselves only have validity in a community of meanings – a plurale tantum.[70] A speaker's wish for Caius

---

Fragestellung nach unbedingter Gültigkeit selber. Evidenzen und Intuitionen können einander widersprechen, d. h. sie können auch irrig sein."

67 Somlo, *Juristische Grundlehre*, § 111: "Überall, wo die Äußerung eines psychischen Vorganges darauf angelegt ist, von anderen aufgenommen zu werden, gilt es, die Kluft zwischen zwei Psychen zu Überbrücken. Es bedarf einerseits einer Äußerung des Innenlebens und einer Enträtselung dieser Äußerung andererseits."

68 Bolzano says that there are necessarily so many kinds of formulations of sentences (thoughts) as there are possibilities for an individual to express itself. See Bolzano, § 21, p. 111: "Es muss nothwendig so viel Arten von Sätzen geben, als dem Geiste Handlungsweisen des Setzens zukommen."

69 Bolzano, *Wissenschaftslehre*, § 22, p. 115.

70 See Somlo, *Gedanken zu einer ersten Philosophie*, p. 25: "Solange einem Sinn noch etwas Tatsächliches anhängt, zieht ihn dieser Erdenrest unerbittlich in die Niederungen des Bedingten hinab. Schlechthin unbedingt sein kann also gar niemals eine Tatsache, sondern nur

to be honest (i. e. that Caius should be honest), will either be valid or invalid depending on a community of other sentences. Facts themselves are always conditional and therefore validity does not pertain to them. Rather, validity pertains to statements. Yet, the validity of the statement above will not depend on any one state of mind, neither of the speaker nor of Caius, but only on the entire normative order in which the speaker and Caius factually act.

Kelsen, along with most other theorists, presupposes the existence of the sovereign. As a result for Kelsen, the sovereign itself is never part of the sentence seeking validation and all that Kelsen can validate in his theory of norms is the proposition: 'Caius should be honest'. Kelsen, Bulygin and many others are correct that such propositions cannot be contradicted with the result that Kelsen must limit himself to the 'relative' validity of a hierarchy of administrative norms. However, the picture is significantly different if, with Somlo, we open our concept of sovereignty. Suddenly, the operative proposition is no longer 'Caius should be honest' but rather 'S wishes that 'Caius should be honest''. Whether S's wish that 'Caius should be honest' is a valid intention depends on a jurisprudential inquiry that will entail determining whether S in this case is sovereign (primary source of law) or speaks for the sovereign (secondary source of law) and, if so, how 'Caius should be honest' fits within the entirety of the legal order, the norm as plurale tantum. The fact that we have grown accustomed to a certain stability when it comes to (i) our identification of sovereigns as well as (ii) our habits of obeying the norms which they issue has more to do with the valor of our sovereign institutions in reflecting the normative plurale tantum of our societies in their laws than it does with any factual priority of the sovereigns themselves. The strength of the Queen in Parliament, to use Hart's frame, is only secondarily that the Queen in Parliament is sovereign, but primarily that the Queen in Parliament issues norms in accordance with and contextualized within the normativity of the legal order.[71]

In denying the possibility of a logic of norms, Kelsen denies that there is a universe of meaning in the legal sphere between subjects. Somlo's work stands for the proposition that a logic of norms is nonetheless possible through the absolute validity of truth which our reason requires. At the very end of his *Gedank-*

---

eine Bedeutung, ein Sinn. Der Sinn oder die Bedeutung muss also sorgfältig von jedem Erhobensein, Gegebensein, Dasein, Existenz, kurz von jeder Tatsächlichkeit losgelöst werden."

[71] The sovereign's skill in the legislation and execution of the laws is not unrelated to the sovereign's status as sovereign. The skill of a heart surgeon is primarily related to how well the surgeon performs heart surgeries. However, the more surgeries the surgeon performs, the better the surgeon will become in performing this task. Similarly, a sovereign who is well-practiced is likely to be much better at legislation and administration than one who is not. When this is status is institutionalized such that the knowledge and skills of sovereignty can grow from one generation to the next, then the expressions of sovereignty should become ever more stable and in accord with the society at large.

en zu einer Ersten Philosophie, in what remains as a fragment, Somlo discusses the requirement of absolute validity bottoming out in the concept of truth.[72] The validity of an expressed norm (Kelsen's *Rechtssatz*) is always conditional upon the fact of its expression and therefore can never be absolute. Kelsen is therefore correct in stating that a norm as norm, even the basic norm, is never absolute. For Somlo though, the actual norm, that which bears meaning, cannot be reduced to its mere factual expression. As a bearer of meaning, the norm exists not as a grammatical sentence, isolated in fact, but rather as a logical sentence, embedded in the context of the plurale tantum. Truth can be predicated of norms within such a system because of their coherence, and then sovereignty because of the generality of the whole. Sovereignty is then but a function of validity and absolute validity would then result in absolute sovereignty.

This conception of normativity as a logical whole is only possible given Somlo's insistence on the existence of logical sentences, or norms in context with other norms connecting issuers and addressees. Because I can never follow an individual norm on its own but only such a norm as part of a whole, the idea of normativity as a plurale tantum has as a consequence the idea that an individual should abandon preferences born out of facticity in favor of normativity (or meaning) constituted by the collective. Phrased in Kantian terms, this means that an individual should only pursue such courses of action that, when generalized, are in conformity with the system of norms, or normativity, generally. The normative plurale tantum shares with the categorical imperative the same admonition: favor meaning (of the collective) over facticity (of the brute), favor order over anarchy. The possibility of creating such meaning and order is the mark of human rationality. The imperative of creating such a system of order and meaning must be the requirement of legal positivism as the science of law.

---

[72] See Somlo, *Gedanken zu einer ersten Philosophie*, p. 104: "Es ist damit nicht gesagt, dass es neben dem Wahrheitsanspruche andere Geltungsansprüche nicht gibt, – soll es sie jedoch geben, so müssen sie sich ihre Bestätigung vom Wahrheitsanspruche aus erbitten… Denn wenn wir nach ihrer Unbedingtheit fragen, was wir zu tun gezwungen sind, fragen wir ja bereits nach einer Wahrheit. Die Untersuchung der Unbedingtheit des Geltungsanspruches: du sollst nicht töten, erfordert bereits seine Übersetzung in den Satz, es ist wahr, dass das Gebot, du sollst nicht töten, unbedingt gilt. Der Gegensatz von 'du sollst nicht töten', wäre bloß: du darfst oder gar du sollst töten. In dieser Schicht lässt sich aber keine Untersuchung der Unbedingtheit führen. Nun steckt aber auch im unbedingten Geltungsanspruch des Satzes, du sollst nicht töten, das Problem, das wir seiner nur als eines von uns erhobenen gewiss sind, und dass er trotz dieser seiner subjektiv bedingten Erhobenheit, ein unbedingter zu sein angibt. Der hierin verborgene Widerspruch lautet also bereits: dieser Anspruch ist kein unbedingter. Das Problem lautet daher doch nur so, ob es wahr ist, dass dieser Anspruch unbedingt ist. Wir haben also unseren unbedingten Sollsatz 'du sollst nicht töten' in den unbedingten Aussagesatz: es ist wahr, dass das Gebot, du sollst nicht töten unbedingt gilt, übersetzt. Der Sinn seiner unbedingten Geltung ist ein Wahrheitssinn. Mithin gibt es gar keine andere unbedingte Geltung als die der Wahrheit."

Chapter V

Facts and Matters of Fact (Logic of Norms II)

Wenn man feststellen will, worin das Wesen des jus non scriptum besteht, wird man sich vor allem über das genus, von welchem es die eine species darstellen soll, d. h. darüber klar sein müssen, was Recht überhaupt ist.[1]

The expressivist conception of legal norms supposes that legal prescriptions are mere *facta*. Analogous to material facts in themselves, there are no factual relations that hold necessarily among prescriptions in themselves. There is no necessary (as opposed to biological) relation between a tree and water and there is also no necessary (as opposed to sociological, psychological) relation between prescriptions taken as mere facts or, for that matter, between the issuer of a prescription and its addressee taken as material entities. In Chapter I though, I point to von Wright's suggestion that it might be possible to expand our logical aspirations beyond prescriptions in themselves to consider the entirety of the relation between sovereign and subject as expressed through legal norms. In so doing, one would develop a theory of legal normativity not as a description of how legal prescriptions are and come to be in mere fact, but rather as uncovering the underlying structure of the legal norm as necessarily relating sovereign to subject. In Chapters I and II, I show that both 'sovereign' and 'subject' are institutionally iterative concepts that depend on a thick web (and long history) of underlying institutional reality in order to be realized. The legal subject is an institutional construct that goes beyond the material world of desire dependence, just as sovereignty has little to do with being the biggest man having the biggest stick. This institutional (normative) reality is not a *factum* of the material world, but rather a construct of our institutional reality that exists first and foremost in our minds.

In Chapter III, I inquire into the nature of this mental construct. In previous times, so the common (and Kelsenian) conception, we thought that our institutional reality was pre-ordained by the omnipotent God and therefore absolutely (formally, teleologically, physically and metaphysically) necessary. Throwing away that notion, institutional reality at most still has a formal necessity (logical validity) with the concept of God or state functioning as a unifying hypostasis of

[1] Somlo, *Juristische Grundlehre*, § 100, FN 1, citing Bruno Schmidt, *Das Gewohnheitsrecht als Form des Gemeinwillens*.

the institutional or legal order. Ultimately though, Kelsen, through Kletzer, also dismisses that holdover with the result of allowing for a new kind of validity that is actually not a validity at all. Chapter IV then opens a new path of inquiry addressing with Somlo the prospect of the legal order not consisting in valid norms as a function of sovereignty ending in a highest, or basic, norm according to the traditional conception, but rather consisting of sovereignty as a function of the validity of legal norms taken as a whole.

Sovereignty in its naïve conception, as a master imposing duties, might seem materially evident. Yet, this evidence dissipates upon closer examination, revealing an immense complex of institutional structures with their implicit normative relations. Somlo recognized that these relations do not exist individually, but rather only on the whole, and that the form of each relation is that of the logical sentence that is dependent on and only comprehensible in the context of all other such sentences (*der Satz im Zusammenhang*). Such a description of logical sentences existing independently of their grammatical expressions and then of normativity as a *plurale tantum* might lead to the suspicion of a hidden premise of an immutable form and therefore, perhaps, of natural law. However, while the law in this conception of the logical sentence is not of the material world, it is nonetheless a direct result of human volition and rationality that can only be applied as the execution (*Vollzug*) of a generalized form. Such forms are generalized, or generic, not as an emulation of divine laws or as the result of the 'nature' of things, but rather as a result of the necessity of individuals cooperating in their actions, thus achieving objectivity in their subjectivity.[2] Just as with Somlo the sovereign does not create the valid norm, but rather the valid norm the sovereign, it is also the case that the logical sentence does not determine validity independent of acting subjects, but only as a result of their actions. It is not strictly necessary that human beings exist in the context of such forms of cooperation – as Hobbes illustrates, it is perfectly possible to imagine a state of human existence in which no such forms are present. However, where such forms *are* present, they will entail relations between subjects and these relations will be the *material* of the law.

But how do legal norms really exist in a world of material objects? One possible response is to say that they don't actually exist, that they are just a façade for the exercise of power – Kelsen comes close to this concession in § 16 of the

---

[2] See Stekeler, *Hegels Phänomenologie des Geistes* (Vol. II), pp. 22: "Hegels *Phänomenologie des Geistes* erweist sich gerade im Geistkapitel als sinnkritische Analyse üblicher Reflexionen auf uns selbst und unsere geistigen bzw. personalen Fähigkeiten. Das sind solche Fähigkeiten, die es den Einzelnen erlauben, in Praxisformen und Institutionen die erforderlichen Rollen richtig zu spielen. Die Richtigkeit der Aktualisierungen von Anforderungen im Rollenspiel definiert die Normativität des Personenseins in allen seinen Dimensionen."

Reine Rechtslehre (quoted above) before then succumbing to the preservation of the law for the sake of tradition.[3] A second answer is to say that the law does not have any existence apart from the material world, but that a legal norm is merely the (psychological) expression of a more or less arbitrary will of a sovereign (i. e. an expressivist conception of legal norms) or that the discourse regarding legal norms, for example in the case of adjudication, reflects simply a psychological or sociological need for acting as if laws exist, even though such norms themselves might ultimately have very little explanatory power. According to such a position, the law does not have an existence apart from the phenomena of the material world, but rather can be reduced to a set of communications, directives or prescriptions. However, to allow that the law consists of communications from a sovereign to a subject, or as a justification for a decision vis-à-vis third parties in the case of adjudication, is already to presuppose something distinct from the materiality of the sovereign and the subject as human beings. Given such a presupposition, the law becomes a volitional expression through the medium of language on the part of one agent to another who is presumed to understand what is communicated. While this may state the obvious, it is not trivial. Logic does not apply to the material world in itself, but rather to statements which we make about the material world at whatever iterative level such a statement might occur. In other words, logic does not apply to the world, it applies to us.

Facts are in the world. The social world includes all of our descriptions and discourse regarding everything in the world. However, the *social* world does not consist of facts so much as *matters* of fact. Sally punching John is a mere fact that is in itself irrelevant and incomprehensible for our understanding. Only once there is a context to such a fact does it become interesting and suitable for our understanding: as a matter of fact, Sally was trying to steal the ice cream from her little brother, John, when she punched him, and therefore was acting like a bully; or, as a matter of fact, Sally was trying to repel the physical assault of her partner, John, when she punched him, and therefore was acting completely within her rights. The context clearly makes all the normative difference.

What about the matter of fact in the law itself? Some jurisdictions might have it such that there is a legal fact that whatever the absolute dictator declares to be the law will, as a matter of law, indeed be the law. A lawyer of that jurisdiction, looking at the letter of the law, might agree that this should be the case given what has been formally instituted as the law in that jurisdiction. But is that which

[3] Kelsen, Reine Rechtslehre, § 16, p. 37: "Die Möglichkeit und Erforderlichkeit einer solchen Theorie ist schon durch das jahrtausendalte Faktum der Rechtswissenschaft erwiesen, die – solange es ein Recht gibt – als dogmatische Jurisprudenz den intellektuellen Bedürfnissen der mit dem Recht Befassten dient. Es liegt kein Grund vor, diese durchaus legitimen Bedürfnisse unbefriedigt zu lassen und auf solche Rechtswissenschaft zu verzichten."

the law says then really the case or does the dictator protest too much? Congress passed the Fugitive Slave Act in 1850 requiring slaves who had escaped to the North to be returned to their owners in the South. However, compliance with the act was limited in fact. The passage of the 14th Amendment requiring that States treat former slaves and their descendants equally under the law was a direct result of the Union's victory in the Civil War. However, this did not become a real part of American institutional reality until well over a half century later beginning in 1954 with *Brown v. Board*. Facts only count within a context of other facts and a normative framework within which such facts become comprehensible for our understanding. Legal norms, too, only count within a context of facts and a normative framework which is always already in existence. This is the actual logic of norms.

1. Naturalism and Realism

"…the common lawyer resists attempts at systematization and prefers to proceed empirically, case by case."[4]

In an illuminating study of the cultural and historical background of American and Scandinavian Legal Realism, Heikki Pihlajamäki suggests that the Anglo-American and Scandinavian legal systems can best be understood in contrast with Continental Europe, where, beginning in the Middle Ages, first in Italy, then in France, the Netherlands and then Germany, law developed much more strongly as a profession, and therewith also as a science.[5] Whereas educated jurists began to steer Continental legal thought by the Early Modern period, the development of law in England and Scandinavia at this time was dominated by the adjudication of everyday cases by laymen, with lawyers receiving primarily practical, trade based training well into the 19th century.[6] Once attempts to formalize and systematize the legal system reached the United States with the advent of law schools predominantly in the second half of the 19th century, there

---

[4] Legrand (1997), as found in Pihlajamäki (2004).

[5] See Pihlajamäki, "Against Metaphysics in Law: The Historical Background of American and Scandinavian Legal Realism Compared" (2004). For example, p. 480: "Cases go before theories, not vice versa. The good old common lawyer solves practical problems, and in solving them proceeds step by step, not within grandiose theoretical frameworks, just like the common law itself."

[6] For a less historical, but more systematic comparison between American and Scandinavian Legal Realism, see Brian Bix, "The American and Scandinavian Legal Realists on the Nature of Norms".

was ample material in the body of relevant cases to make any one assertion of absolute rights or duties in a given case appear as a fool's errand.[7]

In the American legal system, in any case, it all kind of depends. The existence of a right or duty in any given instance is not absolute, but relative. Whether a person may have a claim (or a liability) will often not hinge on an abstract rule as much as on the facts which constitute the case, including such issues as which State has jurisdiction, which law will be applied, whether the trial will be decided by jury or judge and, if it is to be decided by a judge, it is even relevant to know by which particular judge it will be decided. All of this is to say that in American law, and presumably also in English and Scandinavian law, the facts matter. Then again, it is not as if facts do not matter in French or German law. Also, the notion that, for example in France, a case would hinge on an abstract rule, seems to be too superficial. The outcome of a case, regardless of legal system, must actually always depend on the facts of the case. Only once these facts have been packaged in a certain way, sorted into facts that are in some way relevant and facts that are rather extraneous, can a case, through a process of subsumption, be said to be under or subject to a certain rule. This is the same both within the civil and common law systems.

Legal Realism may have developed so strongly in the United States and Scandinavia (principally Sweden and Denmark) as a result of the fact that these countries were very much on the vanguard of social and political science at the beginning of the 20th century, although the similarly oriented *Freirechtsschule*[8] in Germany slightly ahead of the heyday of American and Scandinavian Legal Realism is a testament to the fact that social science was certainly not evolving

---

[7] The fact that the *Sachsenspiegel* (1235), a codification of existing medieval Germanic law, was produced more than five centuries prior to Blackstone's *Commentaries*, illustrates the starkness of the temporal shift at play.

[8] A summary of the position of the Freirechtsschule can be found with Kantorowicz, "Some Rationalism about Realism", p. 1241: "The free law doctrine teaches (if we may sum up an elaborate system in a few words): The traditional sources of the law, the 'formal' law, statutes and precedents, have gaps which must be filled up, must be filled up with law if the decision is to be a judicial decision, and this law must have a general character if equality before the law is to be maintained; the gap-filling material must therefore consist of rules, rules of law. These are 'free' law in the sense that they are not formal law: they have not been formalized but are still in a state of transition like bills, principles of policy, business customs, inarticulate convictions, emotional preferences. Many of them are formulated for the purpose of a concrete judicial decision by the courts, acting within their discretion, through acts of will and value-judgments, and constitute therefore judge-made law. Their validity is far less than that of the formal law and sometimes nil, but their practical importance is even greater, because, where the formal law is clear and complete, litigation is not likely to occur. This free law thesis has been exaggerated by those realists who teach that law consists of judicial decisions alone, and therefore of facts."

solely in America and the Nordics. It could also be the case that the anti-metaphysical stance attributed to American and Scandinavian legal thought is a result of the formative periods of the respective legal cultures occuring during a thoroughly modern moment in the development of Western thought. This can be taken as merely a reflection of a specific cultural context or it can be understood as a harbinger of the potential of legal thought freed from the limitations of ideological constructs which may have become anachronistic. Be that as it may, it seems worth investigating the theoretical commitments of American Legal Realism within the common law system in order to understand what this particular approach to the law can show us regarding the reality of law more generally.[9]

Such a project is at the heart of Brian Leiter's interpretation of American Legal Realism as a proto-naturalist movement. For Leiter, naturalism is characterized by a turn away from apriori methods and toward empirical theories for the resolution of philosophical problems,[10] it is primarily "a methodological view to the effect that philosophical theorizing should be continuous with empirical inquiry in the sciences."[11] Leiter does not necessarily subscribe to "Substantive Naturalism", which he understands to be the view that the only things that exist are natural or physical things.[12] Namely, Leiter allows that reasons, legal, moral and / or political, might very well provide adequate causal explanations for certain phenomena, especially in the case of legal norms and the "internal point of view" acting as "ineliminable features of the causal structure of the social world".[13] However, Leiter holds that when it comes to addressing what the Legal Realists were concerned about, i. e. understanding why judges adjudicate as they do, the psycho-social facts about the judges themselves might have a higher explanatory capacity with respect to a certain holding than whatever reasons, in the form of precedents, statutes or otherwise, a judge may cite as controlling his decision.[14]

Leiter attributes this 'methodological naturalism' to the (American) Legal Realists as a result of what he calls Legal Realism's "Core Claim": "in deciding cases, judges respond primarily to the stimulus of the facts."[15] This seems to be

---

[9] Not only is common law practice marked by a lack of formalization, the conceptualization of the system itself, notwithstanding the legacy of H.L.A. Hart, is characterized by a certain lack of systematization. See Roscoe Pound, *The Spirit of the Common Law*.

[10] Leiter. *Naturalizing Jurisprudence*, p. 31.

[11] Id. at p. 34.

[12] Id. at p. 35.

[13] Id. at p. 4.

[14] For example, p. 57: "Surely, for example, the astonishing rigidity of Justice Scalia's constitutional jurisprudence, especially his fear of "unconstrained" judgment; or Justice Thomas's almost pathological incapacity for – or unwillingness to engage – empathetic feelings, both cry out for psychoanalytic explanations."

[15] Id. at p. 16.

an adequate description of the movement, as loosely organized as it was.[16] Moreover, Leiter's naturalism as a methodology of jurisprudence which seeks to be continuous with the natural *and social sciences*[17] does not appear objectionable in and of itself. However, while a naturalized jurisprudence must allow for the possibility that legal or even moral reasons could provide an explanation for the phenomenon of adjudication, Leiter nonetheless suggests that judicial reference to legal reasons / legal normativity is merely lip service to a perceived obligation on the part of judges to justify their decisions in such a way. In reality, Leiter claims, judicial outcomes can be far better explained by using an empirical model that takes account of judges' respective ideological attitudes plus the facts of the case (the Attitudinal Model) as opposed to merely taking account of the relevant legal sources in a given case (the Legal Model).[18]

Leiter's primary concern in developing a naturalistic jurisprudence lies in developing a descriptive account of adjudication that will provide the information that "works for lawyers", i.e. information regarding how judges actually decide,

---

16 For an extended contemporary analysis of the various wings and centers of the movement, see Llewellyn's 1931 Harvard Law Review article, "Some Realism about Realism", reprinted in *Jurisprudence: Realism in Theory and Practice*. There in the third sentence Llewellyn states: "Before rules were facts; in the beginning was not a Word, but a Doing." Llewellyn's phrasing clearly mirrors Goethe's, in which Faust declares: *am Anfang war die Tat!*

17 Leiter, Naturalizing Jurisprudence, for example at p. 184: "Philosophers, on this approach, are the abstract and reflective branch of empirical science, clarifying the contours and extensions of concepts that have been vindicated by their role in successful explanation and prediction of empirical phenomena. For a naturalized jurisprudence, this same approach would mean taking seriously the enormous social scientific literature on law and legal institutions to see what concept of law figures in the most powerful explanatory and predictive models of legal phenomena such as judicial behavior."

18 Id. at p. 191: "The Attitudinal Model certainly does not understand judges to be lemmings, but rather, political actors advancing an ideological agenda: they do the same thing, to the extent they do, because they share ideological aims. Moreover, they almost all share one behavior in common: namely, the *concealment* of their ideological aims behind rhetoric which involves purporting to take the normativity of law seriously: judges, of all ideological persuasions, claim that they do what they do because they have legal obligations to reach these decisions, not because they feel an obligation to implement their ideology. A complete causal story of judicial behavior would have to explain this striking fact about the practice as well." See Kantorowicz, "Some Rationalism about Realism", p. 1241 for an example of how at least one prominent German Realist would dispute the extent to which Leiter wishes to lean on the empirical sciences: "The sociological school of law teaches that the law must be interpreted according to its aims, that these aims are to be found in its (desirable) effects on social (including economic) life, and that therefore the law cannot be understood nor applied without the aid of a sociological (including economic) study of social reality. This sociological thesis has been exaggerated by those realists who teach that legal science is itself a sociological, and therefore an empirical science."

and will decide, cases.[19] This pragmatic approach was also an aspect of the Realist program. However, it seems that at least the *American* Legal Realists also transcended this pragmatist / empirical motivation in a very important way.

To see the way in which this is the case, let us continue for another moment with Leiter, who, leaning on Quine, insists that the merits of a science are determined by its results. Our physical understanding of the world is justified if we generally manage to keep airplanes in the air[20] and our jurisprudential understanding of adjudication is justified if we are regularly able to predict the outcomes of court cases. In endorsing Quine's approach to epistemological justification, Leiter states:

> The reason all inquiry proceeds from within science is that science works: it 'delivers the goods' one might say. Science, for Quine, is simply on a continuum with common sense, which like science aims to predict the future course of experience in order to facilitate our coping with the world… For creatures like us, it is a pragmatic necessity to figure out what will come next.[21]

It is not clear that the objective of a theory of adjudication is to predict judicial outcomes, any more than the objective of physics is to keep airplanes in the air. Certainly, if the existence of airplanes would contradict the current laws of physics, then there would be reason to revise the laws of physics rather than the existence of airplanes. Likewise, if decisions in the courts regularly contradicted a theory of adjudication, then there would equally be a reason for revising the theory, assuming, in any case, that such decisions were the result of adjudication and not, for example, of corruption. Indeed, this is part of what the American Legal Realism movement sought to accomplish. However, the objective of the Realists was to introduce a theory, not with which lawyers could better predict outcomes[22], but rather by which lawyers (and everyone else) could better under-

---

[19] Id. at p. 52: "…it is a criterion of acceptability for a theory of adjudication for the Realists that it work for lawyers. Work for lawyers, for the Realists, means that it enables them to predict what the courts will do." Compare here Quine in "Two Dogmas of Empiricism", pp. 44, 45: "The myth of physical objects is epistemilogically superior to most in that it has proved more efficacious than other myths as a device for working a manageable structure into the flux of experience." And then: "Epistemologically these (i.e. abstract objects) are myths on the same footing with physical objects and gods, neither better nor worse except for differences in the degree to which they expedite our dealings with sense experiences."

[20] See Leiter, "Normativity for Naturalists", p. 7: "That airplanes work is not an epistemic warrant, but that airplanes work gives us the pragmatic explanation why creatures like usare disposed to treat the epistemology that underlies aerospace engineering as the benchmark of the true and the knowable."

[21] Id. at pp. 147, 148.

[22] As Llewellyn points out in *The Common Law Tradition*, lawyers generally do a very good job of predicting outcomes even without espousing legal theories, which stands in contrast to the rather limited results which the empirically based Attitudinal Model produces.

stand what was happening when judges adjudicate cases. The point of the science of law, as with the science of physics, is to understand the general phenomena, not to engineer specific outcomes.[23]

As such, the approach of American Legal Realism was not so much an early form of Leiter's methodological naturalism understood as a practical enterprise in predicting judicial outcomes as it was an approach that, first and foremost, stood in opposition to the perceived formalism of Langdell that was understood to place legal doctrine above the actual development of the law.[24] While the core claim of American Legal Realism that judges respond primarily to facts is certainly relevant as a theory of adjudication, and despite the trappings of the American Legal Realists' works that suggest a thoroughly practical objective,[25] the American Legal Realists, or at least one of its most central figures, Karl Llewellyn, were actually trying to describe something essential to the phenomenon of law, at least in the United States, on the basis of how the judicial system, and especial-

[23] See Kantorowicz, *supra*, p. 1250: "If, as Mr. Justice Holmes says and all the realists repeat (as if they wished to advertise the one theory of the great judge and jurist which one would prefer not to find in his work), the law is what courts of law do, one could also say: religion is what the churches preach; science is what the universities teach; medicine is what the doctor prescribes; art is what the artist produces; and shoes are what the shoemaker makes. All this is placing the cart before the horse. One cannot define church without religion, university without science, doctor without medicine, artist without art, shoemaker without shoe, and courts of law without law. The law is not what the courts administer but the courts are the institutions which administer the law. For this reason alone can it be foretold what the courts will do. In so far as the lawyer knows the law, and in so far as the judge will follow the law, the lawyer will be able to foretell what the judge will do."

[24] That Langdell is Llewellyn's bogeyman for legal formalism, or *Begriffsjurisprudenz* in the German speaking world, is itself very interesting given the importance that Langdell placed on the case method which necessarily entails a close study of the factual contexts of cases. A likely explanation for the perceived need of a renewal on the part of the American realists could be that Langdell's attempt to systematize the law (for example in the field of contracts), though required in the context of teaching law as a science, necessarily resulted in a loss of nuance that, if a fresh graduate would have attempted to practice solely on the basis of the doctrinal rules put forth by Langdell, would have resulted in a lack of relevant knowledge. Of course, both Langdell and the realists are right: doctrine is surely important, but only as a springboard for properly delving into the cases. See here Llewellyn's statement in *The Bramble Bush*, p. 12: "We have discovered in our teaching of the law that general propositions are empty. We have discovered that students who come eager to learn the rules and who do learn them, and who learn nothing more, will take away the shell and not the substance. We have discovered that rules alone, mere forms of words, are worthless. We have learned that the concrete instance, the heaping up of concrete instances, the present, vital memory of a multitude of concrete instances, is necessary in order to make any general proposition, be it rule of law or any other, mean anything at all."

[25] For example, Llewellyn's main late work is entitled: The Common Law Tradition, *Deciding* Appeals (emphasis added).

ly the appellate system, actually works. I contend that it was, and really still is, a most serious and sophisticated form of legal theory.[26]

"In a comparison of abstract legal systems the common law is at its worst."[27] This statement by Roscoe Pound at the beginning of *The Spirit of the Common Law* is of significant moment: the norms of the common law are based neither on the precepts of a divine law nor on the principles of the enlightenment nor on a rationalistic system composed by experts of the law. Instead of these, the foundation of the common law is mere coincidence – the hodgepodge of cases that happen to have been brought, and to have made it through to judgment, most often through to appellate adjudication, as a result of a variety of factors, such as the occurrence of fluke accidents, the financial wherewithal of the litigating parties, or a pre-existing presence of enmity between such parties, that really have nothing to do with the high idea of law as such. It is therefore not entirely surprising that Pound, a proto-Realist, gives the impression of being self-conscious regarding the lack of a viable theoretical justification for the American legal system. Moreover, Leiter is correct that the proper Realists such as Llewellyn were not necessarily sophisticated philosophers with a fully developed conceptual apparatus for describing the material with which they worked. Leiter is of the view that the American Legal Realists implicitly espoused the theory of law of hard positivism[28], according to which the criteria of legal validity set out by any society's Rule of Recognition must consist in social facts regarding pedigree or sources.[29] According to this position, the Realists espoused the idea that in some cases there would be an enumerated set of laws which were valid on the basis of their pedigree, e. g. as a result of duly passed legislation or binding precedent, but that such laws would be indeterminate regarding the outcome of the case – in arriving at a holding, a judge in such a case would turn to extra-legal sources, for example morality or policy considerations.[30] However, some of Llewellyn's chief writings give the impression that the Realist theory of adjudication did not

[26] Leiter has argued that Legal Realism is precisely not a theory of law, but rather a theory of adjudication, see "Positivism, Formalism, Realism", in: 99 Colum. L. Rev. 1138.

[27] Pound, *The Spirit of the Common Law*, p. 3.

[28] See Leiter, *Naturalizing Jurisprudence*, p. 67.

[29] Id. at pp. 123.

[30] Id. at pp. 72, 73: "What concept of law is being presupposed here in these arguments for legal indeterminacy, a concept in which statutes and precedent are part of the law, but uncodified norms and policy arguments are not? It is certainly not Ronald Dworkin's theory, let alone any more robust natural law alternative. Rather, the Realists are presupposing something like the positivist idea of a Rule of Recognition whose criteria of legality are exclusively ones of pedigree: a rule (or canon of construction) is part of the law in virtue of having a source in a legislative enactment or a prior court decision. The Realists, in short, cannot be Conceptual Rule Skeptics, because their arguments for the indeterminacy of law presuppose a non-skepti-

actually piggy-back off of a hard positivist theory of law, as Leiter contends, but rather that the theory of adjudication that the Realists, or at least Llewellyn, advocated, actually, and despite Llewellyn's own contestation to the contrary[31], contained its own original theory of law expressed *by means of a theory of adjudication*: if we look at how judges, especially appellate judges, actually decide cases, we learn something not just about how adjudication works in the American legal system, but about how American law itself is structured. This insight into the structure of American law, in turn, can be broadened into a picture into the way that law works in general, i. e. a general theory of law.[32]

That Leiter sees this picture differently, i. e. that Leiter sees American Legal Realism as merely a theory of adjudication and not also as a theory of law, I would contest, rests on a misunderstanding regarding the mode in which legal norms, and norms generally, exist. Leiter gives the impression that judges, in deciding within the mold of the American Legal Realists, would actually disregard the law in arriving at their decisions. In attributing a tacit hard positivist stance to the realist movement, Leiter pretends that such judges would have an enumerated set of legal norms at their disposal in any given case and that they would then, in some of these cases, disregard or go beyond the ambit of such norms. In such a view, judges would treat legal norms like letters in a game of Scrabble, as fixed entities to be used mechanically, without reflection. In easy cases, for example in writing the word 'S E T', a judge could simply choose an available 'S', 'E', and 'T' in order to arrive at the required word. In hard cases, though, for example in creating the word 'X Y L O P H O N E' where neither 'Xs' or 'Ys' are left, a realist judge might have to plunder another Scrabble set or simply write down the respective letters on a piece of paper. However, this was not the gist of the realist argument.

The realist claim is not that judges must turn to extra-legal sources in hard cases, but rather that the concrete sentences that are meant to express legal norms, whether found in the Constitution, in statutes or in the holdings of binding precedent, the kind of sentences that are written in hornbooks and that were deemed

---

cal account of the criteria of legality, one that has the most obvious affinities with that developed by Hard or Exclusive Positivists."

[31] See Llewellyn, *The Common Law Tradition*, p. 509–510: "Realism was never a philosophy, nor did any group of realists as such ever attempt to present any rounded view, or whole approach."

[32] For a concurring view, see Kantorowicz' "Some Rationalism about Realism", p. 1240: The Realists "agree on two fundamental postulates, one, a substantive postulate regarding the nature of the law, the other, a formal postulate regarding the nature of legal science […]. The substantive theory is that the law is not a body of rules but of facts; the formal theory, that legal science is not a rational but an empirical science. I do not assert that these theories are simply untrue; I shall try t show that they are exaggerations of the truth."

to be favored by the formalists, that these formulations will often be inadequate in hard cases. Such formulations will fail to properly express the underlying norm in question. For this reason, it was Realists including Llewellyn who put significant effort into the project of the Uniform Commercial Code precisely in an effort to find better, clearer and more suitable formulations of the existing case law than what had existed previously. It was Llewellyn who conducted an extensive study on the law of the Cheyenne tribe, a law which was *unwritten* and *informal* but which is nonetheless considered by Llewellyn to be a form of law.[33] It was also Llewellyn who praises the "Grand Style" of American jurisprudential writing in the 19th century as a style of writing that allows for significant development of the law through an explication of reasons that is especially prone to building consensus within the legal community.[34] What becomes clear in reading Llewellyn's texts is that Llewellyn, but other realists as well, see the actions of American judges, as they exist in practice, to be relevant not just for the adjudication of laws within the United States, but rather for the system of law itself. Within the common law tradition, at least within the United States, the law develops through the judges and this is not an abberation or a systemic flaw, but rather part of the essential economy of the system itself.

2. 'Hard Facts make Bad Law'

To further understand the systematic relevance of this approach to adjudication for the theory of law, it makes sense to dwell on the nature of the relationship between facts and law. Leiter's plea for methodological naturalism in the analysis of judicial activity is based on two observations: i) that what is relevant for our understanding of American jurisprudence is that which actually happens on

---

[33] See Llewellyn, *The Cheyenne Way*, University of Oklahoma Press, 1967.

[34] See *The Common Law Tradition*, p. 46: "The type-thinking of the time is to view precedents as welcome and very persuasive, but it is to test a precedent almost always against three types of reason before it is accepted. The reputation of the opinion-writing judge counts heavily (and it is right reason to listen carefully to the wise). Secondly, 'principle' is consulted to check up on precedent, and at this period and in this way of work 'principle' means no mere verbal tool for bringing large-scale order into the rules, it means a broad generalization which must yield patent sense as well as order, if it is to be 'principle'. Finally, 'policy', in terms of prospective consequences of the rule under consideration, comes in for explicit examination by reason in a further test of both the rule in question and its application. The tone and mark consist in an as-of-courseness in the constant questing for better and best law to guide the future, but the better and best law is to be built on and out of what the past can offer; the quest consists in a constant re-examination and reworking of a heritage, that the heritage may yield not only solidity but comfort for the new day and for the morrow."

the ground; and ii) that the insight of American Legal Realism is that judges actually decide cases based on the stimulus of the facts. However, the facts that are actually decisive for judges are not just any facts, but very particularly relevant facts. These are the facts that determine a particular situation or a form of practice. It is the situation-fact[35] or, in German, *Sachverhalt*, that counts.

Hard facts are said to make bad law because, from the formalist perspective, it is the hard facts, i. e. those which do not fit a textbook fact pattern or which perhaps present a perceived moral conundrum in the face of a clearly applicable rule, that may result in a holding which pushes legal precedent away from a bright line rule towards a grey zone in which it is not clear whether certain behavior is actionable or not. However, the insight of the American Legal Realists and all who over time have been critical of strict formalist positions is that the law is not a static device to be applied with mechanical precision.[36] It is precisely the hard cases which turn the law away from a dry exercise in accounting toward an interpretation of the status quo of the law through focusing a lens on social life.

Llewellyn, quoting the German commercial law theorist, Levin Goldschmidt, records the situation in the following way:

> Every fact-pattern of common life, so far as the legal order can take it in, carries within itself its appropriate, natural rules, its right law. This is a natural law which is real, not imaginary; it is not a creature of mere reason, but rests on the solid foundation of what reason can recognize in the nature of man and of the life conditions of the time and place; it is thus not eternal nor changeless nor everywhere the same, but is indwelling in the very circumstances of life. The highest task of law-giving consists in uncovering and implementing this immanent law.[37]

Holmes' *The Common Law* consists entirely of an account of how the forms and doctrines of private law have developed over time reflecting the historical developments of legal agents' beliefs and practices. His theory of the Common Law which he therein expounds can be summarized in the following:

> The customs, beliefs, or needs of a primitive time establish a rule or a formula. In the course of centuries the custom, belief, or necessity disappears, but the rule remains. The reason which gave rise to the rule has been forgotten, and ingenious minds have set themselves to inquire how it is to be accounted for. Some ground of policy is thought of, which seems to explain it and to reconcile it with the present state of things; and then the rule adapts itself to the new

---

[35] Llewellyn, *The Common Law Tradition*, pp. 113 ff.

[36] See *The Common Law Tradition*, p. 70: "Now the truth is this: only in times of stagnation or decay does an appellate system even faintly resemble such a picture of detailed dictation by the precedents, and even in times of stagnation and deliberated determination to plant feet flat 'upon the ancient ways' movement and change still creep up on the blind side of the stagnators."

[37] Id. at pp. 115, 116, quoting Levin Goldschmidt, *Kritik des Entwurfs eines Handelsgesetzbuchs*.

reasons which have been found for it, and enters on a new career. The old form receives a new content, and in time even the form modifies itself to fit the meaning which it has received.[38]

Holmes describes the legal norm as it develops out of social fact (i.e. the customs[39], beliefs or needs of a time). The legal norm becomes solidified through practice or codification and takes on a life of its own, creating thereby new social fact. It serves as an anchor around which institutions evolve until its existence becomes questioned, at which point the rule itself evolves and takes on a new meaning. The source of the evolution is social fact as interpreted in light of the rule, and the rule as interpreted in light of social fact. This view is essentially one with Llewellyn's view as set forth in *The Common Law Tradition* that the judicial development, or "fashioning" of law is the result of the correct evaluation of the correct understanding of the "facts of life".[40] The formulation of judicial opinions and remedies based on "the present state of things" and the "facts of life" does not consist in a recourse to extra-legal sources for Holmes and Llewellyn, but is rather precisely the stuff of law.

Leiter cuts the cake differently by maintaining, in line with a version of 'hard' positivism, that the scope of legal norms available in difficult cases is necessarily limited, indeed too limited to adequately explain the holdings that are actually made. This allows Leiter to argue for his preferred method of analyzing judicial practice through the lens of empirical science. From the external perspective, law, including judicial practice, consists of social fact and, as such, is certainly amenable to study by the social sciences. However, what counts for law itself is not the sociological (or psychological) external perspective, but rather the jurisprudential internal perspective.[41] Here, the insight of the anti-formalists like Holmes and then the realists like Llewellyn was that also this internal, jurisprudential inquiry depends not just on analysing forms, or norms, but also on analysing social facts, not because the best way to be a lawyer is by being a sociologist, but because the best way to be a lawyer is to take account of the full universe of applicable norms, both in the law books and in social life, and, importantly, as the law books express this social life through a detailed analysis and explanation of the cases.

---

[38] *The Common Law*, p. 5.

[39] Of course, such social facts, including also beliefs and needs, for their part arise out of yet other norms, which, we can assume, arise from still other normatively factual contexts. Here, there is no bottom to the well, nor need there be. Holmes goes back 3000–4000 years and yet, even then, there is no beginning in sight. This merely serves to solidify the impression of interwovenness of norm and fact.

[40] See Llewellyn, *The Common Law Tradition*, p. 119: "Only as a judge or court knows the facts of life, only as they truly understand those facts of life, only as they have it in them to rightly evaluate those facts and to fashion rightly a sound rule and an apt remedy, can they lift the burden Goldschmidt lays upon them: to uncover and to implement the immanent law."

[41] Compare, for example, Hart's Postscript to The Concept of Law, p. 242 ff.

It is the formalists' and, therewith implicitly[42], the hard positivists' perspective which is expressed in the dictum that hard facts make bad law. It is typically thought that, if, in response to a strange fact pattern, an 'activist' judge strays from the letter of the law in order to accommodate a sympathetic plaintiff or his own moral sentiments, then such a judge would be doing a disservice to the legal system, would be making 'bad law' because such thereby newly established precedents would be in accord neither with previous precedent (from the formalist perspective) nor with the chain of command from the sovereign (from the positivist perspective). Such a judge would be both shoddy in his practice (because he fails to abide by the appropriate rule) and acting ultra-vires (making himself the sovereign with respect to that case).

What is missing from this analysis is the following: once the factual record has been established, it is the judge's primary duty to decide what the case, i. e. what the fact pattern or matter of fact, actually is. A court might be presented with the strangest of facts. But if none of these strange facts are pertinent for settling the petitioner's claim, if in reality the case is rather clear cut, then such strange facts will turn out not to be 'hard' facts at all and the judge will be able to reach the decision without referring to new law. On the other hand, a case might present facts that are completely normal prima facie, but which, thanks to a discerning counsel or judge, present a question which is of first impression. The relevant

[42] Cf. Sebok, *Legal Positivism in American Jurisprudence*, Cambridge Univ. Press 1998 and contrast Leiter's strong disagreement with the notion that formalism entails (hard) positivism in "Positivism, Formalism, Realism" as cited above: "What bears emphasizing, though, is that the two central commitments of positivism-to the Social Thesis and the Separability Thesis entail no theoretically substantial claims about the nature of adjudication. A formalist about adjudication might be a positivist, but he could just as well be a natural lawyer. A positivist about the nature of law might think Realism gives the correct description of appellate adjudication. The two doctrines-positivism and formalism-exist in separate conceptual universes." (99 Columbia Law Review 1138, 1150). Contrary to Leiter's assertion, the reality is that positivism in the Austinian form entails that the law issues from the sovereign. As a result, judges, if they are to speak in accordance with the law (univocal with the sovereign) would need to be formalists in practice. This situation remains essentially the same even with the construct of the Rule of Recognition, which, via the veneer of social fact, accounts for why the law possesses the forms that it does, forms that might include such aspects as officials (including judges) adjudicating cases based on statutory texts or binding precedent. Leiter is correct that one can, at least hypothetically, posit a Rule of Recognition which does not tie (all of) its officials to such forms and instead, as Leiter suggests, allows for the possibility of the Rule of Recognition to recognize that judges have discretion in deciding cases contrary to or beyond what a statute or precedent would dictate: "Notice, to start, that it is compatible with the Rule of Recognition being a social rule that, say, appellate judges always exercise discretion in deciding cases (and thus fail to realize the formalist ideal)" (id. at p. 1152). However, such a rule of recognition, devoid of certain hierarchical aspects, which essentially states that the law is "whatever the judge says is the law" becomes so hollow that Hart's model would be hardly of use.

distinction is not between 'easy' facts that would create good law and 'hard' facts that would create bad law, but rather between well established fact patterns that require nothing more than precision in applying the established rule and novel fact patterns which require a new or alternative formulation of existing rules. Of the novel fact patterns, some are surely so idiosyncratic that any resulting right decision will hardly ever practically function as legal precedent. Such a decision might be considered 'bad' law to the extent that the rule which is used to establish the holding is so outside of the mainstream doctrine as to no longer form a coherent picture within the given area of law. On the other hand, if the facts in such a case are really so strange, then the precedential effect is likely to be equally low. Some novel fact patterns, though, are novel not because they are idiosyncratic, but simply because they are new. In such a case, the art of adjudication entails again the use of a rule that is outside of the mainstream doctrine. However, whereas with an idiosyncratic set of facts the resulting heterodox rule is largely irrelevant for the general body of precedent, a novel rule that arises out of a new kind of fact pattern is especially relevant for the legal system as it constitutes a reference on the path of law going forward in accordance with a reflexion on the path of social life. As a result of such reflexion, it is precisely the hard facts which can, at times, make excellent, new law.[43]

3. The Critique of Pure, not Practical, Reason

In "Normativity for Naturalists", Leiter develops in greater depth his approach to analyzing normative discourse through the lens of the empirical sciences.[44] For Leiter, "normativity is simply an artifact of the psychological properties of certain biological organisms, i. e., what they feel or believe or desire (or are disposed to feel, believe, or desire)."[45] To use Leiter's example, the naturalist does not think that Oedipus gouged out his eyes for the wrongful things he had done, but rather that Oedipus gouged out his eyes because he *felt* that the things he had done were wrongful. As such, the naturalist does not seek to understand the rea-

[43] For examples, one could refer to any number of cases that are standardly presented in case books, whether in Tort, Contract, Property or even Constitutional Law. One could also refer to Llewellyn's studies set forth in *The Common Law Tradition*. Indeed, the implied normativity of social fact as it exists inchoately is nearly, or at least has traditionally been, omnipresent in the education and practice of American law.

[44] Leiter, "Normativity for Naturalists" (University of Chicago Public Law & Legal Theory Working Paper no. 527, 2015), p. 1: "By 'naturalists' I mean philosophers who think that what there is and what we know are questions reliably answered by the methods of the empirical sciences..."

[45] Id. at p. 3.

sons for human actions, but rather the causes. Finding adequate causal explanations in subjects' feelings, beliefs, desires and dispositions to so feel, believe and desire, the naturalist, or at least Leiter, would suggest that the 'reasons' that are attributed to actions by non-naturalists are merely superimpositions upon basic psychological states. For example, I provide the goods that I agreed to provide in the contract because I do not desire to pay damages in case of non-performance or because I believe that doing so will be in my long-term financial interest. I might also provide the goods because I *feel* or *believe* that it is the right thing to do. However, on closer inspection, the naturalist claims, I will find that my feeling or belief that this is the right thing to do or that I have an obligation to act in this way will boil down to my own simple feeling or belief, without any objective reference for the propositional content "that it is the right thing to do" or "that I have an obligation".[46]

If the causal explanation for supposedly normative behavior lies in the individual, subjective psychological states of agents, one might wonder how it could be the case that often entire communities or even societies share the same sentiments with regard to a particular course of action or normative proposition. Here, Leiter points to the regularity of our theoretical beliefs, for example with respect to our knowledge of medicine or the physical world.[47] The fact that many of us believe that antibiotics can cure infection is not the result of us following a norm which dictates such a belief but rather that many of us share a common experience in which infected people are regularly cured by antibiotics. Instead of positing normativity, it suffices, at a certain level of explanation, to simply state that our sentiments are shaped by our experiences and, to the extent that we experience things in common with others, it should not be surprising that these common experiences lead to common beliefs and normative attitudes (i. e. what we *feel* to be right or wrong).

Leiter is of the view that such convergence of sentiment does not obtain nearly as well within the area of ethics or practical rationality. Whereas the scientist

[46] Id. See, for example p. 17: "There are no reasons whose existence and character is independent of human attitudes; there are only human attitudes which lead us to 'talk the talk' of reasons. And if real normativity does not exist, if only feelings of inclination and aversion, compulsion and avoidance, actually exist, then that means that all purportedly normative disputes bottom out not in reasons but in the clash of will or affect."

[47] See id. at p. 19: "If epistemology proper, the systematic account of what one 'ought' to believe, gives the appearance of a more robust discipline it is only because its primary data points–namely, the claims of the successful empirical sciences–are clearer and more widely accepted, precisely because of their resonance with our practical interests." Then further: "Let us call a 'Global Humean' about epistemic values someone who notices that creatures like us generally converge in our epistemic attitudes because the norms those attitudes endorse do so well at meeting widely shared human needs and interests, such as predicting the future course of experience [...]"

has a clear roadmap for determining (and agreeing) on beliefs in the theoretical realm based on epistemic norms such as "treat normal perceptual experience as prima facie veridical, honor logical inferences, and employ the inductive method in empirical inquiry",[48] norms that assist in the "successful navigation of the world and prediction of the future course of experience", Leiter's non-convergent view with regard to beliefs in the practical realm, which he attributes to his reading of Nietzsche's interpretation of the Sophists, seems to rest on the view that practices, customs and morals, vary significantly across place and time. Contrary to Leiter, and as an aside, I would maintain that there does actually seem to be some room for norms in the realm of the ethical similar to those that Leiter cites in the realm of the epistemic, e. g. love thy neighbor, or do unto others as …, or do not steal or do not kill, norms which, even though they cannot be 'proven' to be correct, still seem to provide a basic and functional framework in which individuals can share a basic existence in common. However, while such norms do seem to drive a basic convergence in social behavior and legal norms across societies and across time, Leiter's overarching point still stands that even such a convergence in the ethical realm would still not necessarily show normativity, but rather simply a similarity in attitude.

Sans normativity in the epistemic and the ethical, even when the count of sentiments stands 99–1, there is simply no room for argument about what one should do because there is no room for reasons:

> If we have no real reason to believe the same or act the same, and thus we may not believe the same or act the same, given that our underlying psychological states (our attitudes) vary, what follows? What follows is basically what Ayer and Stevenson correctly diagnosed not quite a century ago: where people share attitudes, reasoning about what one ought to do and what one ought to believe is possible; where people do not share attitudes, reasoning is not possible and only force prevails in a dispute, whether that is the rhetorical force of producing a change in attitudes by whatever means are effective or the physical or lawful force of suppressing contrary attitudes.[49]

Ayer and Stevenson's prognosis above, as told by Leiter, relates to practical rationality: what should we *do* in the absence of an agreement on a specific course of action? *How* should we proceed in the face of discord? Ayer's (and Leiter's) disturbing solution to this basic social conundrum is force. The theory of law, though, is concerned with what we can know, not what we should do. And what we can know with the law does not pertain to individuals, but collectives. Consider the following two examples of law addressing the issue of personal liability:

a. The State of New York has a no-fault insurance scheme, according to which all motorists are required to purchase insurance which covers the basic costs of damages. In the event of an ac-

48 Id. at p. 20.
49 Id. at p. 21.

cident, a policyholder simply hands in a claim to his insurance company and will be reimbursed according to a fixed schedule, without the need to establish a lack of fault. In the event of a two car accident, the other motorist will do the same. In most cases, the parties to the accident are precluded from suing each other. The goal of such a scheme is to reduce insurance premiums as well as the burden of litigation in the courts. There is much debate regarding whether such legislative schemes are good policy. However, what is beyond doubt is that this legal construct, i.e. a legal obligation to purchase automobile insurance combined with a sure and certain path to compensation in the event of an accident along with the relative security of avoiding litigation in the future, represents a fairly sophisticated stage of legal development that arose from the recognition by legal scholars and then legislative bodies that automobile accidents and the damages caused by them are not the isolated problem of a few individuals, but at least have the potential of affecting every motorist at some point in time.

b. Holmes references a passage from Exodus: "If an ox gore a man or a woman, that they die: then the ox shall be surely stoned, and his flesh shall not be eaten, but the owner of the ox shall be quit."[50] Though this passage is more complex than Holmes acknowledges in the chapter on "Early Forms of Liability", he uses it as a predecessor to similar laws among the Greeks and Romans and ultimately as a precursor to the doctrine of surrender in Maritime Law, the strict liability of innkeepers for damages suffered by their guests, as well as the liability of the master for damages brought on by his servant (agent). Contrary to this usus being a limitation of liability relative to the owner of the ox, or of the ship, Holmes argues that the practice of offering-up for expiation the immediate cause of damage has its root in the human impulse to seek vengeance against that which has caused pain, not unlike that "which leads even civilized man to kick a door when it pinches his finger".[51]

Which of the above would be in line with Leiter's view that legal science[52] should follow the lead of the empirical sciences? The no-fault insurance scheme is certainly rationalistic, but potentially also naturalistic, to the extent that we assume that this is a case of a hypothetical imperative according to Leiter's diagnosis (attributed to Ayer and Stevenson) that where people share attitudes, it is possible to agree on what ought to be done: since most people wish to not be involved in the hassle and risk of litigation about automobile accidents, it is sensible to create a legal norm which prevents potential litigants from such hassle and risk. At the same time, and despite Leiter's association of 'the holy book' with the dismissal of perceptual evidence,[53] the ox-goring example seems, at least on Holmes' interpretation, to be a very direct example of a norm which reflects very basic human attitudes: if I slam my hand in the door, I might kick the door and if the ox gores my daughter, I would, at least initially, want to kill the ox. If the ox is in the possession of another, I would want it to be delivered to me in expiation or at least

[50] Holmes, *The Common Law*, p. 7.

[51] Id. at p. 11.

[52] Note that, whereas the discussion of Leiter's naturalism has focused on theories of adjudication, no-fault insurance schemes have typically come about through legislation. The difference here should not be material.

[53] Leiter, "Normativity for Naturalists", p. 21.

to know that the other, in whose possession the ox finds itself, has done the same on my behalf.

With respect to the naturalistic view, it is not of particular relevance that the norm providing for the surrender of the ox in the case of a goring forms part of the Torah. The underlying injury is certainly familiar enough in many societies, past and present and does not, to my knowledge, have any particular affinity to the Jewish people. I suppose that a naturalist, like any other lawyer, when learning of this norm, would acknowledge that the norm indeed reflects a very common attitude, but that it is nonetheless, perhaps, from our perspective, a norm which suggests a certain primitive stage of development. From the legal perspective, we might consider the norm primitive because, as Holmes points out,[54] it is not the ox, void of the possibility of agency, that stands at the beginning of the causal chain, but rather its owner. As such, the ox-goring norm represents a significant contrast in the level of abstraction relative to the no-fault insurance norm since the latter looks past not only the immediate cause of harm, in its case the automobile that causes injury, but also even the culpable party in each case in the acknowledgement that all licensed (and therefore sufficiently trained) drivers will ultimately over the course of their driving careers share more or less equal culpability for the harms caused to others and that this liability can be more efficiently shared by collectivizing these costs through insurance premiums.

However, even if we can agree that the ox-goring norm is relatively primitive, it is nonetheless important to acknowledge what the norm itself represents: at the time that this norm was written down in the form that we know it (perhaps in the 6th century BCE), we can assume that it had already existed for many centuries, if not longer, in the oral traditions of the Hebrews and / or their neighbors in the ancient world. This would indicate that even though the norm as Holmes states it is relatively direct in its call for revenge against the physical cause of injury, it is not as if the norm that we have in Exodus is the product of an angry law-giver in the grips of vengeance having recently lost a loved one to an ox. Rather, we must assume that the norm as we have it is the product of centuries of discussion and reflection on the part of early jurists or lawyer-like people with respect to how to properly handle situations of this type. Yet, even this is not the entire story since the norm which Holmes cites to support his theory of revenge being the common ground of "the various forms of liability known to modern law"[55] is only part of the entire passage, which one translation presents as the following:

---

[54] *The Common Law*, p. 11: "An untrained intelligence only imperfectly performs the analysis by which jurists carry responsibility back to the beginning of a chain of causation."

[55] Id. at p. 37.

When an ox gores a man or a woman to death, the ox must be stoned; its flesh may not be eaten. The owner of the ox, however, shall go unpunished. But if an ox was previously in the habit of goring people and its owner, though warned, would not keep it in; should it then kill a man or a woman, not only must the ox be stoned, but its owner also must be put to death. If, however, a fine is imposed on him, he must pay in ransom for his life whatever amount is imposed on him."[56]

The entire passage, which follows shortly after the passage regarding an eye and for an eye, casts a very different light on the state of the respective liability regime. While verse 28, taken alone, can still be read with Holmes as codifying the attitudinal posture of revenge, limiting the object of revenge to the ox and excluding the owner, the other two verses would indicate that verse 28 is indeed a limitation of liability – the owner in charge of keeping the ox must lose his ox, but not his life. That is, unless the owner had reason to know of the ox's "habit of goring people", in which case the owner could fear for his own life. Thus, not only does the passage transcend the raw sentiment of vengeance by limiting the extent to which the vengeance may be taken out, it also introduces the concept of negligence, the advent of which in Anglo-American law is not that ancient at all. Finally, the passage also introduces the concept of monetary (punitive) damages which may be offered in exchange for the owner's life. Nor does the story end there: the Talmud and other rabbinic sources have commented on this passage for centuries, always adding new light to the basic principle in the context of changed situations.

In the end, the two systems of liability, the surrender of the ox in the case of goring, and the recourse to the insurance provider in the case of accident, though the result of differing methodologies in their development, are not as different as meets the eye. It is also true that both systems can be causally explained through the lens of the empirical sciences. However, to claim that the two developments are the mere result of the shifting of attitudes, beliefs and desires among the various stakeholders is like saying that high table at Gonville and Caius is the mere result of a bunch of hungry people trying to satisfy the basic need to nourish themselves. It is certainly that, but it is that as it has developed and been reflected upon over the course of centuries. Social life is indeed in some ways the sum of all of our attitudes, beliefs and desires, especially as we relate to one another. And lawmaking, whether in the judicial or legislative process, is the reflection on that reality which then constitutes the system of norms that we refer to as normativity.[57]

---

56 Exodus 21, 28–30.

57 See Llewellyn, "Constitution as an Institution", p. 17, FN 30: "Some institutions-for instance, our present Constitution-have found words and rules serving them as midwife or even as ancestor; but in the main it is action which comes first, to be followed by delayed perception

"Rabbi Jischmael sagt: Wer weise werden will, der befasse sich mit dem Zivilrecht (Geldurteile), denn es gibt innerhalb der Weisung kein Gebiet für dich, das mehr wäre als dieses, denn es ist eine Art sprudelnde Quelle."[58]

This passage runs parallel to something which Llewellyn says at the end of *The Common Law Tradition:*

There is little use in preaching, and less in indignation. But when I find an economic historian leaping like a tomcat in May upon some colonial court record of 1758, while neither he nor his sociological confrere nor his colleagues in psychology nor even his brothers in government are willing to save foundation money and their own time by exploring from the behavioral side the amazing gathered treasure of the law reports – then I feel I ought at least to point the fact that these ready records, with all kinds of factors "held equal," are there waiting for exploitation. And they are rich.[59]

Why is the civil law within the Jewish tradition an overflowing source and why are the American law reports so rich? The sources certainly contain norms, but the value does not lie in the compilation of norms. It lies in the reporting of social fact, and especially in the reporting of conflicts – conflicting attitudes, desires, feelings and the conflicting actions which arise therefrom. It is the study of these conflicts as matters of fact, and how these conflicts have come to be resolved that lends the study of law its depth, its cohesion, and which provides authority to the law's judgements. As such, the individual judgements are never really concerned with the beliefs or feelings of token individuals, but rather with how such tokens fit-in with the types of norms embedded within society.

4. Objectivity in the Law

What we refer to as the common law (in the German legal tradition, from the historical perspective, *Gewohnheitsrecht*) is not a source of normativity in the law due to its factual existence, but rather due to the role that it plays in shaping the volition of legal subjects. The law does not derive an 'ought' from the 'is' of social fact, but rather an 'ought' from the practice forms of its subjects. As such and also in line with the historical role which the norms of the common law have

of that action, then by rationalization of the action delayed still longer, and finally by conscious normatization of what has been perceived or rationalized. Before these latter processes have been worked out, the lines of the action commonly have shifted. Veblen's eyes were keen: 'A man's ethics are modelled on the conditions of his grandfather's time.'"

58 Mayer, Reinhold, *Der Talmud*, citing Berakhot 63b. My own translation: Rabbi Ishmael says: whoever wishes to become wise should study the civil law as there is no area within the instruction which could be more than this: it is a kind of overflowing source.

59 *The Common Law Tradition*, p. 539.

played in the development of modern legal systems, it seems that the common law is not a special case for the theory of norms, but rather is centrally important for understanding the source of normativity in the law. In order to validate this position, I suggest approaching the question of the common law not through the lens of naturalism but through the lens of objectivity.

There are two senses in which the law can be said to be objective. First, the law is objective in that it consists of general principles or norms of the state which are applied to particular cases as applicable.[60] It is in the very nature of law that it is independent of subjective whim, whether on the part of the lawgiver / enforcer or on the part of the legal subject. *Nulla poena sine lege* first entails that government officials can only punish on the basis of a pre-existing, valid rule of general applicability and secondly that legal persons, lest they become subject to punishment, submit their particular, subjective desires to the authority of the state as expressed in such rules.

However, the essence of law is not fully described by reference solely to its general character. If *generality* is the necessary form of the law, its matter is a composition of a thoroughly *particular* sort. It is the self-interested intention of the individual, structured in generality, that serves as the basis for the legal expression of the civil society, that which Hegel calls the *Not- und Verstandesstaat*.[61] Indeed, the problem of the relationship between the individual and society, the subjective will and the coercion of the law, first arises in the necessity of the individual to realize his thoroughly subjective needs (of food, shelter, wealth, etc.) in the context of a shared life with other individuals. This is the second sense in which the law is objective – in coordinating the pursuit of subjective desires and their satisfaction of subjective needs, individuals must have recourse to something which exceeds their own subjectivity, to a norm recognizing the presence of others or a set of common practices.[62] In its objectivity the law is an enabling structure allowing individuals to maximize the satisfaction of their desires by being able to transcend their own subjectivity.

---

[60] Compare Hegel, *Grundlinien der Philosophie des Rechts*, § 3. In addition to this aspect, Hegel refers in this section to the codification of the law through the state as a 'positive' characteristic of the law. This aspect of codification will be discussed at greater length below.

[61] Id. at § 183.

[62] Compare the Searlean framework as set forth in John Searle, *The Construction of Social Reality* and later works, for example, *Rationality in Action*, according to which institutional reality, which would include law, is epistemically objective but ontologically subjective as a result of Searle's view that such things exist as a result of subjective agreement among individuals. Even for Searle though, the source of such agreement does not spontaneously appear, but rather is the result of individuals making use of a common background of experience and capabilities, including that of reason, which gives this 'subjective' reality a strongly objective flavor.

Hegel expresses well this necessary relationship between the particularity of each individual, each action and each interest, and the generality of the legal form:

> Die Idee in dieser ihrer Entzweiung erteilt den Momenten eigentümliches Dasein, – der Besonderheit das Recht, sich nach allen Seiten zu entwickeln und zu ergehen, und der Allgemeinheit das Recht, sich als Grund und notwendige Form der Besonderheit sowie als die Macht über sie und ihren letzten Zweck zu erweisen.[63]

In this conception, the law lives off of the concrete instances, the facts on the ground, that make-up the flurry of action of its actors. This is also the core insight of the American Legal Realists and also lends credence to Leiter's emphasis on basing legal science on empirical science. However, if we would only focus on the concrete factual, as the American Legal Realists were perhaps sometimes wont to overemphasize[64] and for which Leiter principally argues, the result would be for the law to completely dissolve into subjectivity. Without the objectivity provided by law's normativity, the presumed objectivity of fact would result in the mere subjectivity of the attitudes of each individual. If this were really the case, then all prospect of community, society, government, and, of course, law would be lost. Though not directly evident to empirical science, it is actually the form of generality, here in the law, which allows the subjectivity of the individual attitude to attain objectivity.[65] Reduced to the purview of merely empirical

---

[63] Hegel, *Grundlinien der Philosophie des Rechts*, § 184.

[64] There are many examples, but two from the Bramble Bush will do: P. 12: "What these officials do about disputes is, to my mind, the law itself." Pp. 13–14: "The main thing is what officials are going to do. And so to my mind the main thing is seeing what officials do, do about disputes, or about anything else; and seeing that there is a certain regularity in their doing – a regularity which makes possible prediction of what they and other officials are about to do tomorrow. In many cases that prediction cannot be wholly certain. Then you have room for something else, another main thing for the lawyer: the study of how to make the official do what you would like to have him. At that point 'rules' loom into importance. Great importance. For judges think that they must follow rules, and people highly approve of that thinking. So that the getting of the judge to do a thing is in considerable measure the art of finding what rules are available to urge upon him, and of how to urge them to accomplish your result." I have argued that such statements do not represent the core insight of the American Legal Realists. There are two aspects to this: first, with respect to Llewellyn (and my references are almost solely with respect to Llewellyn) much more weight is given to his late work (*The Common Law Tradition, Deciding Appeals*) than to his earlier, rather polemically oriented work (*The Bramble Bush*). Secondly, the core insight of American Legal Realism is that insight which is most capable of illuminating an interesting legal theory. Leiter focuses on Llewellyn's emphasis on facts and treatment of rules (or formalism) as mere jargon because that supports the naturalism that he advocates. I have tried to show that the far more interesting angle on American Legal Realism is to see how the emphasis on facts and the partial contempt for explicit rules shows us a path to a different kind of normativity.

[65] See here Plessner, *Grenzen der Gemeinschaft*, p. 115, and read 'law' for 'state': "Der Staat ist ein Verfahren und keine Substanz, ein offenes System von Vorkehrungen, die Forde-

inquiry, the individual attitude can be nothing but a psychological state, with neither direction nor cohesion, that, at most, becomes expressed in a movement in the natural world. With the form of generality that is the law, the same psychological state becomes the basis for an action by a person that is embedded in the social structure of the world.

However, and I take this as the real message of the American Legal Realists, it is not as if such objective normativity comes from on high or directly from a sovereign edict, legislative enactment or even a systematic legal treatise. The idea, or *eidos*, is the form taken on by the practices of individuals as they become objectified through cooperation.[66] The objective form comes from us, as we engage in our normal, daily lives. To fail to grasp this form as the complex of implicit norms guiding individual conduct within society would be for the law to fail in its aim of objectivity and to become a merely subjective expression of desires within a mere artifice of objectivity (as conceded by Kelsen in Chapter IV above). In avoiding such an outcome, the purpose of the law within its second general sense must be to capture, express and systematize the forms of cooperation, the common practices among individuals.[67] One of the key issues for legal science is how a legal system can best realize this purpose through its expression of the laws.

5. Knowing the Law

One such systematic method of expressing the law might consist in convening expert parliamentary committees which make recommendations regarding the best potential laws based on a desired output. A second method could lie in attempting to increase democratic involvement in the legislative process. By letting the people themselves decide or by permitting greater opportunity for citi-

rungen der Oeffentlichkeit aus ihrer Unabsehbarkeit und Unbestimmtheit herauszuheben und dem Gemeinschaftsverlangen jedes Menschen, seinem Naturrecht auf Waerme und Vertrauen anzugleichen und die Gefahr bestaendiger Reibungen und Beeintraechtigungen der beiden Sphaeren zu bannen. Staat ist systematisierte Oeffentlichkeit im Dienste der Gemeinschaft, Inbegriff von Sicherungsmassnahmen der Gemeinschaft im Dienste der Oeffentlichkeit."

66 Stekeler, Pirmin, "Eine Kritik juridischer Vernunft". In: Horst Dreier, Dietmar Willoweit (ed.), *Würzburger Vorträge zur Rechtsphilosophie, Rechtstheorie und Rechtssoziologie*, Heft 48, Baden-Baden: Nomos Verlag, 2014, p. 70.

67 See Hegel, *Grundlinien der Philosophie des Rechts*, § 229: "In der Rechtspflege führt sich die bürgerliche Gesellschaft, in der sich die Idee in der Besonderheit verloren [hat] und in die Trennung des Inneren und Äußeren auseinandergegangen ist, zu deren Begriffe, der Einheit des an sich seienden Allgemeinen mit der subjektiven Besonderheit zurück, jedoch diese im einzelnen Falle und jenes in der Bedeutung des abstrakten Rechts."

zens to express their views through elected representatives, one might come to enact laws which attain a high level of correspondence with social norms. A third method, which encompasses both legislation and jurisprudence, lies in a Herbert Spencer style approach to social engineering through legal norms.[68] On this view, embraced to some degree by the law and economics movement today, the law should be used to remove social or economic inefficiencies caused by the conduct of irrational actors. However, if we look at the social practices which form the basis for the objectivity of the law as described above, we must conclude that while such practices can inform each of these alternatives, their methods seem to be less than ideal in achieving the purpose of expressing the implicit ideas (or forms) underlying this reality: expert panels make recommendations based on preferred outcomes; direct democratic involvement operates on public opinion which is highly subject to external influence through various media; and law and economics is based on mere models of economic efficiency.

Hayek claimed in the first volume of his *Law, Legislation and Liberty* that legislated law tends to work against the essence of the "rule of law" by placing in the competence of a centralized planner the task of intentionally creating rules of order which tend to possess a non-systematic character as a result of the ad hoc, purpose driven nature of parliamentary, special-interest based, decision-making. For Hayek, this model of legislation is inherently flawed because the core problem of the legal order, and indeed with all social order, is not in ensuring the freedom of expression, the balancing of interests through democratic elections or even in planning for the social good, but rather in systematizing and ordering the dispersed knowledge of society. Under this view, legal norms exist quite independently of the very finite listing of statutes that are found in the civil code or the constitution. Indeed, legal norms are primarily determined and negotiated not in a legislature or even in a courtroom, but in the banal and quotidian activities of ordinary individuals. In referring to such legal norms, Hayek states: "The result of this development will in the first instance not be articulated knowledge but a knowledge which, although it can be described in terms of rules, the individual cannot state in words but is merely able to honor in practice."[69]

When a common law judge becomes involved in a dispute arising out of such activity, his method of decision-making is key to the persistence and development of this order. In adjudicating contractual disputes, for example, judges seek to determine the rule of conduct which governed the activity in question and then

[68] See Oliver Wendell Holmes, "The Path of the Law", 10 HARV. L. REV. 457 (1897). One of the more famous judicial opinions in this regard was Holmes' opinion for the US Supreme Court in Buck v. Bell, 274 U.S. 200 (1927) in which Holmes upheld a law requiring the sterilisation of the unfit by penning the phrase: "Three generations of imbeciles are enough".

[69] Friedrich A. Hayek, *Rules and Order*.

apply that rule in arriving at their decision. Hayek refers to such rules as being non-purpose driven and abstract: "The chief concern of a common law judge must be the expectations which the parties in a transaction would have reasonably formed on the basis of the general practices that the ongoing order of actions rests on."[70]

In determining these expectations, the judge, in concert with the attorneys arguing the case before the court, does not just probe the minds of the witnesses, but also looks to relevantly similar cases in the past to see how parties similarly situated have acted and which rules were held to govern those situations. The rule of precedent works by the judge, with the help of counsel on each side, finding the "controlling" case or set of cases, i. e. those cases which together cover the essential aspects of the case at hand, and applying its governing rule. This new rule though, will be slightly different from the previous rules because the facts which the rule is adjudged to govern are slightly different from the previous cases. The new holding will nudge the body of law ever so slightly, even if it is never again applied in court. The rule of the case will not be a binding rule in a normal sense, but the case (as a complex of rules applied to facts), especially if it is from a higher court, will be binding. This case, together with thousands of other cases over the course of centuries, will form the body of law which future judges, when presented with a case, will turn to in determining the idea (*eidos*) which will have governed the practice in question. Not articulating a rule which will apply to all future cases (i. e. a rule of general applicability), but rather the rule that has actually governed the action in question, the common law judge articulates a rule that is not generally applicable, but *generically* applicable – it is a mere expression, explication, conceptualization of the implicit form of the conduct in question.

The distinction between a general and a generic rule is essential to understanding the method of the common law. If a judge would base his holding merely on a new legal rule of general applicability, such a rule would satisfy the requirement that the law apply to all persons equally, but it would violate the requirement of *nulla poena sine lege* referenced above. Mistakenly taking the common law to consist of mere general laws, some criticize the common law for being a system of "judge-made" law on the premise that a judge, unlike a parliament, has no democratic legitimacy. However, were it the case that the basis for a judge's holding were merely a rule of general applicability, such a system would be guilty of the far worse feature of punishing a party for violating a legal norm that, at the time of the action in question, did not exist. Such an unjust and arbitrary system could hardly be considered a system of law.

---

[70] Hayek, *Rules and Order*, p. 86.

Instead, the method of the common law makes the assumption that an action in question will have taken place within a normative context of established social practices. If the prosecution or plaintiff fails to assert that the action in question took place within such an established social practice, then the action will be deemed to have taken place where the law is silent and the case will be dismissed. However, if the action in question did occur within the context of established social practices, then the case can be adjudicated on this basis and the legal analysis will consist in determining which precise context applies to the case, which language game the litigants were playing when the cause of action arose.

6. The Mode of Expression

The idea of generic legal norms is not unique to the Anglo-American legal tradition, but has its origin and a very prominent role in the European tradition as well. The *Kodifikationsstreit* between Thibaut and Savigny was precisely about how to best articulate the generic norms of the Roman and Germanic legal traditions with Thibaut in favor of systematizing the current various generic norms into a single and uniform code and Savigny arguing for the necessity of further organic development of these norms, not wanting to cut short the natural progression of the legal system. Hegel in § 211 of the *Grundlinien der Philosophie des Rechts* plays off of Savigny's *Vom Beruf Unserer Zeit*[71] when he writes:

> Einer gebildeten Nation oder dem juristischen Stande in derselben die Fähigkeit abzusprechen, ein Gesetzbuch zu machen – da es nicht darum zu tun sein kann, ein System ihrem Inhalte nach neuer Gesetze zu machen, sondern den vorhandenen gesetzlichen Inhalt in seiner bestimmten Allgemeinheit zu erkennen, wäre einer der größten Schimpfe, der einer Nation oder jenem Stande angetan werden könnte.

The codification debate ultimately revolves around the issue of expedience: is it most expedient to allow for the legal system to continue to develop organically, perhaps even erratically, at the expense of the uncertainty of multiple, sometimes

[71] For example, the Conclusion states: "Auch in der Beurteilung des gegenwärtigen Zustandes treffen wir überein, denn wir erkennen ihn beide für Mangelhaft. Sie aber sehen den Grund des Übels in den Rechtsquellen, und glauben durch ein Gesetzbuch zu helfen: ich finde ihn vielmehr in uns, und glaube, dass wir eben deshalb zu einem Gesetzbuch nicht berufen sind." Savigny's opposition to a code at the time of writing *Vom Beruf Unserer Zeit* in 1814 was principally twofold: first, it would be deeply mistaken as to the essence of law to try to construct a code on principles of natural law that would be valid for every nation at all times (i.e. equating positive law with natural law) and second, it was not an opportune time in 1814 for creating a code since the contemporary jurists would be incapable of properly inserting the principles of Roman and Germanic law into a national code. It was only this second point with which Hegel took issue.

contradictory, lines of judicial opinion; or, after one thousand years of the common law's development, is it rather most expedient to declare the nation fully formed in its generic norms, thereby sacrificing marginal future development but gaining uniformity and certainty. The proponents of codification have in many ways won this debate with even strong movements existing in the United States for Restatements, or non-binding codes of civil law which have strongly persuasive authority. Indeed, there is also a declaratory aspect to codification by which we make something to be the case by taking it to be the case[72], or determine the norm by making it a rule. It is often simply more efficient to declare a binding or even non-binding rule around which social practices can form and become stabilized.

Nonetheless, if we understand the generic form, then we also see that explicit legal rules, at best, can only be generic at the moment of codification and that any generic developments within a codified system are bound to occur in the shadows (penumbra) of the declared rules. In an important way, code-based law is divorced in its methodology from the practices of society while common law is not. It is a top-down approach to explicating norms although the explicandum exists at the depths of social practice. Importantly though, the genericity of social practices is not just negotiated in the court room, but throughout the functions of the society. Therefore, the issue is much larger than simply how the civil law structures its rule making. Indeed, this may be the deeper truth behind Hegel's push for codification – that the civil law reflects only one of many kinds of social practice constituting the republic[73] – I believe that this insight is key in understanding Rousseau's *moi commun* that serves as a basis for the *volonté générale* as well as the 'reason combined with human affect' which Spinoza sees as the guarantor of a stable constitution.

The common law allows learned judges to appreciate actions not as token instances, but as representations of generic norms. However, a well-formed repub-

---

[72] See Searle, *Speech Acts*.

[73] In contrast to this unitary view of the state, American culture indeed tends to place most of its belief in the integrity of the judiciary, strongly elevating the status of judges, and is susceptible to considering the rest of political life to be a free for all, open to the influence of special interests with legislation often openly applicable only to particular groups. Of course, the danger of such a development is that the common law becomes diminished relative to the much larger part of political life that takes place around it. Instead of being defined by generic norms underlying social practice, the society becomes dominated by game-theoretical deliberations about how to best allocate tax resources. In this sense, the American Tea Party was perfectly consequent in analysing the current political situation in the United States: there really is no point in paying taxes or in having a state at all if the state is not governed principally by generic norms, but rather by the whims of special interests consisting solely in collecting taxes and dispersing the money to favored groups.

lic will ensure that the generic norms underlying social practice will be manifested throughout the political sphere, extending, for example, from expert commissions as part of the parliamentary process to labor unions as a check on asocial profit seeking. Indeed, any lobby, if its influence is expressed in an appropriate way, can form an essential input in determining the form of the generic.

Judges have a unique role in the life of the republic due to their responsibility for articulating and systematizing the implicit norms governing the actions of individuals. However, these individual citizens are not just relevant as generic instances in judicial disputes, but rather in all of political life. Whenever individuals act according to a generic norm, they are participating in and contributing to the life of the republic.

Conclusion: Law as Constitution

My objective has been to analyze the state and its individuals as belonging to a normative order as expressed in the law. With Kelsen, I conceptualize the law (or also the state) as an intrinsically normative order which is the product of human activity and is entirely amenable to scientific inquiry. Contrary to Kelsen, I argue that the scope of inquiry for legal science extends beyond administrative action under the guise of hypothetical norms to the actions both of sovereigns and subjects. Extending the scope of inquiry in this way, legal science can no longer be content with hierarchies of norms, but rather must concern itself with the manner of existence of both the sovereign and the subject.

Upon closer examination, the sovereign and subject, at least throughout modernity, are not as far removed from each other as it may seem at first glance. Sovereignty is always an artifice of our own making. However, unlike many of our own designs, sovereignty, at least in the Hobbesian conception, admits of no half-measures: there is no exit-clause or right of reservation in the subjugation of oneself to the sovereignty of the state. The upside to this structure is that the constitution of the state affords the subject its proper agency: in its deontic commitment the subject becomes itself sovereign.

It is not just a manner of speech to attribute sovereignty to the state, nor is it merely aspirational to say that the subject is sovereign. Sovereignty is the mode of political reality as a unity, without which the commonwealth cannot be conceived as a rational order. It is the rational subject that provides the basis for sovereignty. Without individuals acting pursuant to desire independent reasons for action, the state would not come into existence. The state being the realization and personification of the people, it is therefore dependent on the people and the people then must actually be the highest power, the sovereign.

The normativity of the legal order for Kelsen derives from the hierarchy of norms ending in the vacuous basic norm resulting in a normative order that is ultimately devoid of all normativity. In contrast, the normativity of the legal order for the present theory derives from the facticity of human agency and is therefore devoid of the hierarchical structure made familiar by both Kelsen and Hart. It is not the pedigree of the norm's issuance which makes it count as a legal norm, but rather, with Somlo, its belonging to the legal order as such – legal norms exist as plurale tantum. While one can imagine that a norm could be expressed with any given set of words, it is the reflection on the meaning of this expression, i. e. on the logical sentence, within the context of the body of legal norms that provides the expression in question its legal normativity. Legal norms within the traditional conception are dependent on the fact of having been validly issued within a state whose existence is itself always contingent. Thus, they are always contingent. In the present conception, proper legal norms, i. e. the logical sentences, are valid not based on the contingency of material fact, but rather on the certainty of their meaning. The result of this is absolute validity.

The state, the legal order, the subject and even legal norms understood as logical sentences are all kinds of ideal entities that are grounded only in the fact of human agency. But the legal system itself is strongly characterized by the empirical. Libraries are filled with books containing paragraph upon paragraph of statutes and judicial opinions. Jails are filled with inmates, courts are filled with litigants and society is replete with contracts, injuries, property etc. Even the individuals themselves are immediately characterized not by agency, but rather attitudes, desires and predilections. American Legal Realism is correct in holding that the law depends on such facts much more than on the ideas set forth in any number of theories or treatises – the life of the law is the experience of social fact. However, while the source of the law is the factual, it is actually the reflection upon such states of affairs which, when engaged in by officials, judges, lawyers and citizens, comprises the normativity of the law. While such reflection takes place throughout all cultural instantiations of society, the reflective activity of the law is of a special class in that its function lies in discerning the generic forms of common practice and integrating such forms into the existing normative framework. In no part of the law is this kind of reflection more apparent than in the case method of the common law.

Hegel suggests that every people has exactly the political order which it deserves.[1] This is the conservative moment of legal theory. On the other hand, an individual's autonomy is correlative to the complexity of the order of the state in which it exists. This is its liberal moment. The difference in the quality of legal systems relates to the complexity with which each system recognizes its idealized individuals. The more complex such a system is, the more each random individual will be recognized in its token instantiation.

---

[1] Hegel. *Grundlinien der Philosophie des Rechts*, § 274: "Einem Volke eine, wenn auch ihrem Inhalte nach mehr oder weniger vernünftige Verfassung a priori geben zu wollen, – dieser Einfall übersähe gerade das Moment, durch welches sie mehr als ein Gedankending wäre. Jedes Volk hat deswegen die Verfassung, die ihm angemessen ist, und für dasselbe gehört."

Recall that Tocqueville praised the merits of the limited government in place in the young United States of America by pointing to the harmonious, localized nature of its political system:

Chez la plupart des nations européennes, l'existence politique a commencé dans les régions supérieures de la société, et s'est communiquée peu à peu, et toujours d'une manière incomplète, aux diverses parties du corps social. En Amérique, au contraire, on peut dire que la commune a été organisée avant le comté, le comté avant l'État, l'État avant l'Union.[2]

However, a key part of Tocqueville's analysis is based on the role of religion in the everyday activity of American communities. For example:

La liberté voit dans la religion la compagne de ses luttes et de ses triomphes, le berceau de son enfance, la source divine de ses droits. Elle considère la religion comme la sauvegarde des mœurs; les mœurs comme la garantie des lois et le gage de sa propre durée.[3]

Partially due to Tocqueville's account of America, there is often a perception that the 19th century was a paradise of harmonious civil society in which all levels of government were limited in nature and in which all citizens were free to pursue their commercial and personal interests without interference. To the extent that a harmonious unity existed, this was a result of a limited union which devolved the remainder of its powers to the individual States, limited State governments which devolved the remainder of their powers to the counties, limited county governments which devolved the remainder of their powers to the communities and communities which were all united by a common ethos reinforced through strong religious practices. In part by plan of the founding fathers and in part by the fortune of having a relatively homogenous cultural and political belief system, the state of 19th century America was that of limited government characterized by strong deference to the normativity of existing religious practices. Religion was a key unifying source of normativity in early America to the extent that it existed as a state. To the extent that such a unified normativity did not exist, the American society of the time may better be conceived as a mere civil society based on the pursuit of individual needs and was either bound to develop such a normative unity or bound to disintegrate – a dynamic which foreshadows the conflicts leading up to the Civil War.[4] Depending on one's positioning within the American

---

[2] Alexis de Tocqueville, *De la Democratie en Amerique I*, Ch. II., p. 37.

[3] Id. at p. 40.

[4] See Hegel, *Grundlinien der Philosophie des Rechts*, § 185: "Die selbstständige Entwicklung der Besonderheit ist das Moment, welches sich in den alten Staaten als das hereinbrechende Sittenverderben und der letzte Grund des Untergangs derselben zeigt. Diese Staaten, teils im patriarchalischen und religiösen Prinzip, teils in einem Prinzip einer geistigern, aber einfacher Sittlichkeit, – überhaupt auf ursprüngliche natürliche Anschauung gebaut» konnten die Entzweiung derselben und die unendliche Reflexion des Selbstbewußtseins in sich nicht aushalten, und erlagen dieser Reflexion, wie sie sich hervorzutun anfing, der Gesinnung und dann der

political spectrum, the measures which centralized power in the federal government during the Reconstruction following the Civil War and leading up to the New Deal of the Franklin Roosevelt administration are either interpreted as an usurpation of the local sovereignty built around a religious normative framework or a necessary assertion of sovereignty by the union in an attempt to avoid the collapse of American society into self-interested factions with extreme wealth on the one hand and extreme poverty on the other. For the one side, a complete normative order already existed in the combination of a laissez-faire structure of civil society with religious communities and other charitable organizations serving as security blankets for the unfortunate. For the other side, the actions of the federal government were absolutely required to restore an order which, perhaps at one point had existed, but that was present no more.

Civil society is the realm of special, particular interests. Political society, or the state, is the realm of common, general interests. As described in the section above, the organizing factor of civil society must be understood as generic norms or ideas that guide practices and are brought to expression through a kind of Hayekian approach toward equilibrium. If political society does not exist, then man is deprived of his political existence. His share of a common value or heritage with his fellow man is absent and his is a non-political existence of arbitrary endeavors based on carnal or perhaps patriarchal needs. However, if political society does exist, then it exists within a normative framework organized according to the general or common interests of all, expressed through generic forms.

On the one hand, the existence of this normative framework entails not legislating as general that which is merely particular.[5] On the other hand, it entails taking account of the particular in legislating the general.[6] If the sovereign fails in either respect, the actions of the state risk straying from the authority of the

Wirklichkeit nach, weil ihrem noch einfachen Prinzip die wahrhaft unendliche Kraft mangelte, die allein in derjenigen Einheit liegt, welche den Gegensatz der Vernunft zu seiner ganzen Stärke auseinandergehen läßt, und ihn überwältigt hat, in ihm somit sich erhält, und ihn in sich zusammenhält."

[5] Ibid. regarding criticism of Plato's Republic for excluding the possibility of the development of particular interests through the civil society.

[6] Id. at § 260: "Der Staat ist die Wirklichkeit der konkreten Freiheit; die konkrete Freiheit aber besteht darin, daß die persönliche Einzelnheit und deren besondere Interessen sowohl ihre vollständige Entwickelung und die Anerkennung ihres Rechts für sich (im Systeme der Familie und der bürgerlichen Gesellschaft) haben, als sie durch sich selbst in das Interesse des Allgemeinen teils übergehen, teils mit Wissen und Willen dasselbe und zwar als ihren eigenen substantiellen Geist anerkennen und für dasselbe als ihren Endzweck tätig sind, so daß weder das Allgemeine ohne das besondere Interesse, Wissen und Wollen gelte und vollbracht werde, noch daß die Individuen bloß für das letztere als Privatpersonen leben, und nicht zugleich in und für das Allgemeine wollen und eine dieses Zwecks bewußte Wirksamkeit haben."

general will and thereby invalidating themselves. If the state legislates particular interests as the general will, it either becomes oppressive by encroaching ever more into the private sphere of its individuals or corrupt by privileging the interests of certain individuals at the expense of others. If the state fails to account for the particular in legislating the general, it is in danger of legislating on ideology removed from the basis of its authority. The purpose of the positive constitution, both formally and actually, is to provide a normative framework that incorporates the pursuit of particular interests into its general structure.[7]

The common law is a methodology which provides a built-in structure for capturing such particular interests within civil society as they are expressed through the ideality or normativity of forms of practice. Much constitutional deliberation has concerned itself with the implementation of such a methodology regarding the political society. The insight of the authors of the Federalist Papers, as well as that of Hegel, each following Montesquieu in their own way, is that the normativity of the political sphere can be posited by forming the particular structures of society into a cohesive whole through, for example, separation of powers and a system of checks and balances.

However, creating such a normative framework is where the constitutional difficulties begin. If the authorization of the state lies in integrating particular interests into the general objectivity of the law, then it should be easy enough to regularly take polls of the people and then, as Rousseau suggests, balance the competing interests with each other to find the common interest.[8] However, while the opinion of the public may always be correct with regard to general sentiments, satisfaction or the lack thereof, pride or angst, it is often mistaken with regard to concrete actions or means to ends.[9] Moreover, given that organized interests always know what they want and how to make their voice heard (e. g. the industrial lobby or non-governmental organisations), it is most likely

---

[7] Id. at § 261: "Das besondere Interesse soll wahrhaft nicht bei Seite gesetzt oder gar unterdrückt, sondern mit dem Allgemeinen in Übereinstimmung gesetzt werden, wodurch es selbst und das Allgemeine erhalten wird."

[8] Rousseau, *Du contrat social*, Livre II, Ch. III: "Il y a souvent bien de la différence entre la volonté de tous et la volonté générale; celle-ci ne regarde qu'à l'intérêt commun; l'autre regarde à l'intérêt privé, et n'est qu'une somme de volontés particulières: mais ôtez de ces mêmes volontés les plus et les moins qui s'entre-détruisent, reste pour somme des différences la volonté générale."

[9] See Hegel, *Grundlinien der Philosophie des Rechts*, § 317: "Ein großer Geist hat die Frage zur öffentlichen Beantwortung aufgestellt, ob es erlaubt sei, ein Volk zu täuschen? Man mußte antworten, daß ein Volk über seine substantielle Grundlage, das Wesen und bestimmten Charakter seines Geistes sich nicht täuschen lasse, aber über die Weise, wie es diesen weiß, und nach dieser Weise seine Handlungen, Ereignisse u.s.f. beurteilt, – von sich selbst getäuscht wird."

that the "people", as the vague designation referring to everyone else, will not know what it wants.[10] This may be because it is subject to the random influences of the inconsequential and accidental and therefore blind to its own reason. However, being told that it is the source of its own sovereignty, "we the people", believing in its inherent authority, threatens to disrupt the normativity (Hegel calls it *Idealität*) underlying the state by replacing it with the tyranny of the majority.

Such a majority does not see that the existing institutional structures, those familiar to all Western societies such as a free press, an active lobby, social security, a regulatory framework, corporations, non-profits, career bureaucrats and politicians, all have an integral role within the normative framework that is the state. It does not know that the way to increase its sovereignty is to strengthen these institutions and affirm them by ensuring that they are used for objective instead of subjective ends.

In the face of these difficulties regarding the constitution of the republic, it is important that order can neither be created on paper nor in the ballot box if it does not already exist within the people. Were law merely social fact, the position advocated by the reductivists, then, within the sense of nation building, any constitutional structure would be possible and it would be up to us simply to create the positive framework that suits us best. However, if law is inherently normative as I have argued, then any given constitutional structure is determined to be constituted by the law.

Order cannot merely be posited – that is its conservative moment. On the other hand, if one focuses solely on the preservation of order in the conservative moment, one loses track of the possibility of individual freedom in the liberal moment.

How brilliant was the first man who thought of enclosing a piece of land and calling it his own, and how naïve was the first passerby who took him at his word?[11] Of course, it didn't happen quite in that way. Property, like all institutional structures / legal frameworks, must always be considered as part of the entirety of the social construct. We must not think that civil society began upon the first person building a fence, but rather that the first person built a fence once there had already been a civil society that afforded him the institutional framework, and therewith the deontic structure, that allowed him to make the appropriate claim.

Rousseau speaks about the man with his piece of land with tongue in cheek. His irony can be understood as an implicit critique against the Lockean notion of

[10] Id. at § 301.

[11] See Rousseau. *Discours sur l'origine et les fondements de l'inégalité parmi les hommes*, Seconde Partie: "Le premier qui ayant enclos un terrain, s'avisa de dire, ceci est à moi, & trouva des gens assez simples pour le croire, fut le vrai fondateur de la société civile."

the individual who grounds his right to property in his own labor.[12] When several landowners join together to form a commonwealth, it is understandable that each wishes to enjoy the benefits of collectivization, e. g. a common defense, without sacrificing any more than is absolutely necessary with respect to the rights which they have acquired. But acquired from whom? And what does the natural order of things say about the serf who tills the land for the lord, or the unemployed who hopes to get the chance to till the land for the lord? The same deontic structure which affords the lord his fence will also afford the serf his rights, not because it is the way things should be, but because it is the way things are. The serf is not an ox, but a human with rational faculties that allow him to reflect on his standing and that of those around him – he cannot be expected to suffer his underestimation lightly and his resistance weighs deontically.

Upon closer inspection, we might be able to conceive of Locke's natural order as simply the way of the world as it is for us as agents in community with others. This way of our world is another way of saying 'constitution' and of the many constitutional theories, there are two strong theories that shed a particular light on the role of the individual in the constitutional order: Richard Epstein's perspective set forth in *The Classical Liberal Constitution* and Karl Llewellyn's set forth in his 1934 article "The Constitution as an Institution".

Richard Epstein conceives of a natural American order as it was codified in the US Constitution. It is an order that was created by its authors based on the state of the art of physiocratic Enlightenment thought,[13] importantly employing the notion that political order works particularly well through a combination of guar-

---

[12] *Second Treatise*, p. 26: "Though the earth and all inferior creatures be common to all men, yet every man has a 'property' in his own 'person'. This nobody has any right to but himself. The 'labour' of his body and the 'work' of his hands, we may say, are properly his. Whatsoever, then, he removes out of the state that Nature hath provided and left it in, he hath mixed his labour with it, and joined to it something that is his own, and thereby makes it his property. It being by him removed from the common state Nature placed it in, it hath by this labour something annexed to it that excludes the common right of other men. For this 'labour' being the unquestionable property of the labourer, no man but he can have a right to what that is once joined to, at least where there is enough, and as good left in common for others." For a brutally consequent 19th version of the individual assertion of rights, see Max Stirner's *Der Einzige und sein Eigentum*.

[13] Epstein, in putting forth his understanding of laissez faire, approvingly cites Jacob Viner: "I will carefully avoid using the term laissez faire to mean what only unscrupulous or ignorant opponents of it and never its exponents make it mean, namely, philosophical anarchism, or opposition to any governmental power or activity whatsoever. I will in general use the term to mean what the pioneer systematic exponents of it, the Physiocrats and Adam Smith, argued for, namely, the limitation of governmental activity to the enforcement of peace and of 'justice' in the restricted sense of 'commutative justice', to the defense against foreign enemies and to public works regarded as essential and as impossible or highly improbable of establishment by private

anteeing private property while ensuring limited government. Epstein sees his project as neither conservative nor progressive, but as liberal in the proper sense of the term – the goal is to ensure liberty through critically examining instantiations of over-intrusive government, whether this be evidenced by means of the progressively oriented excessive regulation of property rights or the conservatively oriented interference in the free market through the favoring of big business. While government for Epstein is certainly necessary, its chief function is merely to "maintain order without destroying liberty".[14] Epstein refers to Thomas Paine's statement that government is tolerable at its best, intolerable at its worst. However, *The Classical Liberal Constitution* should not be understood as being hyper-individualistic or contrary to republican ideals. In the classical liberal view, the locus of the commonwealth is to be primarily found in the continuation of civil society as an end in itself – where government can aid in that task, it may; where it impedes, it must be criticized. In such a case, the chief object of criticism for Epstein is the Supreme Court in its traditional role as arbiter of constitutional norms. The key historical period which highlights the proper role of the Court in preserving the liberal order is referred to as the Lochner era (from the late 1890s until 1936) when the Court struck down a series of regulations by the States under the rationale that such regulations restrict economic liberties and impede the freedom of contract. This period is distinguished from the New Deal era in which President Franklin Roosevelt, together with Congress, passed other (similar) reforms that the Court then no longer held to be unconstitutional. In Epstein's diagnosis, the Supreme Court lost sight of America's liberal heritage when in the 1936 term:

> a sharply divided Court decisively repudiated what remained of the classical liberal synthesis, which prized both federalism and the strong protection of economic liberties. The progressives did not view government as a necessary evil, but rather as a positive force for good in a wide range of social situations where the comparatively minimalist classical liberal view was said to have faltered.[15]

The Court began to betray the principles of the American constitution in 1936 when it gave way to the democratic impulses of the New Deal expressed in legislative enactments creating entitlements and undue governmental interference. This shift irrevocably moved the country away from the order which Epstein considers best: a minimal amount of government and a maximal amount of freedom. Indeed, such an order is nice to have if you can get it.

---

enterprise, or, for special reasons, unsuitable to be left to private operation." Epstein at p. 582. See Jacob Viner "The Intellectual History of Laissez Faire," 3 J. Law & Econ. 45, 45 (1960).

[14] Epstein, *supra*, p. 3.

[15] Epstein, *supra* at pp. 6, 7.

And the United States of America were indeed somewhat successful in being able to establish this order well into the 19th Century, and then, even despite the New Deal, again well throughout the 20th. The sober observation of American fact suggests that the landholdings which guaranteed the freedom of the landowners at the Founding had actually first been acquired from the natives, and then from the British, and then again from the natives, all the while depending on the labor of slavery in order to secure profits, and with the profits the property and freedom concomitant thereto. In the North, the capital was more in industry than in the land, and the labor predominantly from immigrants, some of whom were then able to become landowners as part of Western expansion, while others did not. In the 20th century, property, and thus freedom, were guaranteed first through the continued suppression of the former slaves and their descendants, then through fighting for freedom in the century's great wars. The freedom attained in war, though, did not primarily come from the lack of subjugation by foreign powers as much as it arose from the rising global economic dominance which American victory ensured: the result was never a return to the *status quo ante*, but rather a continuous striving for more influence, more wealth, more freedom. While some might see in all of this the incessant march of the Constitution's liberal ideals toward realization in the world,[16] you can also see in all of

[16] For example, President Ronald Reagan in his farewell speech to the nation: "I've spoken of the shining city all my political life, but I don't know if I ever quite communicated what I saw when I said it. But in my mind it was a tall, proud city built on rocks stronger than oceans, wind-swept, God-blessed, and teeming with people of all kinds living in harmony and peace; a city with free ports that hummed with commerce and creativity. And if there had to be city walls, the walls had doors and the doors were open to anyone with the will and the heart to get here. That's how I saw it, and see it still." Epstein himself would seem to think that the march of liberal ideals was mostly halted at the transition from the Lochner court to the FDR New Deal Court in the 1930s, see below. With respect to the topos of the shining city on the hill, *Wikipedia* ("City upon a Hill") refers to two other uses, the original use by John Winthrop upon setting sail to settle America in which he refers to his group's future community as "a city upon a hill, the eyes of all people are upon us" and President John F. Kennedy's statement at the beginning of his administration: "I have been guided by the standard John Winthrop set before his shipmates on the flagship Arbella three hundred and thirty-one years ago, as they, too, faced the task of building a new government on a perilous frontier."

"We must always consider," he said, "that we shall be as a city upon a hill – the eyes of all people are upon us." Today the eyes of all people are truly upon us – and our governments, in every branch, at every level, national, state and local, must be as a city upon a hill – constructed and inhabited by men aware of their great trust and their great responsibilities. For we are setting out upon a voyage in 1961 no less hazardous than that undertaken by the Arabella in 1630. We are committing ourselves to tasks of statecraft no less awesome than that of governing the Massachusetts Bay Colony, beset as it was then by terror without and disorder within. History will not judge our endeavors – and a government cannot be selected – merely on the basis of color or creed or even party affiliation. Neither will competence and loyalty and stature,

this the constant struggle of the landowning class to maintain the liberal ideal (*sotto voce*: the arrangement with respect to property as of 1788) in the face of growing pressure. With the exception of Britain which was fought back in successive wars, the American story is also a story of natives and then Native Americans, slaves and then African Americans, immigrants and then the middle class, wives and then women, the third world and then the developing world all eventually coming to assert their rights within the deontic framework of the American landowning class. Just as the principles of the classical liberal constitution have come to pervade the American understanding of political order, it has been equally inexorable that all people touched by its ideals come to raise their hands asking for participation in the freedom which property affords. And the law sees it all.

An incipient recognition of this can be found already with Llewellyn's 1934 article, "The Constitution as an Institution", in which, following Arthur Bentley's 1908 *The Process of Government*, Llewellyn develops the precis of a theory regarding the de facto constitution of the United States of America, as opposed to the theory regarding the formal Constitution, which, for Llewellyn is a theory filled with fictional treatments regarding the applicability of the words of a document that has since out-served its original purpose.[17] While Llewellyn certainly approaches the American constitution from a different angle than Epstein, the latter writing 80 years later, the two approaches are not directly in each other's crosshairs. For example, Epstein's project is not really prescriptive in the sense that he would like for the constitutional structure for the United States to be a classical liberal one, but rather that the underlying frame for understanding the actual constitution of the United States was, at least until 1936, the classical liberal frame and that this frame still imbues much of American political life today. Furthermore, while Llewellyn's primary target is the prevailing constitutional formalism of his day,[18] Epstein sees the US Constitution as being in many ways imperfect and in need of an interpretation along of the lines of the classical liber-

---

while essential to the utmost, suffice in times such as these. For of those to whom much is given, much is required." https://www.jfklibrary.org/learn/about-jfk/historic-speeches/the-city-upon-a-hill-speech (accessed 29 March 2022). The relevance of contrasting the passage from Reagan with those of Winthrop and Kennedy is that, whereas Reagan considers The City on the Hill mainly in terms of entitlement (a tall, proud, God-blessed city in which one can live in harmony and peace), both Winthrop and Kennedy conceive of The City on the Hill primarily as a source of obligation.

[17] See also von Jhering's *Der Zweck im Recht*, which Bentley acknowledges as a principal source for his own work and which functions as a significant predecessor for Legal Realism generally. With respect to Llewellyn's distinction between the constitution as it exists in reality and the constitution as it exists formally, see also Schmitt's similar treatment in his *Verfassungslehre*.

[18] Llewellyn, "The Constitution as Institution", p. 2.

al tradition in order to achieve its full potential. Nonetheless, Llewellyn provides an important counterbalance vis-à-vis Epstein for understanding what the American constitution actually entails.

The basic issue for Llewellyn is the following: "The existing theory of our constitutional law once had some point and value; as applied to a code some century and a half old, it has ceased to serve." For Llewellyn, the US Constitution, as a document, at best aspires to establish a certain state of political affairs. However, whether the document succeeds in establishing this state of affairs or not, the actual constitution of the United States is not to be found in the document, but in the actual state of affairs. While the document, because of its historical influence, may well be a key source for interpreting the current state of affairs, it is ultimately the state of affairs that counts and not the document.[19] Furthermore, this is also the case even if all relevant actors profess being guided in their actions by the formal document. It is not the document, but the actions which count. The document at most has derivative importance.

At a certain level of reflection, everyone can agree that this is the case. Of course, the United States of America *could* do away with its Constitution or entirely replace it with another document, even if the resulting state might only vaguely resemble the former one. It is mostly a background assumption in American constitutional law discourse that the Constitution is, or at least is taken to be, the constitution of the United States. Llewellyn's aim in this article, I take it, is to move the relevance of the Constitution in American discourse from the background to the foreground, especially given the general turbulence surrounding the Court in the 1930s which also Epstein reflects on in his last quote above. Llewellyn's move, in turn, raises the question regarding the purpose of a written constitution as well as the general notion of the constitution itself. Where Epstein would contest that the role of the US Constitution as a formal document is important in order to codify the political philosophy of a classical liberal order, thereby in important ways limiting the development of a federal state, Llewellyn, in his matter of fact way, observes that neither the society nor the government of the 1930s (much less in the 21st century) materially reflects the picture envisioned by the delegates to the Constitutional Convention when the document was drafted. Instead of designating the document as the constitution, Llewellyn suggests: "As an institution of major size, then, our working Constitution[20] embraces the inter-

---

[19] See Llewellyn, *supra*, p. 12: "Wherever there are today practices 'under' or 'in accordance with' the Document, it is only the practice which can legitimatize the words as being still part of our governing Constitution. It is not the words which legimate the practice."

[20] I have chosen to capitalize the document of 1789, as amended (i.e. the US Constitution) and keep in lowercase the general concept of constitution; Llewellyn adopts the opposite approach.

locking ways and attitudes of different groups and classes in the community – different ways and attitudes of different groups and classes, but all cogging together into a fairly well-organized whole."[21]

This dynamic, non-formalist approach importantly mirrors Somlo's conception of the legal norm as *plurale tantum*, set forth above in Chapter IV. The guiding idea is that the legally relevant material, whether in matters of civil society or of the political constitution, primarily consists neither in rules, whether abstract or in some way codified, nor in edicts from a physical sovereign, nor in a Founding Document. Rather, what counts is the *interlocking* of the ways and attitudes of individuals, groups and classes. In Somlo's terminology, it is the context in which norms acquire their meaning; in Llewellyn's terminology, it is the *cogging* of society which establishes the law's objective. For a state's constitution, this cogging will not necessarily be engineered any more than that of a family or a common law partnership. Yet, as Llewellyn points out, one can see in these basic groups, constituted as groups, that the various individuals all have rights and responsibilities that may develop more or less spontaneously.[22] Recording how this cogging works and helping it to advance more efficiently, or with less friction, is the task of the law.

Llewellyn uses the example of a family as a microcosm of the constitution. Families, like many constitutions, start more or less from scratch but with fully formed, i.e. mature and inculturated, individuals as constituent members. It might start with two individuals and nothing but a kiss, but soon money must come to fill the common coffer, dishes must be washed and diapers changed. Llewellyn goes into significant illustrative detail regarding how the ways of a generic family interlock.[23] The father appears at the breakfast table with food and wife awaiting him, he reads his newspaper, departs for work and then brings

---

[21] Llewellyn, *supra*, p. 18.

[22] Llewellyn, *supra*, pp. 18, 19.

[23] Ibid. For the sake of reference, the entire passage is as follows: "Mr. Hubb goes out to work and provides for payment of the bills. When he rises, his breakfast has been attended to; and the bathroom has been left free for his shaving. He, and no other, reads the newspaper while he eats. Before he leaves for his train, he fixes the furnace; and he receives certain instructions as to things to be brought back on his return. There is no need to go on. It is obvious that Mr. Hubb's patterns of behavior are not those of Mrs. Hubb, nor those of the maid, nor those of little Lorna. But it is equally obvious that the patterns of all four intercog like the wheels of a clock, and make a whole go round which we choose to call a 'family', and which is more than and different from the constituent parts. It is obvious, moreover, that Mr. Hubb's behavior lies in good part in patterns, expected and reckoned with by the others. And normatized. If he should fail to come home to dinner, or should forget the ordered purchases, or should gamble away his paycheck at a poker-game, Mrs. Hubb would not only be upset in her cooperation, but would feel aggrieved. Meanwhile, each other member of the family contributes her own quite diverse patterns to the interlocking whole that goes on *as* a whole."

home the bacon: a happy familial institution. What Llewellyn does not further thematize in 1934, but which is quite evident today, is that the institution which Llewellyn describes is one that is thoroughly structured according to prevailing cultural norms. Interestingly for Llewellyn's argument is that if *the* family as an institution really would function according to the normative framework that he describes, then, just as with Epstein's classical liberal constitution and contrary to Llewellyn's argument, it really would be amenable to codification in a similar manner to the US Constitution. However, to the essence of Llewellyn's point, though the family as an institution does often work, it does not necessarily work like *that*. Indeed, just as with the constitution in the 1930s, the institution becomes interesting precisely then, when the prevailing normative assumption (paternalism in the family, limited government in the state) is called into the foreground.

This is the liberal moment of constitutional law. To the extent that the goal of Epstein's classical liberal conception of the Constitution is to call into the foreground ideological assumptions underlying the historical document in order that we may better understand them and consciously work them into the existing constitutional framework, Epstein's project, too, represents the liberal moment. However, the work, especially passages criticizing efforts to allocate property to the previously disenfranchised,[24] can also be read as the family's father above extolling the virtues of paternalism. In such a case, the defense is not of an institution, but of a power structure.[25] On the other hand, Llewellyn's consideration of the constitution as an institution should not be read as the general placet of every status quo that may come upon the union. It is not the individual attitude or event which counts for the law, but rather the interlocking of attitudes, the political body as it cogs. Such cogging occurs not by chance but by exigency (sometimes) and reflected tradition (mostly). In a system with a strong Founding, it should not be surprising that much of that exigency and tradition is provided for in the founding document.

Einen Satz verstehen, heißt, eine Sprache verstehen.[26] That this is the case makes all the difference for the theory of law. If the picture which Rousseau paints were correct regarding the first man enclosing a piece of land, or if Locke's conception of the development of natural rights would hold, i. e. that rights derive from the work that one has done or the value that one has added, then the matter would be

[24] See Epstein, *The Classical Liberal Constitution*, p. 34 ff.

[25] Cf. Stekeler (2018), p. 251: "Die geheime Unwahrheit in einer 'liberalen' Kritik an Marx und Hegel besteht in einer ideologischen Apologetik der faktischen Macht der neuen Fürsten, der Bourgeoisie."

[26] Wittgenstein. PU 199.

different. That understanding a language is implied in the understanding of a sentence, and, as argued above, that therefore the understanding of a legal order is required in the understanding of legal norms, requires an inversion in our understanding of the law.

Bibliography

Alchourrón, Carlos / Bulygin, Eugenio: "The Expressive Conception of Norms", in: Stanley L. Paulson (ed.), *Normativity and Norms*. Oxford University Press, Oxford 1998, 383–410.

Alexander, Lawrence: "Legal Objectivity and the Illusion of Legal Principles", in: Matthias Klatt (ed.), *Institutionalized Reason: The Jurisprudence of Robert Alexy.* Oxford University Press, Oxford 2012, 115–131.

Alexy, Robert: *Begriff und Geltung des Rechts*. Verlag Karl Alber, Freiburg 2005.

Anscombe, Elizabeth: *Intention*. Oxford University Press, Oxford 1957.

Aquinas, Thomas: *On Law, Morality and Politics*, Regen, Richard (tr.). Hackett Publishing, Indianapolis 2002.

Aristoteles: *Metaphysik*. Felix Meiner Verlag, Hamburg 1989.

Austin, John: *The Province of Jurisprudence Determined* (1832). Cambridge University Press, Cambridge 1995.

Bentley, Arthur: *The Process of Government* (1908). Belknap Press, Cambridge MA 1967.

Bentham, Jeremy: *Fragment on Government* (1776). Cambridge University Press, Cambridge 1988.

–: *An Introduction to the Principles of Morals and Legislation* (1789). Athlone Press, London 1970.

Bix, Brian: "John Austin", in: Edward N. Zalta (ed.), *The Stanford Encyclopedia of Philosophy* (Spring 2018 ed.), https://plato.stanford.edu/archives/spr2018/entries/austin-john/ (accessed 07 April 2022).

–: "The American and Scandinavian Legal Realists on the Nature of Norms", in: Mattias Dahlberg (ed.), *De Lege*: *Uppsala–Minnesota Colloquium: Law, Culture and Values*. Iustus Forlag, Uppsala 2009, 85–100.

Blackstone, William: *Commentaries on the Laws of England.* Sweet, London 1836.

Böckenförde, Ernst-Wolfgang: *Staat, Gesellschaft, Freiheit*. Suhrkamp Verlag, Frankfurt am Main 1976.

Bodin, Jean: *Les Six Livres de la République* (1576). Arthème Fayard, Paris 1986.

Bolzano, Bernard: *Wissenschaftslehre*, Vol. 1. (1837). Fromann-Holzboog Verlag, Stuttgart 1985.

Bouriau, Christophe: *Le 'Comme Si': Kant, Vaihinger et le fictionalisme*. CERF, Paris 2013.

Bulygin, Eugenio: "An Antinomy in Kelsen's Pure Theory of Law", in: Stanley L. Paulson (ed.), *Normativity and Norms.* Oxford University Press, Oxford 1998, 297–316.

Carnap, Rudolf: *Der logische Aufbau der Welt* (1928). Felix Meiner Verlag, Hamburg 1998.

Chesterton, Gilbert Keith: *The Thing*. Sheed & Ward, London 1929.

Cohen, Hermann: *Ethik des Reinen Willens* (1904). Bruno Cassirer Verlag, Berlin, 2nd ed. 1907.

Constant, Benjamin: *Principes de politique: Applicables à tous les gouvernements* (1806). Fayard / Pluriel, Paris 2006.

Damböck, Christian (ed.): *Der Wiener Kreis. Ausgewählte Texte*. Reclam Verlag, Stuttgart 2013.

Dörrie, Heinrich: "'Υπόστασις', Wort- und Bedeutungsgeschichte", in: *Nachrichten der Akademie der Wissenschaften in Göttingen aus dem Jahr 1955*. Vandenhoeck & Ruprecht, Göttingen 1955, 36–92.

Dreier, Horst: "Der Preis der Moderne", in: Elif Özmen (ed.), *Hans Kelsens Politische Philosophie*. Mohr Siebeck Verlag, Tübingen 2017, 3–28.

Dreyfus, Hubert L / Kelly, Sean: *All Things Shining: Reading the Western Classics to find Meaning in a Secular Age*. Free Press, New York 2011.

Durkheim, Émile: *Les formes élémentaires de la vie religieuse* (1912). PUF, Paris 1985.

Dworkin, Ronald: *Taking Rights Seriously*. Harvard University Press, Cambridge, MA 1977.

Dyzenhaus, David: *Legality and Legitimacy: Carl Schmitt, Hans Kelsen, and Hermann Heller in Weimar*. Oxford University Press, Oxford 1999.

Edel, Geert: "Zum Problem der Rechtsgeltung. Kelsens Lehre von der Grundnorm und das Hypothesis-Theorem Cohens", in: Simone Zurbuchen / Peter A. Schmid (ed.), *Grenzen der kritischen Vernunft. Festschrift für Helmut Holzhey*. Schwabe & Co, Basel 1997, 178–194.

–: "The Hypothesis of the Basic Norm: Hans Kelsen and Hermann Cohen", in: Stanley L. Paulson (ed.), *Normativity and Norms*. Oxford University Press, Oxford 1998, 195–220.

Epstein, Richard A.: *The Classical Liberal Constitution*. Harvard University Press, Cambridge MA 2014.

Farr, James / Williams, David (ed.): *The General Will, the Evolution of a Concept*. Cambridge University Press, Cambridge 2015.

Finnis, John: *Natural Law & Natural Rights*. Oxford University Press, Oxford 2011.

Friedman, Milton: *Capitalism and Freedom*. Chicago University Press, Chicago 1962.

Fuller, Lon: *The Morality of Law*. Yale University Press, New Haven 1965.

Gierke, Otto von: *Das deutsche Genossenschaftsrecht*. Weidmannsche Buchhandlung, Berlin 1868.

Gilbert, Margaret: *Joint Commitment*. Oxford University Press, New York 2014.

Grotius, Hugo: *On the Law of War and Peace*. Cambridge University Press, Cambridge 2013.

Habermas, Jürgen: *Faktizität und Geltung*. Suhrkamp Verlag, Frankfurt am Main 1998.

Halfwassen, Jens: *Hegel und der Spätantike Neuplatonismus*. Bouvier Verlag, Bonn 1999.

Hare, Richard M.: *The Language of Morals*. Oxford University Press, Oxford 1952.

Hart, Herbert L.A.: *The Concept of Law*. Oxford University Press, Oxford, 2nd ed. 1994.

–: (1999) "Kelsen Visited", in: Stanley L. Paulson (ed.), *Normativity and Norms*. Oxford University Press, Oxford 1998, 69–88.

Hayek, Friedrich A.: *Law, Legislation and Liberty*, Vol. 1: *Rules and Order*. Chicago University Press, Chicago 1973.

Hegel, Georg Wilhelm Friedrich: *Grundlinien der Philosophie des Rechts* (1820). Felix Meiner Verlag, Hamburg 2013.

Heller, Hermann: *Staatslehre* (1934). Mohr Siebeck, Tübingen 1983.

Hobbes, Thomas: *Leviathan* (1651). Penguin Classics, London 1985.

Hogrebe, Wolfram: "'Wer in Mythos lebt…' – Eine Miszelle", in: Gereon Wolters / Martin Carrier (ed.) *Homo Sapiens und Homo Faber*. De Gruyter Verlag, Berlin 2005, 309–322.

Holmes, Oliver Wendell: "The Path of the Law", in: 10 *Harvard Law Review* 457–478.

–: *The Common Law*. Little, Brown and Company, Boston 1945.

Hume, David: *A Treatise of Human Nature*. Oxford University Press, Oxford 1896.

Jellinek, Georg: *Allgemeine Staatslehre* (1900). Springer Verlag, Berlin 1921.

Jhering, Rudolf von: *Geist des römischen Rechts* (1907). Scientia Verlag, Aalen 1968.

–: *Der Zweck im Recht*. 1877. Felix Meiner Verlag, Leipzig 1916.

Jørgensen, Jørgen: *The Development of Logical Empiricism*. Chicago University Press, Chicago 1951.

–: "Imperatives and Logic" (1937), reprinted in: *Danish Yearbook of Philosophy*, Vol. 6. 1969, 9–17.

Kant, Immanuel: *Grundlegung zur Metaphysik der Sitten* (1786). Suhrkamp Verlag, Frankfurt am Main 1974.

Kantorowicz, Hermann: "Some Rationalism about Realism", in: 48 *Yale Law Journal,* no. 8, 1240, 1240–1253.

Kelsen, Hans: *Allgemeine Staatslehre*. Julius Springer Verlag, Berlin 1925.

–: *Allgemeine Theorie der Normen*. Manz Verlag, Vienna 1979.

–: "A Pure Theory of Law, 'Labandism', and Neo-Kantianism. A Letter to Renato Treves", in: Stanley L. Paulson (ed.), *Normativity and Norms*. Oxford University Press, Oxford 1998, 169–176.

–: *Das Problem der Souveränität und die Theorie des Völkerrechts*. Mohr Verlag, Tübingen 1920.

–: *Der Soziologische und der Juristische Staatsbegriff* (1922). Mohr Verlag, Tübingen, 2nd ed. 1928.

–: "Die Rechtswissenschaft als Norm oder als Kulturwissenschaft" (1916), in: *Veröffentlichte Schriften 1911–1917*, Vol. 3, *Hans Kelsen Werke*. Mohr Siebeck Verlag, Tübingen 2010.

–: *Hauptprobleme der Staatsrechtslehre* (1911). Mohr Verlag, Tübingen, 2nd ed. 1923.

–: *Reine Rechtslehre* (1934). Scientia Verlag, Aalen 1994.

–: *Secular Religion: A Polemic Against the Misinterpretation of Modern Social Philosophy, Science and Politics as "New Religions"*. Springer Verlag, Vienna 2012.

–: *Was ist Gerechtigkeit?* Reclam Verlag, Stuttgart 2000.

–: "Zur Theorie der juristischen Fiktionen. Mit besonderer Berücksichtigung von Vaihingers Philosophie des Als Ob", in: *Annalen der Philosophie*, Vol. 1 (1919), 630–658.

Kersting, Wolfgang: "Neukantianische Rechtsbegründung. Rechtsbegriff und richtiges Recht bei Cohen, Stammler und Kelsen", in: Robert Alexy et al. (ed.) *Neukantianismus und Rechtsphilosophie*. Nomos Verlag, Baden-Baden 2002, 23–68.

Kervégan, Jean-François: *La raison des normes – essai sur Kant*. Vrin, Paris 2015.

–: *Variazioni kelseniane*. Editione Scientifiche Italiane, Naples 2016.

Kletzer, Christoph: "Absolute Positivism", in: *Netherlands Journal of Legal Philosophy* 2 (2013), 87–99.

–: "The Normative Jinx", in: 37 *Oxford Journal of Legal Studies* 4 (2017), 798–813.

Kolman, Vojtěch: "Wittgenstein and die Meistersinger", in: *Estetika: The European Journal of Aesthetics* 57, no. 1, 44–63.

Kramer, Matthew H.: *In Defense of Legal Positivism – Law without Trimmings*. Oxford University Press, Oxford 1999.

–: *Objectivity and the Rule of Law*. Cambridge University Press, Cambridge 2007.

Kubeš, Vladimir / Weinberger, Ota (ed.): *Die Brünner Rechtstheoretische Schule (Normative Theorie)*. Manz Verlag, Vienna 1980.

Kutschera, Franz von: "Aufgaben, Probleme und Grenzen der Ethik", in: Johannes L. Brandl, Beatrice Kobow, Daniel Messelken (ed.), *Analytische Explikationen und Interventionen*. Mentis Verlag, Paderborn 2021, 173–189.

–: *Grundlagen der Ethik*. De Gruyter Verlag, Berlin 1999.

Lagerspetz, Eerik et al. (ed.): *On the Nature of Social and Institutional Reality*. University of Jyväskylä, Jyväskylä 2001.

Legrand, Pierre: "Against a European Civil Code", in: 60 *Modern Law Review* 44.

Leiter, Brian: "Normativity for Naturalists" (March 29, 2015), in: Ram Neta (ed.), *Normativity, Philosophical Issues* (supplement to Nous), Univ. of Chicago, Public Law Working Paper no. 527, https://ssrn.com/abstract=2586814 (accessed 07 April 2022).
–: *Naturalizing Jurisprudence – Essays on American Legal Realism and Naturalism in Legal Philosophy*. Oxford University Press, New York 2007.
–: "Positivism, Formalism, Realism", in: 99 *Columbia Law Review* 1138, 1138–1164.
Llewellyn, Karl N.: *The Bramble Bush*. Oceana Press, New York 1960.
–: *The Common Law Tradition – Deciding Appeals*. Little Brown & Company, Boston 1960.
–: *The Cheyenne Way*. University of Oklahoma Press, Norman OK 1967.
–: *Jurisprudence: Realism in Theory and Practice*. University of Chicago Press, Chicago 1962.
Locke, John: *The Second Treatise of Government* (1689). Cambridge University Press, Cambridge 1963.
MacCormick, Neil / Weinberger, Ota: *Grundlagen des institutionalistischen Rechtspositivismus*. Duncker & Humblot, Berlin 1985.
Madison, James / Hamilton, Alexander / Jay, John: *The Federalist Papers*. Penguin Group, New York 2012.
Meggle, Georg: "von Wrights Understanding of Actions" in: *Acta Filosofica Fennica*. Philosophical Society of Finland, Helsinki 2016, 293–312.
Mayer, Reinhold: *Der Talmud*. Orbis Verlag, Munich 1999.
Montesquieu: *De l'esprit des lois* (1758). Garnier-Flammarion, Paris 1979.
Moore, George E.: *Principia Ethica*. Cambridge University Press, Cambridge 1993.
Özmen, Elif (ed.): *Hans Kelsens Politische Philosophie*. Mohr Siebeck Verlag, Tübingen 2017.
Paulson, Stanley L.: "Four Phases in Hans Kelsen's Legal Theory? Reflections on a Periodization", in: *Oxford J Legal Studies* 18 (1) (1998), 153–166.
– (ed.): *Normativity and Norms*. Oxford University Press, Oxford 1998.
Pavčnik, Marijan: *Juristisches Verstehen und Entscheiden*. Springer Verlag, Wien 1993.
Perez Paoli, Ubaldo Ramon: *Der Plotinische Begriff von 'ΥΠΟΣΤΑΣΙΣ und die augustinische Bestimmung Gottes als Subiectum*. Augustinus Verlag, Würzburg 1990.
Pihlajamäki, Heikki: "Against Metaphysics in Law: The Historical Background of American and Scandinavian Legal Realism Compared", in: *The American Journal of Comparative Law* Vol. 52, no. 2, 469–487.
Plato: *Symposium*, Avi Sharon (tr.). Hackett Publishing, Indianapolis 1998.
Plessner, Helmuth: *Grenzen der Gemeinschaft* (1924). Suhrkamp Verlag, Frankfurt am Main 2018.
Posner, Richard: *The Problems of Jurisprudence*. Harvard University Press, Cambridge, MA 1993.
Pound, Roscoe: *The Spirit of the Common Law* (1921). Beacon Press, Boston 1966.
Proust, Marcel: *À la recherche du temps perdu, Du côté de chez Swann* (1913). Gallimard, Paris 1919.
Pufendorf, Samuel von: *De officio hominis et civis iuxta legem naturalem libri duo* (*Über die Pflicht des Menschen und des Bürgers nach dem Gesetz der Natur)* (1672). Insel Verlag, Frankfurt 1994.
Quine, Willard Van Orman: *From a Logical Point of View*. Harvard University Press, Cambridge MA 1980.
Rawls, John: *Political Liberalism*. Columbia University Press, New York 2005.
Raz, Joseph: "Authority, Law and Morality", in: *The Monist*, Vol. 68, no. 3, 295–324.
–: "Kelsen's Theory of the Basic Norm", in: Stanley L. Paulson (ed.), *Normativity and Norms*. Oxford University Press, Oxford 1998.

Reinach, Adolf: *Zur Phänomenologie des Rechts – die apriorischen Grundlagen des bürgerlichen Rechts.* Kösel Verlag, Munich 1953.

Repgow, Eike von: *Der Sachsenspiegel* (ca. 1230), Clausdieter Schott (ed.), Ruth Schmidt-Wiegand, Clausdieter Schott (tr.). Manesse Verlag, Zurich 1984.

Rödl, Sebastian: "The Idea of Practice", in: Pirmin Stekeler-Weithofer (ed.), *Wittgenstein: Zu Philosophie und Wissenschaft*. Felix Meiner Verlag, Hamburg 2012, 190–202.

Ross, Alf: "Validity and the Conflict between Legal Positivism and Natural Law", in: Stanley L. Paulson (ed.), *Normativity and Norms*. Oxford University Press, Oxford 1998, 147–164.

Rousseau, Jean-Jacques: *Discours sur l'économie politique*. Paris, Vrin 2002.

–: *Du contrat social* (1762). Reclam Verlag, Stuttgart 2010.

Shields, Christopher / Schwartz, Daniel: "Francisco Suárez", in: Edward N. Zalta (ed.), *The Stanford Encyclopedia of Philosophy* (Winter 2016 ed.) https://plato.stanford.edu/archives/win2016/entries/suarez/ (accessed 07 April 2022).

Schmidt, Bruno: *Das Gewohnheitsrecht als Form des Gemeinwillens*. Duncker & Humblot, Leipzig 1899.

Schmitt, Carl: *Der Wert des Staates und die Bedeutung des Einzelnen* (1914). Duncker & Humblot, Berlin 2004.

–: *Der Leviathan in der Staatslehre des Thomas Hobbes: Sinn und Fehlschlag eines politischen Symbols.* Hanseatische Verlagsanstalt, Hamburg 1938.

–: *Die Diktatur* (1921). Duncker & Humblot, Berlin 2006.

–: *Verfassungslehre* (1928). Duncker & Humblot, Berlin 2010.

–: *Politische Theologie, vier Kapitel zur Lehre von der Souveränität* (1922). Duncker & Humblot, Berlin 2009.

Searle, John: *The Construction of Social Reality*. The Free Press, New York 1995.

–: *Rationality in Action*. MIT Press, Cambridge MA 2001.

–: *Speech Acts*. Cambridge University Press, 1969.

Sebok, Anthony: *Legal Positivism in American Jurisprudence*. Cambridge University Press, Cambridge 1998.

Simmonds, Nigel: *Law as a Moral Idea.* Oxford University Press, Oxford 2007.

Smend, Rudolf: *Verfassung und Verfassungsrecht*. Duncker & Humblot, Leipzig 1928.

Somlo, Felix: *Juristische Grundlehre*. Felix Meiner Verlag, Leipzig 1927.

–: *Gedanken zu einer ersten Philosophie*. Felix Meiner Verlag, Leipzig 1926.

Spade, Paul Vincent / Panaccio, Claude: "William of Ockham", in: Edward N. Zalta (ed.), *The Stanford Encyclopedia of Philosophy* (Winter 2016 ed.), https://plato.stanford.edu/archives/win2016/entries/ockham/ (accessed 07 April 2022).

Spinoza, Baruch de: *Tractatus politicus* (1677). Felix Meiner Verlag, Hamburg 2010.

–: *Political Treatise*, Samuel Shirley (tr.). Hackett Publishing, Indianapolis 2000.

Stammler, Rudolf: *Wirtschaft und Recht nach der materialistischen Geschichtsauffassung* (1906). De Gruyter Verlag, Berlin 1924.

–: *Die Lehre von dem richtigen Rechte* (1926). Wissenschaftliche Buchgesellschaft, Darmstadt 1964

Stekeler, Pirmin: *Eine Kritik juridischer Vernunft*, in: Horst Dreier / Dietmar Willoweit (ed.), *Würzburger Vorträge zur Rechtsphilosophie, Rechtstheorie und Rechtssoziologie*, Heft 48. Nomos Verlag, Baden-Baden 2014.

–: *Hegels Phänomenologie des Geistes. Ein dialogischer Kommentar*. Felix Meiner Verlag, Hamburg 2014.

–: "Eigentum und Selbstbestimmung. Hegels Idee personaler Freiheit in republikanischen Institutionen", in: Pirmin Stekeler-Weithofer / Benno Zabel (ed.), *Philosophie der Republik*. Mohr Siebeck Verlag, Tübingen 2018, 226–251.

Stekeler, Pirmin / Zabel, Benno (ed.): *Philosophie der Republik*. Mohr Siebeck Verlag, Tübingen 2018.

Stirner, Max: *Der Einzige und sein Eigentum* (1845). Reclam Verlag, Stuttgart 2008.

Strauss, Leo: *The Political Philosophy of Hobbes, its Basis and its Genesis*. University of Chicago Press, Chicago 1952.

Tocqueville, Alexis de: *De la Democratie en Amerique I*. Paris 1835.

Tönnies, Ferdinand: *Gemeinschaft und Gesellschaft*. Wissenschaftliche Buchgesellschaft, Darmstadt 1979.

Tuomela, Raimo: *The Importance of Us: A Philosophical Study of Basic Social Notions*. Stanford University Press, Stanford 1995.

Tuck, Richard: *The Sleeping Sovereign, the Invention of Modern Democracy*. Cambridge University Press, Cambridge 2016.

Vaihinger, Hans: *Die Philosophie des Als-Ob*. Felix Meiner Verlag, Leipzig 1922.

Viner, Jacob: "The Intellectual History of Laissez Faire", in: 3 *The Journal of Law & Economics*, Oct. 1960, 45–69.

Vinx, Lars: *Kelsen's Pure Theory of Law*. Oxford University Press, Oxford 2007.

–: *The Guardian of the Constitution: Hans Kelsen and Carl Schmitt on the Limits of Constitutional Law.* Cambridge University Press, Cambridge 2015.

Weber, Max: *Wirtschaft und Gesellschaft*. Mohr, Tübingen 1925.

Weinberger, Ota: "The Expressive Conception of Norms: An Impasse for the Logic of Norms", in: Stanley L. Paulson (ed.), *Normativity and Norms*. Oxford University Press, Oxford 1998, 411–432.

Wittgenstein, Ludwig: *Werkausgabe*, Vol. I: *Tractatus logico-philosophicus / Tagebücher 1914–1916 / Philosophische Untersuchungen*. Suhrkamp Verlag, Frankfurt am Main 1984.

Wright, Georg Henrik von: "Is and Ought", in: Stanley L. Paulson (ed.), *Normativity and Norms*. Oxford University Press, Oxford 1998, 365–382.

–: *Norm and Action*. Routledge Press, New York 1963.

–: "Pilgrim's Progress", in: *The Tree of Knowledge and Other Essays*. Brill Publishers, Leiden 1993, 103–113.

Zabel, Benno: "The institutional turn in Hegel's Philosophy of Right", in: *Hegel-Bulletin 36.1*. Cambridge University Press, Cambridge 2015, 80–104.

Index

Rechtstheorie · Legal Theory

edited by
Thomas Gutmann, Tatjana Hörnle, and Matthias Jestaedt

The new series *Rechtstheorie · Legal Theory* collects innovative contributions on the "grammar" of the law. The mounting complexity and pluralisation of legal orders on the one hand and their increasing interactions and dependencies on the other mean that fundamental knowledge of functional law is of ever greater importance.

ISSN: 2629-723X
Suggested citation: RTh

All available volumes can be found at *www.mohrsiebeck.com/rth*

Mohr Siebeck
www.mohrsiebeck.com